The T.V. Personalities

PLUS

the wicked kitchen staff

RED SQUARE

Pig Posse hi fi IN THE GROOVE

10 till late
£1 CHEAP!

THE AMBULANCE STATION

THIS SAT.
MAY 12th

306 Old Kent Rd. SE1. (Bus: 1,53,63,177, N 74. ⊖ Elephant & Castle)

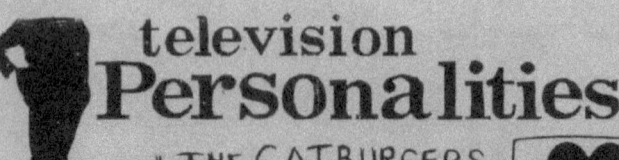

Benjamin Berton

Dreamworld. The fabulous life of Daniel Treacy and his band Television Personalities

Translated by David Marshall

'THE ROOM AT THE TOP'
upstairs at
The Enterprise
haverstock hill n.w.3
CHALK FARM TUBE
SATURDAYS
£2·00 ub40 £1·50

8:30 p.m. 1st Act 9:00

8TH	THAT PETROL EMOTION + GOD!! service
15TH	the pastels + Buba and the Shopassistants + The Palookas
22ND	TELEVISION Personalities "Concert for Peace" + The Walking Floors
29TH	BRIGANDAGE + FRIENDS
July 6TH	The JuneBrides and GOD service
13TH	THE MEMBRANES + Mighty Lemon Drops

Benjamin Berton, born in 1974 in northern France. He received the prix Goncourt du premier roman in 2000 for his debut novel "Sauvageons". He has written a ten novels, which have been translated into various languages. He lives and works in Le Mans and writes for the French-language music press.

© Ventil Verlag UG (haftungsbeschränkt) & Co. KG, Mainz, 2022
Use of this material, in full or in part, is only permitted with expressly agreement of the publisher. All rights reserved.

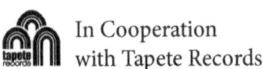 In Cooperation with Tapete Records

First edition, May 2022
ISBN 978-3-95575-178-4

Design & layout: Oliver Schmitt
Layout picture gallery: Kai Becker
Print & binding: Maincontor

Ventil Verlag, Boppstr. 25, D-55118 Mainz
www.ventil-verlag.de

INHALT

The King's Road 1977 11
The kidnapping of Paul McCartney 25
Geoffrey Ingram (1) 32
Part Time Punks 42
Clarendon Hotel Ballroom 52
…And Don't The Kids Just Love It 67
Seven years 74
Nico 89
Bright Sunny Smiles 105

Picture gallery 129

Geoffrey Ingram (2) 145
With Emilee 167
Opening the show 184
Alison Wonderland 193
Happy ending 208
Black hole 215
Butterfly 217
Millennium Dome 234
The Picture of Dorian Gray 245

Chronological markers 255
Acknowledgements 261
Photo credits 262

To Ian and Daniel, who is named after the hero of this book.

THE KING'S ROAD 1977

The King's Road is the epicentre, the snake and the ladder, a fragment of DNA that has encrypted modern life. There would have been no story to tell at all if this ancient royal thoroughfare along which, until 1830, only the King of England could travel, had not seen the coming together, the establishment and the encounter of people and places altogether weightier and more significant than wars or epidemics. The King's Road is the epicentre, the tale, and the refuge.

At the outset, the King's Road is merely a private lane used by King Charles II to go to Kew gardens, one of the most wonderful, verdant spaces in London. In the course of time (things change) the upper classes obtain the right of way and houses spring up, so that by the beginning of the 19th century, the road has become a veritable walk of fame. The King's Road stretches along a little less than two miles, from Sloane Square in the East, on the fringes of Belgravia and Knightsbridge. Then, running through Moore Park, touching on Chelsea and Fulham, the King's Road crosses Stanley Bridge and joins Waterford Road, to give rise to New King's Road. In fact, the same road has several names and stretches even further, to become Fulham High Street and Putney Bridge, before ending its course due West in the borough of Hammersmith and Fulham. The King's Road is an upper-middle-class road, an opulent road, a road in which for a very long time now not just anybody can buy a flat. You either need to work in a bank, or have well-born parents to take up residence there. But we're talking of a time when Chelsea was not yet quite the Chelsea of today. Four decades ago, just a handful of years, but more than enough for things to change, it was a very different place.

At the time we're speaking of, the King's Road is truly the centre of London, and in its own way, the centre of the world. It is 1977 and Daniel Treacy has just walked past the boutique which, a few months earlier, Malcolm McLaren, manager of the Sex Pistols, renamed for the umpteenth time. Daniel Treacy just turned 18 in May. He's wearing a pair of cheap jeans and a checked blue on blue shirt. His only touch of originality, as far as his clothing is concerned, is a leather cap, pierced with small metal studs, covering his hair which is fairly short for the time, but which falls in untidy locks over his neck. The summer has been lousy. Just the opposite of the previous year's scorching weather. It has rained a lot and the streets have never really dried out. Treacy walks past the window and looks at the changes which have been made to this punk hangout since the beginning of the year. The cheap clothes shop has radically changed: from a temple of trash clothes to a trendy boutique, it's now a high-tech zone with ridiculous little lights and screens on the side walls. The punk movement is really weird. Daniel doesn't really know what to make of it all. There are interesting things, but he is suspicious of the people pulling the strings behind the scenes. Too many movements which originate within these walls smell of opportunism and social climbing. People come from all over to buy Westwood's rags and wear them as if they were in disguise. Some of this gear costs a fortune, but that doesn't discourage the customers. How do they do it? How can they be so young and yet so well-off? Daniel doesn't understand, so he's on his guard. They are the same ones that you find these days at the concerts, in the pubs: they go out at weekends then scarper back home to their parents, or to their university. You'd think they were part-time punks.

Originally, 430 King's Road was home to a boutique equipped with a juke-box, called the *Paradise Garage*. Malcolm McLaren and Vivienne Westwood changed the name to *Let It Rock*, then *Too Fast To Live, Too Young To Die*. It became *SEX* in huge capital letters, between 1974 and 1976, but now it's called *Seditionaries*, partly because McLaren's status has changed enormously over the last few months. During the winter, the Sex Pistols had hit the headlines by signing with EMI and taking the piss out of presenter

Bill Grundy who had interviewed them on the BBC in December. Bill Grundy had been particularly inept in suggesting to Siouxsie Sioux, one of the leading lights of the Bromley Contingent, to have it off with her after the show.
— I 've been just dying to meet you, she said ironically on the set.
— Filthy sod.
— Dirty fucker.

Bill Grundy's career was ruined. And the Bromley Contingent more or less deserted the Pistols' concerts in the months that followed. You just can't say things like that during a live broadcast. The punk movement has really taken off over the last few months and now has a considerable following. Daniel doesn't quite know where all that might lead. There isn't enough music in there, not enough songs, not enough lyrics. On top of all that, he doesn't like their repudiation of the 60's. You can't just cross out the Kinks. The *Seditionaries* window is sparsely furnished as always. It's one of the few shops where the proprietors have deliberately stopped anyone from seeing inside. Jordan doesn't seem to be there today. She's by far the coolest girl that Daniel knows. Jordan comes from Seaford. She's the best dressed punk around and not only because she can now borrow McLaren and Westwood's clothes whenever she likes, in order to promote them. Jordan's real name is Pamela Rooke and she has just recorded a song with Adam and The Ants. Daniel hasn't listened to it yet, but she told him about it the other day. They are more or less friends with each other.
At present, his mum has told him to deliver this bundle of laundry to number 42, Oakley Road. Daniel carries it on his shoulder. It weighs no more than three pounds. It's practically nothing. It's already been paid for by Marley's assistant. Once he's delivered his package, Daniel will walk up the King's Road to go to work. It's been several months since he gave up school. His mum had insisted that Peter Grant, the boss of Swan Song Records, take him

on for a trial period, and he does odd jobs for them. There's no need to hurry: there's rarely anyone who turns up before 11 o'clock, and even then, only on a good day. So, Daniel takes his time. Why does he get up so early? When he's older, he's convinced that he'll sleep as long as possible under a thick eiderdown from which he will only emerge to write songs and make love. Daniel isn't quite sure whether it's better to make love under the eiderdown or on top of it. He arrives at Bob Marley's house. It's a really big place, but nobody answers, as if the assistants have taken the day off, or haven't arrived themselves yet. Marley lives there with his group, The Wailers, so it's really surprising that there's not a soul around. Daniel rings again, his bundle of laundry on his shoulder, full of freshly starched fashionable clothes. He doesn't usually just leave a delivery on the doorstep. Mum is one of the best laundresses in West London. She has a good reputation and the important people in the area have no hesitation in sending her their dirty washing. The laundry is always impeccable, which speaks for itself. The firm never lets you down. Marley knows the address. He used to deal there even before he was famous. Now that he seems to have settled permanently in London, his assistants are constantly bringing every soiled item he has to the laundry, as if he had undertaken a major cleaning-up operation upon arriving from his home country. From what Daniel could gather, the singer had had a lucky escape from an assassination attempt. That's why he's left Jamaica and prefers to live here like a Mogul, along with his band, his cook, and his friends.

Daniel is still waiting when the door finally swings open. He's stunned by the vision before him. The most gorgeous girl he has ever seen in all his life is standing in front of him, wearing only a tee-shirt and what looks like pyjama shorts. He blushes instantly and grabs his bundle as if to protect himself.

— Hi there, she says. I'm sorry, but I didn't hear the bell.
— I've come to deliver Mr Marley's laundry.

— Great. Come in for a moment and leave that in the hall. I'll be back in a tick.

The girl turns to go and Daniel can't keep his eyes off her buttocks, thrusting up between the shorts and the raised tee-shirt. She's quite simply perfect, so dark-haired, so young, so white-skinned. Her hair is long and free as the wind. She's bare-foot and gives the impression of gliding over the tiled floor like an angel. When she comes back, Daniel is in the hall. Before him sweeps a wide Victorian staircase, a bit grubby, but quite majestic. The house is full of plants, packing cases, musical instruments. One of the doors off the entrance-hall leads into a sort of living-room furnished with pouffes and sofas. On the coffee table lie the remnants of a party, and ash-trays, and a pungent smell of weed sticks in your throat when you go into the house. You'd only need to breathe the air of this place for ten minutes to be completely stoned, he thinks. The girl comes back. She's been to get a purse, but Daniel would have preferred her to have put on a dressing-gown.

— My name's Cindy. You English?

— Ye..yes, he stammers. Are you the only one here?

— Of course not. But I don't know where the cook is. And the others are still at the studio.

— They start early.

— They didn't come home last night. Are you interested in music?

— A bit. I play in a band.

— Really?

Cindy Breakspeare realises that she is talking to a young guy and that she shouldn't encourage him. Bob has warned her about this. She is far too naïve. In Jamaica, she couldn't easily have this sort of conversation, but abroad, she's not so much on her guard and always on the lookout for distraction.

— I hope your band works out. Here, this is for you.

She hands him a five-pound note.

— It's already paid for.

— Keep it as your tip.
— It's far too much. It's more than the price of the laundry.
— Doesn't matter. That's all I've got.
He tries to give her the note back in order to have the opportunity to brush her fingers again, but she moves away. He looks at the bundle of washing lying at his feet for the last time and takes a step backwards. The girl's eyes make him feel giddy.
— Thanks, he says again as she walks him to the door. Very nice of you.
— See you again.
Her lips are red, just as lips should be, and slightly shiny. Her cheeks are still flushed from the night and her look is so clear that it sparkles like a Coke. Daniel is convinced that he has seen the most beautiful girl on the planet. He doesn't realise how right he is. Cindy Breakspeare had been elected Miss World the previous year. She's Canadian, but has lived most of her life in Jamaica.
Just as she's about to close the door behind him, she hesitates and takes a step forward. Daniel almost shudders. For a fraction of a second, he thinks that she's going to come up and kiss him. He doesn't know why, but this thought flashes through his mind and his heart almost skips a beat. And then he hears the sound of car doors sliding open, and men laughing, as they approach the doorway.
— What's up, Cin? You got company?
They laugh. Two, then four guys come down the steps. Black, tall, dressed in bizarre clothes, well, like reggae musicians. Some have short hair, others an afro style piled up like a wedding cake. Daniel steps aside and the Wailers file past him and go inside, laughing and determined, like a phalanx of legionaries.
At the back, last to get out of the car, Bob Marley closes the ranks. He's tall and walks with a slightly solemn gait, supple and elegant. He's wearing a sandal and a bandage on his left foot instead of a sports shoe. Daniel looks at his face, worn out by a night of

recording. His hair is dishevelled and his shirt gapes open over his chest. He's got a guitar in his hand. He walks past Daniel without so much as a glance and goes down two steps to throw himself into Miss World's arms. He kisses her greedily, a hand low on her hips, sliding between her fantastic buttocks, then he pulls away from her with an ease which surprises Daniel. The Wailers have disappeared and Marley takes the big staircase which leads to the living quarters. The door closes and it's over. He's the invisible man. Daniel thinks to himself that there is a huge difference of appearance between the leader of a band and his musicians. He's not sure that that is a good thing. What is it that makes some people superior to others? He thinks of his own band. It seems to him that Ed and he work more or less on equal terms, even if he has the last word because he is the best composer, the coolest and the most motivated. Ed has his own priorities, a band of his own, so it's not quite the same thing.

It only takes him a few minutes to reach the offices of Swan Song Records. The King's Road is filling up with people. Cars, pretty girls, people coming and going. There are office workers and punks, students and bankers, a whole world coming to life and drifting by, in an ordered ritual. The record label created by Robert Plant and Jimmy Page in 1974 is still in its early days, but has already mounted several hugely successful operations. In 1975, four of the albums produced by the label had reached the Billboard 200, the weekly chart of the 200 best-selling albums in the United States, and remained there for significant periods. Swan Song Records has signed up Bad Company, Maggie Bell, and obviously releases Led Zeppelin's recordings under their label. Page and Plant dream of providing all sorts of artistes with an environment where production and marketing aren't a substitute for inspiration, and artistry is in the making. Swan Songs will perhaps be the long-awaited El Dorado. The god Apollo, borrowed from William Rimmer's painting, *The End of the Day*, which is the label's logo, can well brandish his fists in the air: In London, and soon in New York, Swan Song Records is a long way from singing its own swan song. Behind the scenes, parties and orgies are legion as, so rumour has it, is the practice of black magic, urged on by Jimmy Page. He now lives a good part of the year on the shores of Loch Ness, in Aleister Crowley's old place, the accursed manor of Boleskine House. His drug consumption is worrying and, according to what the staff at the King's Road says, he rarely makes an appearance at the office. Nobody complains. Most of the employees are afraid of Jimmy Page. They say that when he comes into a room, the temperature immediately drops by several degrees.

When his mother had announced that she had managed to get him this first job by threatening Peter Grant, the label's boss, not to return Robert Plant's trousers and briefs, the whole family had had a good laugh. Daniel doesn't know himself how much of this story is really true, but nothing surprises him when it comes to his mother. He knows that she would do anything in her power to help him achieve his aims in life. Music has become a sort of obsession. He thinks about it all the time. He would have liked to paint, but music is the in thing at this time. You can't get away from it. At present, he has enough money to think about recording something. His father has loaned him the extra eighteen pounds he needs. It's only a question of weeks now. But all the same, he thinks, is it wise to work for Led Zeppelin given everything they say about them?

— Mister Grant is charming, his mother replied. And I've been laundering Jimmy Page's jeans for more than ten years. I've never seen the devil jump out of his underpants! It's perhaps the only thing that ain't jumped out of them, if you ask me, she said, bursting out with laughter.

— I don't think I want to hear the rest, his father sniggered.

The young man's first days had been easy going. He had spent most of the day chatting with the assistants, drinking tea, and practising the guitar on the sofa. A few people had crossed the main office from time to time to discuss things with Grant. Daniel had talked a bit with Maggie Bell, whose music he knew, and whom he found very pleasant.

Once or twice, Grant had come out of his office and had asked him to deliver a parcel to Maida Vale, to the BBC studios or to two or three other places of his choosing. The packets were carefully wrapped in brown paper and tied tightly with string. Daniel had assumed that they contained cassettes or tapes. On the second day, Grant had asked him to withdraw a little money for him, and then the following day to do just the opposite by depositing an envelope of cash at the bank. The work was as easy as that. He had crossed Robert Plant's path before the band's departure on tour, but the singer had not spoken to him directly. And then there had been that period of particular upheaval: Grant had joined the band and the label's centre of attraction had shifted to the United States. Led Zeppelin was in the process of touring America. The label was devoid of its managers, nearly all of whom had made the journey to support the four musicians who were its driving force. This period had been even quieter than the previous one for Daniel, whilst thousands of miles away, Led Zeppelin were about to enter a dark stretch, accumulating difficulties and slowly sinking into the blackest time in their history.

It was usually one of the female employees of Swan Song Records who passed on to Daniel the main news from the other side of the Atlantic, and it was almost invariably bad. The band had been very ill prepared to embark on this tour. They were surrounded by a large number of disreputable friends, who trailed violence and many other esoteric incidents in their wake. Peter Grant and John Bonham themselves were interviewed by the police about a racist attack during a concert at Oakland in California. The concerts generally lacked inspiration and the road team was permanently under tension. Going on tour in the United States can quickly turn into a nightmare when you lose control of things. And that was exactly what was happing to Led Zeppelin.

The news that was to bring this inevitably disastrous tour to a tragic end did not, paradoxically, come from over there, but from England. Just before a concert in New Orleans, Robert Plant got a call from a member of his family telling him that his son Karac was ill, followed several hours later by the news that he had died. His world crashed about his ears. Minutes later, Plant wrote a communiqué which he got Associated Press to publish, putting an official end to the tour. He returned home on the first flight out, devastated. His son had died of an infection due to a stomach virus.

When the news reached the London offices of Swan Song which, of course, didn't take long, all of the three or four employees still present were shaken with sincere grief and an understandable anxiety. What would become of the label if Robert Plant were not to get over this stroke of fate?

Daniel exchanged one or two words of reassurance with the other employees. And then Peter Grant and the others turned up, exhausted and haggard, worn out as much by grief as by the life they had been leading over the last three months or so. You could see the terror in their eyes. Plant obviously had gone home. Some joined him a few days later to attend the funeral. And it was then that Page turned up again. It was the first time that Daniel had come across him in the label's offices. Whether it was before or after the funeral, he didn't recall, but he remembered his first impression when setting eyes on the best guitarist in the world. He had said to himself that he didn't look human. Page had turned to Unity McLean, who was drinking her coffee in the staff room while reading the newspapers, and had just asked, while hardly giving him a glance:

— Is he the new odd-job boy?

The young woman had said yes and added nothing more.

Page had gone into Grant's office and come out a good hour later, accompanied by the boss of the label. They had crossed the main office, and then gone up the spiral staircase which led to what Daniel had taken to calling the forbidden room. It was a room which was double locked and to which only certain people had the key. It was evident to everybody that this room hid something fishy and was used for some clandestine activity linked to Swan Song Records. Nobody really thought that it involved fraud or any criminal activity. No, it was more a case of some sort of occult business, in association with the Devil.

Daniel had tried to question Unity who, of all the girls, mainly secretaries, working for the label, was the one with whom he got on best. But the young woman had pretended not to know anything, or perhaps she really didn't know what went on there. But that day, Daniel was surprised that Unity McLean was not only already at work, but that she asked him almost straightaway to go upstairs with her to help clean the room.

— Just the lad I need, she greeted him. I thought you were never going to get here. There's work for you to do.

Daniel just smiled at her.

— Guess who I saw this morning?

— I don't know.

— Bob Marley.

— Oh yeah? Cool.

Unity was the daughter of a former English cricket star. Her father had got her into a job as a secretary at CBS where she had worked until 1975, forging friendly links with several celebrities who regularly haunted the studios. She had notably been very close to Johnny Nash, one of the Jamaican's protégés, whose cover of *Stir It Up*, one of Marley's titles, had ensured his fame. Unity wasn't just your common or garden secretary. She knew people and had even invited Keith Moon to her wedding. Daniel liked her ability to mix with people, her conversation, and her slim legs.

Unity was exactly the type of girl he would have liked to marry, sparkling and full of energy. To him, she was the incarnation of the best that swinging London had to offer. But she paid him no attention. No attention of that sort, at any rate.

— Stop daydreaming, and come with me.

She led him upstairs and took him to the reception room which was open and devastated. The furniture was overturned, pushed back against the walls. The floor was covered with rubbish, glasses, paper and what looked like hair cuttings. In the middle, was an eiderdown with a red and brown blood stain of twelve inches or so in diameter. Daniel was taken aback.

— What's been going on here?

— Nothing serious, don't worry. There are things that it's best not to know about.

Daniel moved forward to have a closer view of the blood stain which, having dried, was no doubt less impressive than it must have been a few hours before. The sheet was stained by what appeared to be a mixture of faeces and semen. A little further off, he discovered the head of a chicken and on the other side of the room the corresponding body stuffed with hmmm.... On one side of the room the place was littered with condoms, some full and others half emptied onto the floor, on the other side there were little bits of aluminium foil, blackened spoons, and fag ends. On the wall, somebody had drawn esoteric symbols, a stylised he-goat busily sodomising what looked like a sort of giant snail with pear-shaped tits.

Daniel didn't utter a word. Unity opened a big bin liner and began filling it with everything that was lying around. She rolled the sheet and the eiderdown into a ball, stuffed them into another bin liner and told Daniel that he should take them to his mother's. He nodded and helped her to get rid of everything that was more or less compromising, and would have prevented the char ladies from cleaning the room.

— You wanna take the chicken home with you? He laughed, waving the headless animal about.

Cleaning up took a good half hour. Daniel used soapy water to erase the sodomite goat from the wall. It had been drawn with a mixture of shit and lipstick and actually stunk like a real goat. Daniel asked Unity why there were just the two of them this morning and why there was nobody else around.

— I don't think anyone has the heart to work at the moment. You know that Jimmy didn't go to the kid's funeral. He just didn't go. You know what that means?

— For the band?

— We don't know the ins and outs of it all, but if you were someone's best friend, don't you think that you'd go to his son's funeral, if he died?

— Suppose so.

— Well, only John went. And Peter and the others of course. But not Jim. That says a lot about their relationship.

When they had more or less finished, Unity made sure the door was closed, while Daniel took the bags of rubbish downstairs. They both came back to the main office to make themselves some tea. The kettle had hardly started whistling than the door opened. It was Jimmy Page. He looked terrible. He was livid and carrying a guitar in a dark case.

— Is Peter here? he asked, without so much as a hello or anything else.

— No, there's nobody here today, Mr Page, replied Unity politely. Daniel pretended to busy himself with brewing the tea. He secretly hoped that Page would not even notice his presence.

— Make me a cup of tea.

Page didn't even bother to take off his leather jacket. He sat down on the sofa and pulled the guitar from its case. He began to strum on it quietly as you do when you just want to pass the time. He played a traditional series of chords which he often altered after the second or third time by inserting a note which shouldn't have been there. As if he were looking for something. And evidently, he was looking for something.

— You can sit down, you know. I don't bite.

Daniel and Unity settled into an armchair next to him and sat back to wait patiently for the tea to brew. After maybe three minutes, Unity poured the brown liquid into the cups. Page was still playing. They listened in awe. Daniel had made huge progress on the guitar and watched Page's fingers running over the neck of the instrument. He played with a delicacy and an agility that Daniel was far from capable of. His own movements were clumsy and sometimes he missed the strings with his fingers or didn't manage to hold them down completely. Page allowed the tea to cool for a few minutes before setting aside the guitar and sipping it slowly without a word.

Daniel thought that it was almost impossible to be surrounded by people for so long without saying anything. It was something that he'd never managed to do. He thought of breaking the silence, but didn't dare. Unity got up to go to the toilet. Page took up his guitar again and then he stood up and left the offices of Swan Song Records.

Later, Daniel would pretend that they had discussed things together and that the two of them had had a jam session. He would tell this story in the course of two or three interviews, but with nobody there to check it out. On another occasion they were even supposed to have spent the evening together and had a few drinks. What would Jimmy Page have thought about *14th Floor*, the first song that Daniel had written? Would he have seen some merit in it? Nothing is less sure.

In one single day, he had encountered Bob Marley and Jimmy Page. And there was no getting away from that.

THE KIDNAPPING OF PAUL MCCARTNEY

— You all sure you wanna go? It's gonna take us ages.

— We don't even know if he'll be there.

In the gang, nobody really remembers who thought up the idea. Daniel knew that it was him, and that he had managed to get the others to accept it without seeming to be interested. That was his technique. He would suggest things and go off somewhere after having said enough for the others to take the idea on board and then be persuaded in the end that it was their idea. That day, there were John, Gerard, Joe, Edward and finally Daniel. You might say it was the Oratory gang as they had all gone, or still went, to the Oratory School situated a little way off. But it would have been an exaggeration to consider them as forming a gang. They indulged in no illicit activities, apart from smoking cigarettes and drinking the occasional beer, playing music, and talking about girls in a great conspiratorial fashion. They were at most a group of friends, just boys, not quite yet men, but nevertheless with ambitions in life, dreams and everything which goes along with them.

— Quite honestly, remarked Gerard, I don't see how we're gonna manage it. There will obviously be folk around and we don't have no plan to speak of.

— Gerard is right, went on John, in the same tone as his brother. It's obvious that it's not gonna work. You tell 'em, Joe, they'll listen to you.

Joe said nothing. He was the most intelligent boy in the gang, the brainiest one, the one who was a good scholar and the most reasonable. The future would prove it in a certain way. But Joe often reacted slowly, as if the problems submitted to him were not of sufficient substance for him to resolve them straightaway.

— That's why we gotta do it, explained Edward. Do you wanna write songs or not? McCartney must 'ave a secret.

— Yeah, let's stop talkin' about it and let's go.
— I ain't even got a bike.
John and Gerard had one bike between them and Daniel and Ed the same. Joe trotted along behind them. Their plan was simple. They would ride to Saint John's Wood, hang about outside 7 Cavendish Avenue, wait for Paul McCartney to come out and, when he turned the corner, they would surround him and take him to some waste ground on the corner of Wellington Road and Circus Road, to interrogate him.
— You got the masks Daniel?
— What masks?
— The masks for God's sake. Don't tell me that you 'adn't thought about that. D'you want us to be recognized?
— Sorry.
— Stop looking for excuses not to go. It's the middle of August. There won't be nobody around the Hospital, interrupted Edward. Get pedallin' instead.
Joe was having trouble keeping up. He was already trailing more than a hundred yards behind when he waved to indicate that he was giving up. He thought a moment about taking the bus to Regent's Park, but he preferred to go back home. His instinct told him that this escapade would lead to nothing. He didn't want to ruin everything now that they had just passed their final exams a few weeks earlier and were about to start earning their living. The Bennett brothers had been taken on in an armoury. He was still looking for a job. Daniel had not turned up to take the exams. He had left school a few months earlier with the blessing of his parents. He had done odd jobs, worked for charitable associations and other businesses. None of them had any idea what to do with their lives. They all liked to play music and laze about. Daniel and Ed wrote songs but they didn't know what to do with them at that point. They liked sitting there at the corner of the street, watching the world go by. You have to admit that they were well

placed to witness the changes taking place in Britain. Cavendish Avenue was at the other end of the world, a couple of steps away from the Abbey Road studios. Their universe was populated by stars and personalities. They had already come across Anita Pallenberg and Keith Richards, Brian Jones, and a few others. Ed's aunt was friends with the daughter of Mervyn Peake, the writer, and everybody knew exactly where Syd Barrett lived when he came up to London.

Getting to Paul McCartney's house was another matter. You had to cross Hyde Park from south to north, skirt around Paddington Station, via Little Venice and then head in the direction of Saint John's Wood. It took about an hour and a half, and was a journey with which they were not very familiar. Despite their bravado, the five friends, now reduced to four given that Joe had let them down, were a bit diffident this far away from their stamping ground. They were exploring unknown territory. The cars seemed more aggressive than on the King's Road, where people drove slowly in order to admire the mannequins and the shop windows. Around Paddington, the streets were narrower and the whole world seemed to be closing in. The people themselves were not as flamboyant. Everything seemed dirtier and damp. It was not a question of social class. The people were just not as cool. They were normal, workaday, and not so good looking.

They stopped several times to get their breath back, smoke a cigarette and have a drink of water. It was a fine August day. There was no rain and the sun made a few shy appearances from behind the lofty clouds.

— And what if 'e ain't there?

— Well, we'll leave it at that.

— And what if 'e comes out wiv a friend?

They had no means of knowing whether Paul McCartney was even in London or away on holiday. The former Beatle had bought the house at 7, Cavendish Avenue in 1965. He had moved in in 1966, taking an opposite stand to the other Beatles who had deserted the centre of London in order to isolate themselves and live far from the madding crowd. McCartney had chosen to do the reverse, as he had fallen in love with this three-storey Regency style building, which wasn't up to much on the outside, but which he had adapted to his tastes over the years. Evidently, the first stage had been to enclose the house by a wall and to equip it with a security system which sheltered the musician from the persistent solicitations of the public. He'd had a few changes made later on, some fittings, a small extension to the rear, but nothing which made it very different from what it was when he'd bought it. Cavendish Avenue had never been turned into a bunker. McCartney had regularly allowed photographers in and you could see him in the garden with his family, if you stood at a spot slightly overlooking the wall.

Daniel and Edward had had long discussions about what they'd do with McCartney once they'd got their hands on him. They had thought of several ways of getting him to reveal his secrets of composition, the most efficient of which was to remove his heart and brain, to render them down in a liquidiser and then drink the juice. They'd thought at one point of cutting off his hands and having them grafted in place of their own, on the basis that it was the hands that composed the melodies and that it was quite probable that even grafted onto another body, they would still remember how to write songs. The memory of hands. Transubstantiation. According to their research, it sounded like a workable plan. They didn't have a car in order to take McCartney out into the country and interrogate him. They didn't think that coercing him into composing masterpieces was a viable method. To tell the truth, they weren't at all sure that their plan had any chance of success, and so they were relieved when, approaching 7 Cavendish Avenue, they saw that the street was crowded with people, cars and journalists mounting the guard.

— Oh shit, exclaimed John. Looks like it's gonna be complicated.
The four boys dismounted and leant their two bikes against a wall. They got their bottles of water out of their rucksacks and took a swig sitting on the pavement.
— Sod it. Looks like we ain't chosen the right day.
They looked at each other in disbelief, their eyes bulging with the effort of getting there. Something must have escaped them. The street was crowded with people. There were vans from the BBC and other major Northern networks, one from an American network and journalists with perches and muffed microphones waiting impatiently, their eyes fixed on the front door of number 7.
— Do you think he's dead?
— Nah, said Daniel. There'd be undertakers. Something else must be up. In any case, the kidnapping idea is done for.
— Just as well.
— Defeatists.
Ed plucked up his courage and moved towards the house, clearly determined to know what was going on. The three others followed him. Their hair was awry and stuck to their heads with sweat. Their shirts were open and the bottom of their trousers still rolled up to prevent them catching in the bicycle spokes. Ed went up to one of the journalists and asked her what was going on.
— Elvis, she replied. Elvis is dead.
The four boys looked at each other while moving towards the house, weaving in and out of the groups of avid journalists.
— They're waitin' for a declaration from McCartney. That's all.
— Elvis, for God's sake
As they made their way, a journalist held up a microphone to George to interview him.
— Are you a fan of the Beatles?
— Yeah, replied George, slightly dazed.
— What does the death of Elvis Presley mean to you?

— 'e was fat 'n flatulent. Partic'ly towards the end. But 'e was Elvis Presley all the same.

They burst out laughing. Fat and flatulent. That was it all right. What did they care about the death of Elvis? And what would happen, now that he was dead? Everyone could play rock music. Daniel had known for some time now that you only needed a few quid to release a record, and that for little more you could record for hours in a studio, and you could do all that even if you hardly knew how to play. That would be the aim now. He'd had a guitar now for what? Six or eight months, not much more. That was no handicap. Elvis couldn't play anything either after all. All the same, it was a pity he was dead. Daniel's father did a good imitation of Elvis Presley. His mother enjoyed his records and he was convinced that she had fallen in love with his father partly because one day he had done his imitation of Elvis for her. Just for her. It was true that his voice was irresistible. Elvis's that is, not his father's, even if his imitation, which he sometimes did at a few well-oiled family meals, was a pretty good one. Perhaps there was an idea for a song in all that. The day Elvis had died, she had cried her eyes out, because it reminded her of when she was young and when her lover had sung just for her like Elvis Presley. Her love had died now, and Elvis had taken his leave too. Life's a bitch.

They waited for more than half an hour to see how things would turn out. Whenever journalists stopped them for an interview, they all said the same thing. "'E was fat 'n flatulent. Partic'ly towards the end. But 'e was Elvis Presley, all the same". They all thought that it was the most brilliant analysis of the subject.

Just after four o'clock, Paul McCartney came out of the gate to his house and went up to the journalists to say a few words. He was wearing casual clothes, a white short-sleeved summer shirt and a pair of cream canvas trousers. They moved closer to get a better view of him, but he was surrounded by the crowd of journalists. McCartney related one or two anecdotes about the day that Elvis had invited the Beatles to his house in Hollywood. It was twelve years ago, day for day. The Beatles had been on a promotion tour of their film Help! which was about as bad as the junk which Elvis had been appearing in for years. Elvis had welcomed them in person. He had just said "Hi guys" and they had drunk whisky and *Seven up* (Elvis loved *Seven up*) on the biggest sofa they had ever seen, a sofa as long as a freight train. Then Elvis had played *I Feel Fine* on the guitar and had more or less forced them to play along with him. They had played each other's songs out of respect. The ones who knew how to play the guitar at least, and that had lasted all evening and a part of the night, playing, and drinking *Seven up*, talking among equals. At that time, the Beatles were more fashionable than Elvis, who no longer produced anything noteworthy and had decided to put an end to his public appearances. This meeting was more than just handing over to a successor. Some have said that Elvis dreamt of working with the Beatles on a whole album, but that Lennon had told him where to get off. Fat and flatulent towards the end.

Elvis is dead. Long live Ringo!

You could see such placards at the time and laugh at them. It wasn't so funny now that Elvis was really dead. But there was a place to be filled.

So, it was time to go home and start working on it seriously. They got on their bikes and told themselves that perhaps the idea wasn't such a good one after all. The kidnapping of Paul McCartney had been a fiasco, even if it had taught them a thing or two all the same.

— I know where Syd Barrett lives, laughed Daniel on the way home.

— And David Bowie.

— And Malcolm McDowell.

GEOFFREY INGRAM (1)

Geoffrey Ingram was not the easiest of the protagonists in this story to track down. This was as much due to the fact that he was a fictional character, as to his absence from public life since the end of the 80's. In his own way, discreet and benevolent, Geoffrey Ingram nevertheless remained in permanent contact with Daniel Treacy since their first encounter which can be traced back to around 1974, until the years when the singer effectively vanished from the scene (we'll come back to this episode later on), that is to say between 2000 and 2005. Geoffrey Ingram and Daniel Treacy were in touch with each other for three decades in the most discreet and almost secretive manner, so much so that none of Daniel Treacy's friends or relations was able to give me the slightest information either about how close they were, or estimate the importance of the relationship between the two men beyond the title of the song that bears the name of the protagonist and which figures in the Television Personalities' catalogue. Geoffrey Ingram is portrayed very advantageously and seemingly endowed with almost supernatural powers which allow him to defy the laws of nature (such as the rain) and the rules of society (such as gaining access to *select* places).

Once I managed to locate Ingram, everything was obviously much easier. The man is now aged 64 (don't ask me why he's only 64 despite being aged something like 20 in the early 60's) and was paradoxically delighted by the fact that I had gone to some trouble to find him, and pleased to see me. It's more exact to say that he invited me to meet him one evening at his club which is situated at the exact location 40 years ago of the former café-concert, The Living Room. The Living Room is a place which has a certain importance in the history of the Television Personalities, as the band played there several times when it was starting out. It was precisely here that the Scotsman, Alan McGee, met Daniel Treacy and also Joe Foster, and precisely here too, that he created the style of promotion which would enable him later to found the Creation Records label and to launch successively the careers of such important bands as the Jesus and Mary Chain, Primal Scream or, much later, Oasis. The fact remains that Geoffrey Ingram was patiently waiting for me in a sumptuous and exaggeratedly wide armchair when I arrived. He was sitting a little forward, his legs crossed and his chin leaning to the side to indicate how much he was relaxed and pleased. You could tell, even in this position, that his lanky silhouette had not got the slightest bit stouter in several decades. He recommended me a cocktail based on gin and guava juice, which was probably the most delicate and delicious drink that I had ever tasted until then, before launching into the story of his acquaintanceship with Daniel Treacy. Geoffrey Ingram spoke with a clear and perfectly London accent. His voice had not changed much since the film by Tony Richardson in which he appeared alongside Rita Tushingham. She was juvenile and boldheaded, full of authority, demonstrative and yet at the same time, infused with a sensibility that made her captivating. To tell the truth, Ingram didn't seem to be any more of a queer than he had been thirty years earlier. His long hands waved about in the air when he spoke and he had a few pouting expressions which might have given him away, but nothing indicated that he had become any more exuberant or effeminate than before.

Daniel contacted me in 1974 if my memory is exact. It was at that time that he had first seen the Tony Richardson film, an adaptation of the play by Shelagh Delaney. *A Taste Of Honey* had a considerable impact on many adolescents in those days. It's something I can't explain, because the film came out in 1961. It was very successful at the time, but it was actually twelve or fifteen years later when its revival began to make a real impression on kids like Steven Patrick Morrissey and Daniel Treacy. It's possible that their living conditions, which had slumped with the economic crisis and were certainly not likely to get any better, found an echo in the film: the poverty, the black and white environment, the carefree yet cruel and ultra-realistic world of the kitchen-sink dramas. Daniel Treacy had both an idealised vision of the 60's, the music of which he adored, and a good perception of the reality of that period: life was difficult, but not necessarily as violent and aggressive from a political and social standpoint as it would be later on. We didn't have all today's mod-cons and I think that Tony Richardson managed to portray that perfectly in the film. Above all there were lots of aspects that were going to take shape later in the Punk movement: the assertion of the adolescent girl or the young man when they discover their sexuality, the place of the woman at the centre of the game, the synthetic beauty of working-class culture and the urban industrial landscapes, the distress of being excluded, all these things. Manchester and London were not such cool places as they are today, you know. When we first met, Daniel was surprised that I was still the spitting image of Murray Melvin, the actor who plays the GI in the film.

"How can it be possible? was his first question. In twelve years, you haven't changed."

Daniel didn't know that fictional characters don't age in the same way as real people. We drift easily into forgetfulness, but age has no real grip on us. Our facial features are moulded by the memory that the public retains of our most significant roles. Age is only one aspect of our make-up among others.

I know that's what you were thinking when you saw me in this armchair. "This bloke must be over 70 now, yet he seems barely 50." Am I right? We laughed, because he referred to the *Picture of Dorian Gray* by asking me if I had a portrait at home somewhere that got older instead of me. I said: "Naturally, I'll show it to you someday if you insist". And then he talked to me about what he wanted to do, about his music and his passionate interest in films of the early 60's. I think I disappointed him in that respect. It's

not as obvious as all that in the film, but I am not necessarily an extremely modern chap. I am liberal, cultivated, whatever you like, but I've never had any particular liking for what Daniel and you certainly call the "alternative cultures". Technically, I'm a war baby, you know.
— You were already a doctor when you met Daniel Treacy?
— Yes. I finished my internship in 1973. It was long after the end of the film you know. A pretty bad end, I'm sure you'll agree, as far as I'm concerned. I disappear and everyone seems to be happy with that.

I tried to remember the last scenes of the film. Helen, Jo's unworthy mother, who is heavily pregnant by an American sailor, finally achieves her goal. No doubt thrown out by Peter, her companion, Helen turns up at Jo's with the intention of moving in and lashes out at Geoffrey. She inundates her daughter with advice and attention, but doesn't succeed for all that in getting her to abandon her friend. In the end, it's Geoffrey who comes to a decision and moves out while Jo is asleep. He slips away in the dark with the intention of protecting his friend by not standing in the way of a possible reconciliation with her mother. And that's the end of the Geoffrey Ingram character and his friendly shoulder.
— A strange ending, you're right. What did you do next?
— I studied medicine. I patched up things with my own family and then I left Manchester for London. It did me a world of good. I got married in the late 60's and even had two daughters.
— Married?
— I know. You find it hard to believe too, don't you? Oscar Wilde was married as well. And he had two magnificent children, just like me. It's something that you could imagine doing at the time. I have no regrets whatsoever. Women have the most astonishing grace and intelligence, don't you think?
— Of course. It's just that I didn't see you as being married.

— It lasted fifteen years. I even had time to cheat on my wife with a woman she was friends with, if you want to know the whole story. Daniel laughed himself silly at that, at the time.
— What about Rita Tushingham?
— She was a charming girl, but she was nothing like Jo in the film, you know. Her father had three shops, grocery shops, I think, in Liverpool. Neither she nor I were really working class. That's what creates the style of the film. We stood out from the crowd.
— How did your relationship with Daniel Treacy develop?
We talked quite a lot about *A Taste Of Honey* during our first meetings. He was very respectful and asked me a lot of questions about the 60's, about my life, what I'd done between the film and let's say the rest of my existence. He was surprised at the very idea that I could have had a life other than this role. He was looking for that original aestheticism. He wanted to understand. And then our relationship evolved. He talked to me about what was important to him and we quickly became friends. I mean real friends. He would ask me for advice. I was a little older than him. I moved in very different circles. My profession as a doctor brought me into contact with people about whom he knew practically nothing: middle-class people, dignitaries. I lived in West London. Despite the fact that it was quite close to his home ground, Daniel had a complex about his origins, his shyness. Just the opposite of me. To him, the middle-class was the incarnation of England and its traditions, but it was an environment to which he was denied access and which frightened him. In all modesty, I was his role-model and his guide. I think he expresses it well in the song that he dedicated to me.
— Did he tell you about this song before performing it on stage?
— No. He gave me a copy of his band's first record. That's where I heard this piece for the first time.
— What did you think of it?
— It made me laugh quite a bit. The vision it gives of me is exces-

sive. You know what character it makes me think of? Gladstone, you know? Donald Duck's lucky cousin. The one who gets everything without trying. He finds money lying in the street, or stoops to pick a four-leaved clover. He avoids disaster. He is very well-dressed. He's always perfectly at ease in society.

— Is there any truth in all that?

— Yes. I consider myself to be lucky. Life has served me well, even if like everyone I've had my share of problems. It's true that I got Daniel into the Marquee for a concert by The Jam and that really impressed him, as the tickets had been sold out for ages. But there was nothing magic about it. One of the bouncers happened to be a friend of mine, if you know what I mean. Would you care to have dinner with me?

— I don't know. I wouldn't like to put you out or take up all your time.

— That doesn't bother me. They haven't had a chef here for the last ten years or so, but they do quite good salads.

Geoffrey Ingram summoned the waiter who was hidden behind a partition and ordered a Caesar salad for each of us. He was really a very refined and elegant man, and I could easily understand how Daniel Treacy would have fallen under his charm.

— You know that the song was inspired by one of the Kinks' titles? Of course. I'm very fond of Ray Davies. Daniel told me everything about this song and I think that to some extent what happened between us, must have been similar to what happened between David Watts and Ray Davies at the time, even if, of course, Daniel and I were neither school mates nor of the same age.

The Television Personalities' song *Geoffrey Ingram* embraced fairly closely the rhythm and lyrics of one of the Kinks' minor successes dedicated to one of Ray Davies' school mates, on whom he had probably had a crush, or at least for whom he had had great admiration. Ray Davies would say later that this was not the case, but that David Watts, which was his real name and who now worked as a concert organiser, had been attractive to him because he had always led a gilded life. David Watts was gay, by the way, and was said to be in love with Ray's brother Dave.

Geoffrey Ingram is really a song "in the manner of". Some consider, because of this similarity and a few other borrowings, that several songs by the Television Personalities are clearly inspired by the Kinks. What is certain is that Daniel Treacy was an unconditional fan of the band and its chief composer. It may also be that he had been familiarised with the Kinks' song, which nonetheless goes back to 1967, by a revival of it by The Jam, in 1978, in the album *All Mod Cons*. It's an amusing piece, as the lyrics are sung by Bruce Foxton, the bass guitarist of the band and not by Paul Weller, the usual vocalist.

— Under what circumstances did you meet up with Daniel again after that?

— It was usually he who contacted me. By telephone most times. He would call my surgery or drop in on me unexpectedly …

— Were you his general practitioner?

— No. I examined him only once and it was long afterwards. He was already suffering from all his problems. I had found him extremely tired and he had asked me to give him an honest evaluation of his general state of health. He thought that the other doctors were lying to him and that he was not in such bad shape as all that. I told him that his days would be numbered if he carried on as he was doing.

— That was in what year?

In the late 90's, perhaps. It wasn't a good time. Besides, he vanished shortly afterwards. We would usually see each other in a pub, or here at the club. We would spend the evening together or go to a concert. Daniel liked to go out every night. He liked to go to exhibitions, to the cinema. We shared a form of cultural bulimia. He talked incessantly about films from the 60's and anything to do with music, obviously, from the great classics of the past, to all the contemporary pop. I couldn't always follow him on that subject but you should have heard him talk about *Ray Of Light*.

— Madonna's album?

— Yes. He adored *Ray Of Light*. He talked to me about it for hours after its release.

— You always talk about Daniel in the past tense. When did you stop seeing him?

— There were several times in his life when he stopped coming to see me. Maybe he was ashamed at certain moments or perhaps it just didn't cross his mind. And then he would turn up again and things would go on as before. We would talk just as if we had seen each other the day before, you see. I remember once when he came and rang my doorbell. One of my daughters answered. The younger one. She must have just turned eighteen at the time. There was Daniel on the doorstep and my daughter called me because he was in a dreadful state. He was filthy. He fell into my arms in tears. I think that he had just gone through a romantic break-up. He was homeless. He spent the evening at my house. It's the only time I ever really helped him out. He asked me several times to give him prescriptions, but I never wanted to get involved in any of that. I'm not Doctor Benway.

— Have you seen him recently?

— A few months ago. But we weren't able to talk as I'd have liked to. He could hardly recognize me.

— Did you know that on certain sleeve notes, Daniel had written texts signed Geoffrey Ingram?

— No. But I'm not as surprised as all that. When you are friends with someone, it's often because that person embodies a quality or something which is lacking in yourself and which you envy in a certain way. Social skills, audacity, beauty, wealth.

— Is that what you were for Daniel Treacy?

— I suppose so. I was successful in the 60's. I've always been at ease with people. My personal life is fulfilled. Please don't think that I'm being pretentious. In many respects my life was similar to the life he would have liked to have.

— A life of fiction?

— Of course, but they're all like that, these lives that we'd like to live and which we'll never attain. What makes the difference between successful people and the others? Only the depth of their regrets.

Geoffrey Ingram asked me if I wanted to have a cigarette with him in the smoking room. I said that I didn't smoke, but that I would be glad to accompany him. We walked across the club to reach a small comfy room panelled in cherry wood. It looked like a swanky smoker's den, luxurious like everything here. Geoffrey took the pack from his pocket and lit up. His hands were unduly long and white. He held the cigarette by his finger tips and drew on it in a certain mannered fashion.

— I've allowed myself one cigarette a day for the past thirty years. All in all, that's the equivalent of two months' consumption for a chap who smokes a packet a day. Over such a period, the effects of tobacco are harmless and even rather beneficial for the skin.

It was late and we had been talking non-stop. Geoffrey Ingram had ordered me three cocktails and they had made me slightly tipsy. As for him, he seemed just as fresh as at the beginning of the evening.

— You should stop by my house one evening. I still have a lot of memories to share. In particular, I've a few videos which you might find interesting.

— It would be a pleasure.

Thus, he brought our first interview elegantly to an end. I agreed to give him a call when I had made progress with my work. And he disappeared. The atmosphere of the club faded away, so that I found myself in Conway Street in a state of almost total confusion. Before my eyes, the building which had been an aristocratic club a few minutes earlier and which in 1983 had been the venue of one of the first concerts given by the Television Personalities now bore the dashing sign of a modern-day pub: The Lukin, in gold letters on a black background. The locality had become residential and no concerts were allowed in this area. In the past, the Television Personalities had appeared alongside another band, Miles Over Matter, before an audience of about 150 people. Shortly after, the police had closed the place down because of the noise, and The Living Room gigs had had to find another haven in a pub near Tottenham Court Road. When I got home, I did a bit of research into the history of the place and found a few of its former uses. It had housed a folk club in the middle of the 70's called Dingles. After The Living Room, the club had changed its name. It had been called O'Neill's, and finally The Lukin since 2009, in honour of the name of the owner's grandfather. You could also read into this name a play on words "Look In": literally "Come and take a look inside".

The change of venue for the gigs organised by the founder of the Creation record label, Alan McGee, gave an opportunity for the Television Personalities to appear on several occasions before a wider audience, but its lasting renown was mostly due to its having seen the advent in 1984 of The Jesus and Mary Chain. It was in June, the 8th to be precise, in front of scarcely fifteen people, at the same place where, in the summer of 1965, young Davey Jones had auditioned before manager Ralph Horton, accompanied by his band The Lower Third. Davey Jones would later take the name of David Bowie and everybody would forget that he had ever played in this place. That's the way things go, they overlap.

PART TIME PUNKS

August 1977

There were few who instantly realised that the incident between the Sex Pistols and BBC presenter Bill Grundy was one of those decisive moments which define a cultural era. Daniel Treacy was one of them.

The first single by the Television Personalities was released at the beginning of 1978. Daniel Treacy had noted a few months previously that certain relatively unknown bands that appeared in clubs on the punk scene had managed to find their way into studios and record titles for next to nothing. That's how he started looking into the cost of hiring a studio and brought his schoolmates round to the idea that setting up a band would enable them to make good use of their spare time, now that the majority of them had left school. It was obvious that they'd soon get fed up with the jobs which they had each found for themselves, and that the life mapped out for youngsters of their age by the dying labour government of Welshman James Callaghan, was a dead end.

The end of 1977 was a busy time. The little gang is working away, operating almost simultaneously in several different configurations. Daniel and Edward are probably the first to record a single consisting of two titles: *14th floor* and *Oxford Street W1*. Daniel had borrowed eighteen pounds from his father to complete the outlay necessary for this first session. According to what he would say later, the owners of the studio ripped him off and made him pay a bit more than what was due. These were not strictly speaking punk songs but you can feel the same vengeful energy and that disabused clarity with which society is viewed. *Oxford Street* is a song which emphasises the rejection of the way of life associated with the middle classes, referred to almost constantly as a "phoney" life, made up of "phoney jobs" and "phoney love". The scansion is half sung, half spoken and characteristic of the solemn and peremptory tone of the punks of the day. The melody is simple but executed enthusiastically. *14th Floor* attracts attention much more acutely because the lyrics are constructed in a more original manner from the standpoint of a narrator perched on the fourteenth floor of a block of flats. At the time of the recording, Daniel Treacy and his family were living on the King's Road in a tower block quite similar to the one described in the song, but only on the 7th floor. Flat n° 26. From this height, daily life seems quite small, crushed by the perspective, and a dead-end. The song harbours no anger and expresses perfectly in two minutes the sensation of imprisonment of the lower middle class. Daniel Treacy briefly describes the neighbourhood: neighbours that he doesn't know, the presence of a Jamaican "who could just as well have been an Irishman". Here resides the punk resignation, but above all the preoccupation with social realism that Daniel Treacy imports directly from the cultural universe in which he is immersed: punk music naturally, folk music from the 70's, but also British cinema. From the outset, the vision is quite strange: the depiction is on ground level, in black and white. The text is full of allusions, but precise and refers explicitly to the lives of the protagonists.

The jacket of the single is concocted scrap-book fashion from fairly coarsely sliced-up newspaper cuttings. The single is signed Teen78, which presumably is the name of the band. On the same layout appears the title of two pieces, *14th Floor* and *Oxford Street*, but also a few adverts including one for a gay dating phone line. The record bears the handwritten signature of four people on the left of the jacket.

N. PARSONS
B. FORSYTH
H. GREENE
R. HARTY

The names are difficult to make out. The record is published in limited quantities and sold in local shops. A test sample is sent to John Peel, the already well-known radio presenter who is the only major DJ to dedicate a prime-time slot to alternative music. In 1978, John Peel has been hosting his own show on Radio 1 for almost ten years. His show has changed formats several times before coming back to something rather classic and original at one and the same time: it's a show where, in some respects, the presenter is the hero, a show where his own tastes are the subjective but accurate benchmark of what is to be broadcast. The DJ has ousted those colleagues who had initially been put to work with him when the radio was launched and imposed an ever more personal format where he presents a diversity of music, including even some poorly-regarded styles such as reggae and hip-hop and of course punk, which he gallantly supports. John Peel programmes the song *God Save The Queen* by the Sex Pistols, despite a ban by the BBC. He was the first to broadcast the song *Anarchy In The UK* a few months earlier and now he has between his fingers this sort of home-made record, the A side of which he is to broadcast and praise to the skies. We can assume that Peel listened to both pieces a little earlier in the day while preparing his programme. He knows exactly what is at stake and has perhaps already given some thought to the record's creators.

"It's an oddity, but the record is signed in pencil by Nicholas Parsons, Bruce Forsyth and er ... Russell Harty. It's marked Teen78. But these are obviously television personalities. From West London, the Television Personalities".

The band has got itself a name. On the other side of the radio set, hardly a few hundred yards away, Daniel Treacy has a smile on his face. This is it. Peel has broadcast the song, with a favourable commentary. The orders are going to come pouring in for sure. So, his own band will be called The Television Personalities. It's a good name and Daniel is delighted. He's Nicholas Parsons, Ed is Bruce Forsyth. That's how it'll be. There's no question of them thrusting themselves into the limelight or unveiling themselves. The mystery is part of the promotional campaign and would be kept up for a whole year when the first requests for interviews and meetings with the Press (well, let's say punk fanzines, articles by students or enthusiasts) were to start coming in. Daniel Treacy would miss no opportunity to introduce himself as Nicholas Parsons.

In 1978, Nicholas Parsons is 58 years old and one of the most popular men on British television. He would carry on broadcasting for more than 60 years with his flagship programme called *Just A Minute*, launched in 1967, a sort of rather comic chat show in which Nick interviews actors and entertainers. The guests are invited to talk on a given topic for a fixed period of just 60 seconds, hence the name of the show. Nick featured in the Benny Hill show for three or four years. He hosted light entertainment shows in the style of *The Price Is Right*. He is an incredible ham that people have warmed to. A special programme to celebrate his 50 years of broadcasting was mounted in December 2017. It's reasonable to suppose that Daniel watched it from wherever he is living. Nicholas Parsons is a lively 94-year-old man. He doesn't seem in a hurry to step down.

Bruce Forsyth was not so lucky and died in the summer of 2017, aged 89, which is not as bad as all that. He had one of the most remarkable careers in British television, to the point of featuring in the Guinness Book of World Records as the male TV presenter having had the longest entertainment career in the world. His moustache and white toothy smile, his slightly idiotic look, are very much part of the period. But which period in fact? Bruce Forsyth is an entertainer, a comedy actor known as much for his one-man shows as for his hosting of emblematic television game shows in the 80's. Ed Ball is Bruce Forsyth. The capitalist presenter with white teeth and short on ideas.

The Bennett brothers are doubtless the two other television stars. Hughie Green is a TV game show presenter and an incredible womaniser, with the look of a sales representative, who happens to be the grandfather of, you'll never guess who: Peaches and Pixie Geldof. His own daughter would discover, only once she was an adult, the name of her father from the tabloids. Russell Harty is a well-known interviewer specialising in cultural gatherings. In 1972, Daniel remembers the day when Harty interviewed Marc Bolan then at the height of his fame, flamboyant and magnificent. Marc Bolan is sitting in a fireside chair and Harty asks him where he will be and what he will be doing in forty or sixty years' time. Bolan runs his fingers through his hair and replies:

— I don't think I'll live long enough to give you an answer.

The moment is deliciously melodramatic, but Marc Bolan would die before reaching his thirtieth birthday in September 1977. His death had a huge impact on the British cultural scene. Such things happen. At about the same time, that is to say in the autumn of 1977, Russell Harty did a second interview of French star Claude François with whom he is on the warmest terms, since having publicly emphasized the fact that the song *My Way* popularised by Frank Sinatra and written by Paul Anka, had been largely inspired by the Frenchman's *Comme D'habitude*. Much later, Russell Harty would be pilloried in The Sun, accused of having contracted the hepatitis that would kill him in 1988, by hiring the services of young boys.

This first broadcast of the single on the John Peel show marks the launch of the Television Personalities' career. At least, that's the official version. The single of *14th Floor / Oxford Street* runs up sales of several hundred copies. 847, according to some sources, which enables Daniel Treacy to cover his costs, a fact which he proudly announces to his parents. His father, of Irish origin, and who knows the value of money for having grafted all his life, is impressed by the manner in which his son has handled this business. He wouldn't have bet a halfpenny on the success of the undertaking and has to face the facts: Daniel is not just a dreamer, but has a real talent for writing.

After the first broadcast of the single on the 11th of May 1978, John Peel does a second one the following August. The show is celebrating the first anniversary of the death of Elvis Presley. Well, how about that? The broadcast of the Television Personalities is preceded by that of *Ça Plane Pour Moi* by Plastic Bertrand, a song which the DJ doesn't dwell on. Peel explains that he would have liked to have played the title *East Sheen* by "O" Level, the band formed separately from the Television Personalities by Ed Ball and the Bennett brothers, but that it includes a swear word which prevents it from being played on this network. He moves on quite quickly to the Clash and *Jilted John*, an extremely popular parody pop band which Daniel Treacy found quite pleasing. Behind *Jilted John* lurks the shadow of Graham Fellows, writer of a cycle of second-degree songs where an adolescent John is deserted by his girlfriend for a guy called Gordon who is "better looking, cool and trendy", a sort of moron version of Geoffrey Ingram. John Peel is the first to play *Jilted John* and to extol its merits. He does it so well that Fellows is then signed up by EMI International which transforms his first song into a hit reaching fourth place in the British charts.

Impressed by the success of this first attempt at making records, Daniel Treacy's parents provide him with the funds to record another title. Daniel goes back to the studios and records a song inspired by the encounter between Bill Grundy and the Sex Pistols. On the A side, he adds a second title, *Part Time Punks*, which remains to this day the band's best-known work. *Happy families* and *Posing At The Roundhouse* complete the EP. Just like the first time, Daniel makes a miscalculation. He underestimates the recording costs and studio expenses. So much so, that when he leaves the Shepherd's Bush studios with two test copies under his arm, he has absolutely nothing left with which to pay for the production of the records. Undeterred, he nevertheless sends a copy to John Peel who would have fun with it on the air. On the 20th of December 1978, Peel does a first broadcast of one of the songs on the EP: *Happy Families*. Less than two weeks later, he programmes the second title on the B side, *Part Time Punks*, which he would play again four times in the twelve following months.

"It's a pity that the band couldn't release the title properly", explains John Peel to the listeners. "It's a one-off pressing. In two copies. Good luck to you". On the sleeve there is an address which he reads out. Daniel Treacy gets a few telephone calls after the first broadcast. *Part Time Punks* has made an impact and is an immediate success. The song is awesomely evident, intelligent, mocking, and full of wit and irony, the sort of qualities which would characterise many of the Television Personalities' subsequent releases. To tell the truth, *Part Time Punks* is an amusing song, and this would haunt the band for the rest of its career.

The song mocks what has become of the punk movement. Its decline, which Daniel had lived though on the King's Road, was almost immediate, if you could say that there ever was such a thing as original punk purity. The Pistols brought a new type of animal to the genre, kids from the posh areas, kids dressed up, superficial guys who swell the ranks of a part-time legion, students in the daytime, daddies' boys in the afternoon and operetta punks in the evening and at weekends. Treacy and Ball know their sort by heart. These are the kids who will soon fill the concert halls, transforming an authentic movement of social rebellion and anger into a pantomime for trendy journals. The boss of Rough

Trade is one of the few people who try to contact Daniel Treacy to offer him their services. He discusses things with Daniel over the phone. He's ready to lend the young man the money needed to release the record. Treacy accepts and two days later receives his order for 1000 copies. It's a homemade production. Daniel receives whole box loads at his home for which he and Ed prepare and assemble the jackets with some help from his family. The first 1500 copies are put together by hand. There are four different sleeves which Daniel has concocted himself. On one of them you can see a headless guy in a suit, on another a black square with a glimpse of the Beatles in the background. The most elaborate one features a close-up of Shane MacGowan, one of the first punks and future singer in the Irish punk folk band, The Pogues. Only a few days after the first order, Rough Trade asks for another 1000, and things don't stop there. *Part Time Punks* is technically one of the first independent phenomena, the first "home-made" single to sell more than 10,000 copies.

The Treacy household is in turmoil and the requests for interviews flood in. Daniel accepts them all but refuses to give his real name. When journalists call, it's always Nicholas Parsons who answers. Rough Trade is delighted and Geoff Travis, its boss, signs up the Television Personalities for another single. There's no talk as yet of an album. When they cross the threshold of 355 King's Road, the journalists often find themselves facing a fifty-year-old man.

— Nicholas Parsons?

They know perfectly well that this bloke in a shirt is not the television presenter. They also know that it's hardly likely that the man who has opened the door is the one who has written *14th Floor* or *Part Time Punks*. The man greets them politely and then turns towards the corridor where he calls out in a calm and composed manner:

— Son, your appointment has arrived, as if he were some sort of butler.

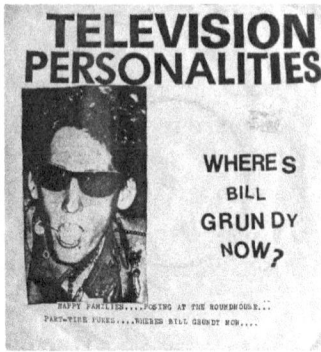

— Thanks dad.

Daniel Treacy's father is a road construction worker. It's the modern term which underlines the technical aspects of this difficult job. You have to know how to drive machines and implement complicated processes. In English at the time, they called him an "asphalter", a bloke who spreads tarmac on the road in all weathers and sometimes after dark so as not to hinder people's comings and goings. Daniel Treacy comes out of his room, guitar in hand. He is frail and seems two or three years younger than his 19 years.

— Nicholas Parsons? asks the journalist

— If you say so, smiles Daniel. I've shaved off my moustache.

Daniel has got into the bad habit of answering journalists with absolute honesty. These guys who come to see him seem quite pleasant and most of them seem to harbour the best of intentions. All his life he would stick to the idea that the Press were on his side, and that journalists were friends to whom he could confide his bouts of depression or health worries. They are the ones who make people famous. In some ways, this slightly naïve attitude would not cause him any harm. The Television Personalities would never be famous enough to find themselves in the eye of the hurricane. Those who were to come and see him, after the early years, would do so because they liked his work and would turn a blind eye to the peripheral details.

Daniel talks about the beginnings of the band, Joe, Ed, the Bennett brothers. He talks about punk culture, the London Oratory School and everything which we already know, spicing it all up with half-truths and real lies. John Peel, Led Zeppelin. At the beginning of the story, there is no real story as yet. When Daniel has finished his account, the guy facing him has a moment of hesitation.

— And what if you became a huge pop star, he asks the kid, just to clear up any doubt. What then?

Daniel laughs and then the butler knocks at the door with a mixture of deference and authority common among the press attachés of Hollywood stars and says to his son:

— Daniel, Mum's home. It'll soon be dinner-time.

The kid says "Dad, not now".

He turns back to the journalist and concludes:

— You can write that my name's Daniel Treacy and that I live with my folks.

CLARENDON HOTEL BALLROOM

The songs had come into being in Daniel's bedroom a few days before each recording session. Ed Ball had been the first to listen to them, in the way bands did things in those days. He had sat himself on the bed, sipping a cup of tea and Daniel had grabbed his guitar and pretended to play in a clumsy fashion, chords which he had already practised well over a thousand times.

Ed and Daniel had really known each other for only a couple of years when everything began. It was a short time, but an absolute eternity on the time-scale of their adolescence. The Ball family had moved from Gloucester Road to Beaufort Street, just a step away from the Treacys' flat, which had strengthened their ties. Within their group of friends, Ed Ball and Daniel Treacy could easily seem to have very different temperaments, even if they had a number of things in common such as having developed an immense musical culture and a deep-seated taste for the cinema.

Edward was a born leader and was constantly urging his friends to develop new experiences and projects. He wrote songs at the drop of a hat to provide material for their practice sessions. Edward wrote plays, regularly gave them draft outlines of projects which would mostly never see the light of day, instructions for them to do such and such, or work towards some goal or other. Daniel was the very soul of discretion. From his earliest youth, he only mixed with others to find shelter or a little solace. Daniel was often silent or pensive, which didn't stop him from writing succulent little texts, short stories full of life and humour which were the admiration of almost everyone. Daniel worked alone and was less inclined than the others to seek the approval of his mates. They had completely different creative modes. Edward liked to be in the limelight and lead the debate. Daniel only sprang into action when he felt the need to, and the rest of the time he stayed in the background. But this was no obstacle to his determination and intransigence. Ed and Daniel had two very different ways of knowing where they wanted to go and how to get you to follow. To his friends, Daniel had always seemed to have an intriguing side to him, and to be possessed of a strange abstinence which made you feel that he harboured a contagious melancholy.

At school, Daniel was shy and introverted, on the rare occasions when he attended, that is. According to the files of the London Oratory School, he reached the summits of truancy during his last school year, setting a record in the matter, according to his schoolmates. Yet, Daniel was by no means a mediocre pupil. He was simply incapable of concentrating enough during lessons to obtain good results. His essays in literature and humanities were top of the range, without him having to make any special effort, and testify to his doubtless above-average creative talents. He had mathematical skills that many of his schoolmates would describe even years later as prodigious. Daniel was particularly gifted in arithmetic and solving problems. But most of the time, he chose not to go to school, to such an extent that, having attended for once, his teacher, a certain Mrs Crouch, had taken it into her head to introduce him as a new pupil. So the teacher said:

— Now boys and girls, we've got a new boy in our class today. He's called Daniel and I'd like you all to make him welcome.

Daniel smiled. Mrs Crouch had simply never clapped eyes on him, or, if she had crossed his path once or twice, had never sufficiently noticed his presence to recognise him as one of her pupils. It was a fine result for two academic years. After two sessions, he had vanished again. Daniel was too busy with everything that was happening outside the school walls. There were such goings-on in the streets and so many things to see. Since 1976, the police had regularly raided certain pubs which were havens for punks and junkies, especially the Roebuck whose boss, Fat Jack, had only one eye and was a bald as a coot. The cops would come charging in from Chelsea and surge in a huge wave of 50 or 60 units, leaving a trail of destruction in their wake. After they'd gone, the ground would be littered with rubbish. You could find drugs hastily thrown away before the onslaught, but also trendy clothes and loads of other things worth gleaning, abandoned by the poor routed punks. The King's Road was such an inspiring world, that school seemed to have very little to offer in exchange. There was a strange atmosphere, however. People of different generations mingled together. Daniel Treacy's eye was particularly attracted by the subtle sedimentation of the cultural and historical strata, and by the way in which one movement or moment in time was swept away by another.

If the country had been suddenly submerged by a volcanic eruption as was Pompei, archaeologists a thousand years later could have scraped away the crust of lava and managed to identify traces of Swinging London, a sort of golden age of elegance and recklessness, traces of the declining and ridiculous hippie movement, now reduced to its most garish and grotesque attire, and traces of punk, scarcely more robust. They would have dug out trendy suits and bags, inherited from old Victorian fashion, and all of this would have suggested that not only all these signs of human life had perished at the same moment, but had occupied for an instant the same time-span. Could some men have seen the dinosaurs? Had the punks, hippies and mods joined up in downing a few jars together at one point? Had they talked about life and black-and-white cinema? Had there been love affairs and brawls between them?

Witnessing these changes alarmed and worried Daniel. You could say that this feeling of the fading away of fashions and eras reminded him of his own mortality. His anxieties were all linked to the passing of time, to the way in which he himself was getting older and thereby being divested, by this mysterious draining phenomenon of age, of everything which he thought to possess someday. Daniel Treacy was nostalgic for his childhood toys. He was nostalgic for the 60's, even though he had never lived through them. He was nostalgic for old television series, but also for the 1001 ways in which the inestimable riches that were music, Elvis, pop, books, poetry, TV and film stars had thrust themselves upon his young adult life. Daniel Treacy was nostalgic for his mother's face and the look which she would bestow upon him when he was four years old. He was nostalgic for his father's outbursts of anger and the littered streets. He was nostalgic for the small shops and the colourful clothes that people used to wear. He sometimes even felt regret for the punks who had disappeared as quickly as they had sprung up. Daniel was a mod before being a punk. He was a mod before the others were mods, devoted to a culture that had become obsolete almost before it was invented. The first mod wave had died out between 1967 and 1968. It had been ousted by the hippie movement, before re-emerging, in a different form, almost ten years later, in the wake of the expiring punk movement. Who really cared anything about these movements and what name they went by? There had been a time on the King's Road, when the lines were blurred. Daniel belonged to that time. He was just as much psychedelic as he was mod, or rock or punk. He was everything and nothing all rolled into one. He was serious, yet frivolous as the wind. He liked to laugh and cry at the same time. He liked melodies and downright noise. His gods were the Kinks and the Velvet Underground. He preferred the Byrds to the Sex Pistols, at least that's what he would have been prepared to swear to under oath in order to avoid Joe Foster sticking one on him.

The Television Personalities would sing of nostalgia and loss, but also of the pleasure of first experiences. Daniel would be the eternal child who sadly suffers the vision of death before his eyes and blocks out the beauty of the world. Their works would stand as a great history of modern times, a testimony for future generations to surroundings which had passed on and to the sensations and the imprint which they had left in men's recollections.

After the success of *Part Time Punks*, Daniel had signed up with Rough Trade, but seemed to have lost a great deal of his interest in music, or either had been faced, in his own way, with a minor crisis of inspiration. We can't be certain, nor can we say that there was an eternity between the release of *Part Time Punks* and that of *Smashing Time*. The recording of the tracks which make up the band's third record was done at the end of 1979 in London and would take place several months before the release of the band's first album. It's likely that Daniel was already under a lot of pressure and that he had difficulty in shouldering it. But his talent as a composer prevailed over his doubts and enabled him to fuel what was seemingly to be a promising work.

Smashing Time, Daniel's new song, is like a post-card or one of those nostalgic memories that we tote around for years on end. The narrator relates in a rather trivial fashion devoid of any serious issues, the weekend spent by his cousin Jill, who has come up to the capital for a few days. The singer lists the local attractions during an excursion as magical as it is stereotyped and unsurprising. Between Mme Tussaud's waxwork museum, the London Dungeon and the Tower of London, everyone is agreed on the incredible nature of this moment spent together. A Smashing Time. The trip ends with ice-creams in Hyde Park and a little stroll, that is also described as fabulous, between Carnaby Street and the King's Road. As in his previous pieces, Daniel suggests that this enchanting vision of London, since it is too good to be true and reserved for folk up from the provinces, is not as real as it appears to be. As in previous works, it's not the singer, nor the song itself, which lifts the veil on the reality of things, but rather the suspicion aroused by the far too innocent form of the picture painted of it. One of Daniel Treacy's recurrent approaches would consist in giving, through the music and the lyrics, a glimpse of things which he would almost always refuse to reveal in full. This technique would be used again much later in the famous song *I Know Where Syd Barrett Lives*, the mechanism of which would rely precisely on the hypothetical revelation suggested by its title (a revelation which would be made only once, on stage, and in an inevitably scandalous manner). A pop song is always at its best when it gives the impression of hiding a secret.

The flip side of the single *King and Country* brought about a major change for the band. The track was sinister. The rhythmic section and the singing kept up a semblance of gaiety, but there could be no mistake: it was clearly a gloomy song. We can't totally discard the possibility that Daniel Treacy was inspired by his own father, who had served in the army, but the vision of veterans conjured up by the narrator and the expression of their war memories is a typical throw-back to the hippies' antimilitarist theories. The song is a perfect example of balance between the vision full of respect for the soldier carefully burnishing his medals and putting a gloss on his glorious deeds, and the questioning of the young man (perhaps his son?) who watches him and can't understand what it's all about. The revelation comes quite quickly when the song suggests (even though it's only a simple question that is posed) that the veteran wakes up at night screaming, for he had no doubt turned and run off in the midst of the battle. Did the hero really exist other than in his own version of events? Does his story have any other purpose than that of masking fear and dishonour? *King and Country* is a chilling song and the perfect counterpoint to the flippancy of *Smashing Time*. The single sold moderately well, but didn't make the headlines. The B side, which nonetheless illustrates the rich diversity of Daniel Treacy's topics and his growing ambition, went by totally unnoticed. In the run-up to the release of their first album, The Television Personalities remain associated with the frivolous and bitterly ironic image of their first singles. What is expected of them is that, as in *Jilted John*, they criticise with a smile and denounce the sham world with typically British spirituality and touch.

Behind the scenes, the gang of five is bubbling over in turmoil. Different groups continually come together and disband to such an extent that nobody really knows who plays with whom. The Bennett brothers have a central role and take part in almost all the gigs. The Television Personalities, "O" Level, Teenage Filmstars. Joe Foster is never far away and everybody is busy releasing singles. Ed Ball pursues his own interests. 1978 and 1979 are wonderful and confused years. But just like the others, Joe Foster wonders what Daniel's real motives are. The singer is both the most ambitious and the most reluctant when it comes to consolidating his position. Nobody can understand why Daniel has not taken better advantage of the breach opened by the unexpected success of *Part Time Punks*. It takes Foster a few sessions of persuasion to convince Treacy that the time has come to get down to the practical work and to give a concert at last.

— We're a studio band, Treacy replies at first.

— A studio band? Your sound is lousy Dan, and you do everything single-handed. You ain't no studio band. Don't make me laugh. You ever listened to any of the Beatles' records?

— You gotta point. But doin' a gig is useless. Nobody will come and we can't even play.

— Nobody c'n play. Could the Pistols play?

Foster is afraid to say that he thinks his friend is scared shitless. Something holds him back, the idea that if his hand were forced, Daniel could easily skyrocket and drop everything. After much insistence, Treacy agrees and, as he was to do later on behalf of Alan McGee, Joe takes matters in hand.

A first concert is planned at the Jeannette Cochrane theatre, a hall run by the Central School of Art and Design, which hosts gigs and other events likely to interest the students of that London establishment. Ed Ball and the Bennett brothers are not available for the concert and seem completely taken up by the work on the *Teenage Filmstars* recordings. At Joe's suggestion, the band enrols young Mark Sheppard on drums. Barely 16 years old, Mark Sheppard is the son of a relatively unknown British actor who has appeared in TV series such as Star Trek or MacGyver and had minor roles in a few films. Mark is a young musical prodigy who, at 15, already had a technique which many professional drummers might envy. Once embarked on the fabulous adventure of the Television Personalities, he is immediately confronted with a supernatural world which he would later revel in during his Hollywood career. As a member of the band between 1980 and 1983, Mark Sheppard would effectively follow a rather unusual path. Drummer for the Television Personalities, then for other artistes such as Robyn Hitchcock or The Barracudas, Mark

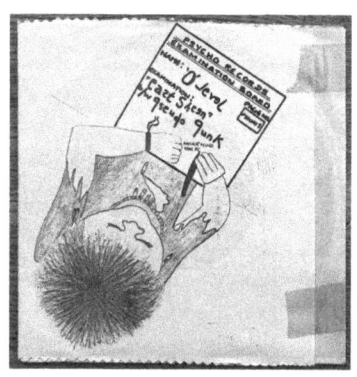

Sheppard leaves for the United States at the beginning of the 90's and reinvents himself as a television and theatre actor. He becomes fairly quickly a star of TV series (*Battlestar Galactica, Supernatural, X-Files, Warehouse*) and has a multitude of appearances and roles in several productions, notably those of Joss Whedon, a close associate of his (*Firefly, Dollhouse*). He still has a successful career and now leads a quiet and flourishing life in Hollywood with his second wife, Sarah Louise Fudge, the rich heiress of an Australian family mining business.

On the stage of the Jeannette Cochrane theatre, Mark Sheppard, Joe Foster, and Daniel Treacy are overawed. The audience which they had imagined to be small has changed into several hundred attentive observers. The concert has attracted quite a few fans from the ranks of the punks and no mercy will be shown. The show is enhanced with ropy lighting effects and slide projections which the band has prepared in order to divert attention from themselves. But things go awry. The sound is bad and Daniel is swiftly overcome with dizziness. He is incapable of singing and struggles to hold the centre stage. His guitar lapses into silence. Nobody remembers the songs that were played that night. Joe whispers into Daniel's ear:

— What's goin' on?

And the singer heads for the wings. Joe goes back-stage to try and bring him back, but Daniel has already left.

— I think some geezer spiked my drink. I've been drugged. That fucker put acid in my drink. I'm seein' things. My 'ead's spinnin'. I can't go back on stage.

Joe doesn't know which fucker is supposed to have done that. Daniel points to a Yankee waiter with a crew cut, wearing the sort of white tee-shirt that American athletes wear. It's fairly unlikely, and it makes no real difference to the situation.

Daniel is as white as a sheet. He's having one of those off-days, a mixture of distress and feeling out of touch with reality. It's one of the first occasions on which he adopts that posture of withdrawal into himself which would become a habit with him many, many times afterwards, as if he were trapped in an infinite dialogue with himself, locked up in a personal made-to-measure prison. Daniel gets up and makes a quick exit from the theatre. Joe and Mark go on with the concert as a duo. Ten minutes or so later, the singer Jowe Head looks in and realises that the two men are finding it hard to hold down the audience. The atmosphere is electric. Daniel Treacy has been gone for a long while now. He and Jowe Head had met two years before. Jowe Head, the brothers Nikki Sudden and Epic Soundtracks and a few others form a group with variable contours called Swell Maps, the first records of which, released at the same time as those of the Television Personalities, had attracted Daniel's attention. *Read About Seymour*, one of their leading songs came out in 1977 and two years later, the Swell Maps reached number 1 in the independent charts with their first album *A Trip To Marineville*. In 1978, Daniel had invited Jowe Head to come and see him, so he turned up for a cup of tea at the family flat. It was their first encounter. At home. Jowe Head and Daniel Treacy find that they have much in common. They both like fragile voices, childlike characters and that mix of musical dilettantism and self-confidence backed up by a booming bass which would become characteristic of the music of their respective bands, and then become a reference for the DIY movement, (that do-it-yourself music made with few resources and played as if at home). Jowe is struck by Daniel's shyness and modesty. He can't believe at first that this guy has the ambition to lead a band towards success, and even less that he has worked for those raging madmen called Led Zeppelin. And then he is won over by Daniel's determination and soon perceives the energy and conviction lurking behind the contradiction. This guy is not at all what he seems.

Faced with the three or four hundred impatient spectators, Jowe Head and Nikki Sudden have no intention of letting their colleagues sink further into the mire. They come on stage and do what they can to help Joe and Mark calmly finish their set. The Television Personalities' first show, if it can be called that, given the absence of Daniel, is a fiasco and a disaster.

Joe doesn't waste time in trying his luck again and the band is scheduled for the 22nd of May 1980 at the Hammersmith Clarendon. Built in the 1930s, the hall is part of a hotel complex, the Clarendon Hotel Ballroom, the architecture of which is in remarkable Art Deco style. The building would be completely demolished in 1988 to make way for a shopping centre. Immortalized in the album *Paisley Shirts & Mini Skirts*, the Television Personalities' performance is much more convincing than the first one, which is hardly difficult, and positively impressive if you think of it as their first concert. The three men play it safe. Joe is on bass guitar, Daniel is lead singer and guitarist and Mark is on drums. The set lasts almost 50 minutes, which is fairly long for the time, and includes thirteen songs, some of which will never be performed again. The record which was to immortalize what became, historically, the first real concert given by the Television Personalities, comes out in 1995, devoid of any other information. The Overground Records label confirms a little later, that it is at the origin of this rather unrefined release (the sound is anything but perfect) but which is so important for the fans. We can assume that the tapes were handed over directly by Daniel from his private stock at a time when he was on the look-out for easy money to finance what you might call his "life-style". The jacket of the record is magnificent. Entitled *Paisley Shirts & Mini Skirts*, the vinyl disk is presented on a red background, in the centre of which is a black and white photo of a smiling, long-haired, sexy young girl wearing shorts, taking a kick at an old-style football. The setlist is remarkable and bears witness to the already formidable repertoire brought together by the band on the basis of its three official singles. Between an amusing version of "*Frère*

Jacques, dormez-vous?", entitled *Hello Edward*, Daniel lines up half a dozen instant references such as *I Remember Bridget Riley, La Grand Illusion, Magic Playground* and, already, the song *I Know Where Syd Barrett Lives*, which we will come back to later.

The concert is enhanced, like the previous one, only more successfully, by the projection of various arty gimmicks, which immediately place the band in a very different universe from the one in which punks or post-punks roam at the time. The Television Personalities are unrefined, but sophisticated. There's no mistaking it, such are the pains that Daniel has taken to plant his cultural markers all over the place. Alongside Syd Barrett and the traditional London references, you find a subtle and nostalgic reference to Bridget Riley, a painter aged 45 at the time, and who was known for her works based on geometrical motifs, often in black and white, usually associated with the Op Art (as in Optic Art) movement. Bridget Riley, apart from being a painter who quits the scene in 1970 to go travelling, is a pretty dark-haired young woman of iconic beauty when she emerges in public with her first exhibitions in the early 60's. The homage paid to her by Daniel is discreet and sincere, interwoven with the drama and charm of past celebrities. The song is the first of a series of portraits which would be made of obscure figures of British cultural life: black and white actors, past and present, from the world of television, painting, cinema or, like that pretty secretary Christine Keeler, involved in political scandals.

Late in the evening, with *Girl On A Motorcycle*, Daniel offers one of the most beautiful pieces on the setlist, in a similar register. The song refers directly to a film entitled *La Motocyclette* in the French version which features Marianne Faithfull and Alain Delon in a story filled with eroticism and chrome. Faithfull's character, Rebecca, is married to a boring, pale figure of a man. One night, she slips a full leather combination on over her underwear, straddles a gleaming Harley Davidson, and roars off to meet

her lover (called Daniel and it's a fortunate coincidence) played by Alain Delon, who at that moment is in Germany. Presented in the official selection at Cannes, the film directed by Jack Cardiff, is an adaptation of an erotic novel by André Pieyre de Mandiargues. Caught up, however, in the midst of a social and political crisis*, the festival is interrupted and we shall never know whether the film deserved an award or not. The dramatic issues are tenuous, but the erotic issues between the two actors, Delon and Faithfull, sublimated by her leather outfit, are phenomenal and, fifty years later, are still well worth watching.

The concert is a triumph. The band immediately imposes its unique character and, despite a few hiccups, due more to stage-fright than the still quite approximate dexterity of its members, brilliantly reveals a world composed of phantoms of the 60's, of still-born dreams of glory and an insidious form of sadness. The music is lively and betrays a willingness to drive headlong into a wall with a smile on your lips. *Magic Playground* is a song with irresistible romanticism which can be linked as much to British psychedelia as to Lewis Carroll. At intervals of several years, Johnny Marr and Morrissey would each revive, with much greater success, the ingredients put together by Daniel Treacy on his own: the aesthetics of the 60's set up as a model of nostalgia, the borrowings from the major figures of pop art, the obsession with celebrity, art for art's sake and the infra-cultural references. No band could afford to leave aside such an unbeatable song as *It Had To Happen*. It seems however, that that was its one and only performance. This fatalistic song could have had its importance but, like many of the Television Personalities' other creations, would be forgotten once performed. Daniel has no memory for his compositions. And this would only get worse over time. Some

---

* Translator's note: The protests in France of May 1968

are lost, some are forgotten, and he sometimes massacres the ones which he remembers. But it's not out of negligence or stupidity. For him, music refers to the present moment and to movement. The truth is, that music is nothing other than an unstable moment in time.

With these first two concerts, Daniel Treacy really becomes himself and, whether consciously or not, defines slightly better the ambitions which he has for the band. From now on, the place of the Television Personalities will be here: between two moments in time and at the heart of emotion, a perfect alternative structure to everything that exists, predictable and precarious, but also brilliant and indispensable.

...AND DON'T THE KIDS JUST LOVE IT

The record is the band's heartbeat. It's the band's reason for living and what fixes its place in history. The record is the alpha and the omega: it's what unifies and captures the moment. In the Television Personalities' history, the record will have served many purposes: first to come into being, then to bear fruit. Later on, the record is also a means of keeping the band together and continuing to exist, before becoming simply an odd way of paying off debts, buying drugs and repaying friends. The record is the real owner of the songs. It has the power to be immense and to change people's lives, but also to make a laughing stock out of you, and go unnoticed. The record is hope and disappointment. It's the instant and the moment rolled into one. The record is the singer's rival. It robs and annihilates him.

It's possible that towards the middle of 1980, the idea of recording an album for Rough Trade represented something important for Daniel Treacy. In all likelihood, Daniel prepared himself for it in his own way, by accumulating enough items so as not to be lacking in raw materials and by practising the songs enough times on his own for them not to have any secrets for him once in the studios. Many think that the Television Personalities' first album *...And Don't The Kids Just Love it* is their best and most significant one. It's probably the one for which they are still best known and technically, the one which brings together the greatest number of their iconic songs. From an artistic point of view, it is a total success, starting from the jacket down to the last note of the record's fourteen songs. Daniel Treacy shows that the whole of Britain can fit into a nutshell, as the saying goes, of some 37 minutes or so.

The success of the record relies on a mix of several things which we have already mentioned: the punk dynamics, a pop benchmark "substrate" which is tremendous and largely borrowed from the 60's, but also a production technique which was new at the time and which can be deemed to be a precursor of the lo-fi movement and more widely of all that would become the intimistic and electrified pop music of the decades to come. It's always quite simple to underline everything that is good in a record with the benefit of hindsight, but the originality of ...*And Don't The Kids Just Love it* speaks for itself. Let's just remember the age of the protagonists playing on this record and the perfect compatibility between the music and what it says about the period to which it belongs. Daniel Treacy is only 20 when most of these songs are written. Mark Sheppard is barely 17. These are kids from West London who have almost no experience and have hardly ventured beyond their own back yard. They have been fed on memories and witnessed the Fall of the British Empire over a span of just a few short years. Margaret Thatcher now occupies 10 Downing Street. The steel works are closing down and the first strikes are hitting the headlines. Month after month, unemployment reaches unprecedented levels since the post-war days, whilst monetarist policies drain the country's consumer economy. Charles and Diana aren't yet married and John Lennon has been assassinated the previous December. ...*And Don't The Kids Just Love It* is released against the backdrop of a heap of rubble in the making. The album is the assertion of the British stiff upper lip and a collapsing soufflé. You discover it, like entering a secret passage, through the expression of harsh and brutal latent anger, *The Angry Silence*. The genial band of the early days has disappeared, and only peeks its nose at you again on the B side. In the meantime, the father shouts at the mother and threatens to pack his bags and leave; the brother is anorexic, the sister is a barmaid in a club. The teenager is afraid to leave his room and wallows in poetic love for a girl who doesn't share his feelings. For Daniel Treacy, the family circle is psychotic and doomed. *"It's hard to disagree in today's society"* Daniel sings.

"Can you hear this angry silence?" The Television Personalities' music maintains a certain rhythm and dynamism which lighten the pessimism of the lyrics. The bass is buoyant and the percussion as light as a drum roll. The production is deliberately slapdash and clipped. Drowned out by the sound effects, the vocals are distant and often scarcely in tune. *Glittering Prizes* talks about starting out in working life and the boredom which quickly besets everyday existence. Anyone who has listened to The Smiths will be surprised to see that the TVPs chart the same seas as Morrissey, but several years ahead of time. Here, the expression is more direct, less glorious and incarnate. Daniel Treacy embodies the youth of the day who are devastated and sacrificed, before even having started to live. All resistance is futile. You can see it in the tragic fate of Pauline Lewis, an unknown teenager with such a British name, found dead on her bed, curled up alongside her dreams. The song is like a fairy tale gone wrong, where nobody can wake up the princess. Lost in her imaginary world, the young girl dies, like an inverted Narcissus, drowned in her own reflection

after looking at the photo of a sophisticated model in a fashion magazine.

The World Of Pauline Lewis is the first of a series of portraits of drifting young women, seductive and fragile like pre-Raphaelite spectres. These Lolitas run away (*Silly Girl, La Grande Illusion*) or flee from a dull husband (*Girl On A Motorcycle*), but rarely find happiness. In such escapades, it's rather the feeling of liberty and risk-taking which is expressed, be it at the cost of an unfortunate outcome. In *A Family Affair*, Daniel Treacy keeps up the festivities with a deceased husband, a mother whose children have been taken into care and another young woman ditched by her boyfriend because she is pregnant. The conclusion is summed up magnificently: *"I telephoned God today. But all I got was the answering machine. Please help me."* This one verse summarises the band's whole story. God's answering machine, of course. A gigantic telephone call during which humanity records its miserable existence in one aesthetic and transcending act which scoffs at itself.

Daniel Treacy's irony and the determination of the musicians prevent this first album by the Television Personalities from being weighed down and despairing. Its impeccable jacket serves to remind us that it's only a game, a pop-art smoke-screen and a reconstruction of reality through the prism of the author's artistic sensitivity. For the illustration showing Patrick McNee, star of the *The Avengers* series, and the top-model Twiggy, Daniel delves into the archives of a famous photo session of the 5th of January 1967. Directed by the renowned photographer Terry O'Neill, the session with Twiggy aims not only to promote the 5th season of the well-known show which would be screened a few days later, but also to promote the collection of clothes by Alun Hughes and Pierre Cardin, worn by John Steed and Emma Peel throughout the series. Twiggy's skinniness is perhaps no longer the fashion today, but the photo session (filmed by British Pathé for a documentary) is a moment of infinite grace. Other celebrities such as the racing-driver Graham Hill (Damon's father), the weight-lifter George Manners and the boxer Billy Walker are also brought in to broaden the cast. We can't say whether, when choosing the album's cover, Daniel had access to other photos, or, as is likely, the photo simply appealed to him as being patently pop, while leafing through a magazine some 10 years later. By her second notable appearance on a record sleeve, after having adorned David Bowie's *Pin Ups* in 1973, Twiggy acquires a kind of iconic trendiness which would stand her in good stead during her come-back in the 90's. It's effectively hard to imagine anything more glamorous and truly British than this standard-bearing cover, which instantly gives a lighter touch to the content of the album.

The flip side opens up a new landscape of hope, where happiness can be obtained by recourse to imagination or good fortune. One or two magical reminiscences take us back to the innocence of childhood and an escape from an unduly grim reality. Geoffrey Ingram's luck is proverbial. The emblematic figure of Syd Barrett, half bewildered father, half Peter Pan, hiding out on his mountain, his whereabouts known only to us, seems to want to redeem men's sins. With *Jackanory Stories*, Daniel conjures up the world of Lewis Carroll in which the stories we make up are the fabric of real life. Only imagination and art can redeem the world and propel daily routine into a sort of alternative reality. The mansion-cum-art-gallery of the *Picture of Dorian Gray*, with its paintings and cucumber sandwiches, is like the Grand Meaulnes' enchanted house. In the course of its adaptations, Daniel would embellish it with various traits each more marvellous than the others. *...And Don't The Kids Just Love it* ends as it begins in raised voices. In place of anger, you now find a sort of regret and repentance, the notion that a purge has taken place and you can move on and go back to the real world and have a good time (*Parties in Chelsea*). *Look Back In Anger* is a gentle song, devoid of all animosity. It is the perfect conclusion of an album which is more of a hatch-out than a blow- out.

...*And Don't The Kids Just Love It* receives a few mostly lukewarm reviews which criticise the poor quality of the recording, the out-of-tune vocals, but recognise the quality of certain songs. The critics recognise the pertinence of the lyrics and certain brilliant bits of repartee, but consider the slow or mid-tempo songs to be more or less botched. Several years would go by before what was considered to be a fatal flaw would come to be seen as a quality. Little by little, the album is re-evaluated and deemed to be an essential landmark in the evolution of post-punk music by the future idolaters of so-called anorak pop. This term generally refers to people literally obsessed with a single subject and for whom each detail gives rise to an in-depth study. The *train spotters*, the first examples of such nerds, would hang about on British station platforms spending hours peering at their surroundings, like cows watching the trains go by, dressed in ... anoraks. The anorak became an analogy for a fan of independent music, capable of mobilising all his energy into dissecting the work of some obscure band, or snubbing public radio to pick up pirate offshore broadcasts on some makeshift device. The anorak is as much the symbol of fans of indie rock music as it is of a sort of avant-garde geek or Otaku. The movement would be particularly widespread in Scotland and the North of England from the middle 80's until the emergence of Brit pop. In this very ritualised world, Treacy's obsession with pop culture personalities becomes a testimony filled with unsuspected riches, giving rise to the systematic detection of all the references to be found in his work. In this respect, ...*And Don't The Kids Just Love It* is an album which offers an almost unlimited playing field stretching from its jacket to the literary or cinematographic origin of almost all the tracks. What with Renoir (*La Grande Illusion*), Geoffrey Ingram, *The Picture of Dorian Gray* and Syd Barrett, but also *Look Back In Anger*, the title of a work by gay playwright John Osborne, or *Diary Of A Young Man*, the title of a TV film directed by Ken Loach in 1964, and *The Glittering Prizes*, a novel by Frederic Raphael about the lives of Cambridge students, Treacy turns his songs into a treasure hunt strewn with Easter eggs (Mary Quant, designer and creator of the mini-skirt is mentioned in *Pauline Lewis*) and a form of name-dropping which would delight both *diggers* and fans of intertextual references.

The album sells moderately well, but its critical and economic performance is way below the enormous hopes raised by the surprising success of *Part Time Punks*. As often, and not without cause, Daniel Treacy blames Rough Trade for not having promoted the album enough. One or two adverts, a few inserts and that's it. The desire for independence does the rest. The Television Personalities pack their bags and set up their own label, called Whaam!, borrowed from the name of one of Roy Liechtenstein's most famous pictures, painted in 1963 and inspired by the comic book *American Men Of War*. Like a slamming door, Daniel Treacy leaves Rough Trade and turns his back for good on the early days and the carefree time of the first singles.

SEVEN YEARS

Success is no easier to explain than disaster. Neither of them is ever certain. They only come about if you really believe in them and often at a cost of considerable effort. Just like in a game of hide-and-seek or blind-man's-buff, a sound or a glimpse tells you they're there, then they slip away or change their appearance, revealing themselves in the end for what they are: the same sort of capricious conquest.

...And Don't The Kids Just Love It, is an undeniable artistic success, but one that attracts little acclaim, and turns the Television Personalities into a band whose fate would be quickly sealed. The possibility of thunderous recognition slips away almost as fast as it had arisen. Hardly eighteen months would pass between the release of the band's first album and their third (in August 1982) which Daniel would name with his characteristic sense of timing, provocation, and lucidity: *They Could Have Been Bigger Than The Beatles*.

It would take only eighteen months for the show to be over. That wouldn't prevent things from continuing to be taken seriously nor playing with the big guys, but there would be few to keep on believing in the Big Night. Daniel Treacy's attitude towards success is at the heart of the fault lines which split the members of the band, or what's supposed to be a band, at the beginning of the 80's. It's a lucky man who can say what the singer has in mind and what he really wants to achieve. Daniel's level of commitment is obvious, but the success of the first singles seems to arouse in him a sense of insecurity which would long haunt him. In a film about the band made by Swedish TV in 2009, Daniel and Ed Ball are sitting outside a pub discussing rather cheerily the band's early days. Daniel, beer in hand, is relaxed and smiling when, in mid conversation, Ed insinuates that his friend took fright when success came their way.
— It's just a feeling I 'ad, he tells him. That's when your problem started, ain't it?

Daniel Treacy's face crumples in an instant. The expression in his eyes changes.

— No way, he replies. Nothing to do with that. No. No.

The singer gets ups and walks about nervously. He's not violent. Just lost, and in pieces, he shelters behind the miniature palms installed to decorate the place. The smile gives way to a look of distress which, at this precise moment, is not only heart wrenching but upsetting. Daniel Treacy is no longer available for anyone. Shooting is interrupted. Cut.

The first bout of depression comes on at the age of fourteen. Daniel Treacy's childhood was filled with joy and tenderness. He grows up pampered by his two elder sisters and has all the advantages of being the youngest child. The family's lifestyle is modest, but the Treacy's live fairly comfortably all the same. They listen to music. Sometimes they go to visit their family, even travelling as far as Ireland. They enjoy themselves. The 60's float by as if in a dream. Daniel sometimes rides across town on a scooter huddled against the solid and friendly back of one of his family. He likes going fast and feeling the wind bringing tears to his eyes. He sees the London streets rush by and gets high on the pleasures of the town. London is a theatre of pretty women and extravagance. It's an open-air museum which breathes modernity and youthfulness. Daniel likes the lights and he likes the grey colours which glisten in the rain. Reality is like a film. When he recognises the face or the gait of someone famous in the street, he thinks the whole world is famous.

The first episode of depression comes on at school. There's this big lad who insults him and corners him during break. He's blond and built like a Yankee. He's as big as a mountain. Square-jawed, he's called Big Boy, like in the films. There are times when he just says *"Treacy the pussy"* or *"Treacy the laundry"*, a reference to his mother's job. If it were only that. The guy starts bringing dirty socks and underpants which he stuffs with slimy dogs' turds. He throws them in his face, and Daniel is enveloped in the smell and incapable of avoiding the shit-filled socks that bounce off him and land at his feet. "You can wash those for me", Big Boy belches, sharpening his predatory grin. *Brush, brush!. The Laundry!* Few are laughing, but the guy has one or two supporters who clap, and look on with smiles on their faces in case the bully decides to pick on them. Daniel keeps his distance, but the harm is done. From now on he would speak to nobody.

Then one day the bully is waiting for him outside school. Daniel never speaks to him. Neither to him nor the others. Big Boy emerges out of nowhere and belts him one. Daniel doesn't see it coming. He hasn't time to run away. He sees the fist coming at him as if out of the wall. It's a child's fist, but as powerful as a gust of wind. The ambush is perfect. He sees the fist and then the smiling face just behind it. He follows the swing of the arm and collapses under the impact. Daniel passes out for a second or two, before coming to with a pain in his nose which throbs like a heartbeat. He feels as if everything that he has known until now is slipping through his fingers and draining away from him. He's in swimming trunks, building sand castles on the beach. He's holding a spade in his hand, kneeling the way children do. The fist hits him again, but this time as if it'd been propelled from inside. He's opening his presents beneath the Christmas tree. And then he realises what has happened and the recollection of it spreads out there on the ground amidst the others and contaminates his happy memories. Big Boy is gone, but lingers deep inside him. In 2006, it's exactly this feeling that another punch might land at any moment which is expressed in the most explicit song that Daniel would dedicate to this episode. *And Then A Big Boy Came And Knocked It All Down.* The title says it all. Against a backdrop of funereal organ music, the phantom of Big Boy has never been so present, the original bogey man and eternal persecutor.

In the bus which he sometimes catches, Daniel is the prey of other boys acting on orders from Big Boy. The big bully sometimes gets on the bus with them. Whenever this happens, Daniel usually gets off at the first stop and continues his journey on foot. One day, a young woman with an extravagant look who works at the SEX boutique sticks up for him and takes the adjacent seat to protect him. She is four years older than him and there is no ambiguity in their relations, even if he would love to kiss her. Pamela is bigger than him. She is wearing provocative black leather pants with cream knickers over them, and a top with VENUS picked out in silver studs, and dozens of badges pinned all over it. But it's mainly her peroxide platinum blonde porcupine hair-do which makes her supernatural. Her make-up is outrageous with wide bands of colour that trace a triangle from the point of her chin to her temples. She might just as well have come from another planet or out of a Moebius comic book. Big Boy and his gang look at Treacy and Jordan sitting next to each other, as if hypnotised. Pamela Rooke could demolish them with a single look, but her superiority over these young idiots is such that she doesn't even deign to cast them a glance and just turns to watch the street gliding by, taking Daniel's hand in the palm of her own.

— Don't worry, she says to him. I'm here.

He's fourteen, but he's trembling.

— You'll always come across twats like them. They can't harm you. Believe me, they don't even exist.

Jordan's power comforts him, because they've both been through the same things, but Big Boy is never far away, since he's found a hidey-hole deep inside Dan's inner being.

When I'm on my way to work, there are people who take my photo. I've sometimes travelled first class because the ticket inspector wanted to protect me from the mockery of the other passengers. I love travelling first class.

Daniel doesn't have any eccentric clothes. He doesn't understand what difference it makes. He likes to wear a woollen bonnet on his head.

— When I'm at the boutique, I'm a sort of star. There's a guy who's asked me to make a film and I quite often do stage work. That's the place to be.

Her voice is the most comforting thing he has heard in all his life. He still suffers when she is not around.

— You can be whoever you want to be, believe me. Absolutely anybody you want to be.

Then the curse comes back to plague him every seven years. It's the rule. Every seven years Daniel Treacy falls victim to vagueness, a severe depression, a juvenile fear which comes and demolishes everything he's tried to build. If he were a mountaineer, it would be like losing your grip, an inability to cling on and hold the rope. The body would slowly detach itself from the rock face only to fall and suddenly vanish, depending only on the resistance of the rope which ties it to the anchor bolt, or to the rope-team. The possibility of a fall never leaves your mind. Being swallowed up by the abyss is one of the risks that gives things their permanent fragility. Friendly figures like Jordan do what they can to keep Daniel on the straight and narrow and stop him from losing his foothold, but they are not usually strong enough to compete with fate and all that it unleashes. At present, everything happens inside him. The enemy is within, reinforced by all the mistakes, the betrayals and the lies, the failures and Daniel's lost dreams.

The first of these disturbances, following the one caused by Big Boy, comes over him around his 21st birthday. It's the one to which Ed Ball was referring and which, just thinking about it thirty years later, causes that frantic reaction during filming for Swedish television. There would be many others, more acute and lasting. The curse sometimes opens up chasms which engulf

Daniel and isolate him from his friends for years on end. Nobody knows what he does during this time. Better to get high as a kite on drugs rather than let the flaw in your make-up swallow you whole. It's better to get stoned. And that's saying something.

But at this stage, these things don't count for much, faced with youth and the desire to get on with things. The period following the release of the first album is a time of intense activity, the pace of which defies the doubts which assail the singer. At the beginning of 1981, Daniel and Edward set up their own label—Whaam!, which gets off to a roaring start with The Times' first single, then the first offerings of a new band, The Gifted Children, which at the time might well have been thought of as a replacement (in name) for the Television Personalities. The Gifted Children, consisting of Daniel, Mark Sheppard, and the bass guitarist Bernie Cooper, record a few titles which would be later reattributed to the Television Personalities. *Painting By Numbers*, accompanied by *Liechtenstein Girl* comes out in May 1981 and marks the double apogee of the psychedelic era and the band's obsession with pop-art. Whilst in the first song, after having met Frank Sinatra and Andy Warhol, Daniel colours in the whole world, including the Kremlin, the second song describes the beauty of a young girl who looks like a painting by Roy Liechtenstein, before being transformed by sadness into the figure of a young girl who has drowned.

The artist is inspired to paint his picture Whaam! by his years spent serving in the army during which he had flying lessons. The message (a combat plane shooting down another) sublimated by the spelling of the title, is rather ambiguous. Is it, as some think, an anti-war painting after the manner of Guernica, or rather an epic rendition of a victorious battle? From whatever angle, the image is perfect and symbolises wonderfully the dazzling and conquering character of the new label. Daniel Treacy and Ed Ball have great ambitions for Whaam! which should allow them not only to produce with total freedom the music that they write, but also to sell it without worrying about the uncertainties of the moment.

The Television Personalities' time with Rough Trade has left Daniel with a feeling of unfinished business and he is convinced that the label had other priorities and sabotaged the promotion of his last single and the entire album. The label's activity, between 1981 and 1984, given its resources and financial coverage, is a minor miracle which owes everything to the inventiveness and ingenuity of the two men. Devoid of business premises, but with an abundance of ideas, Whaam! would leave a legacy of 15 singles and almost 10 albums, amongst which one or two gems by artists other than the duo. Whaam! would pride itself on having released the first record by The Pastels, *Songs For Children*, or on having discovered (and almost laid to rest) the excellent Jed Dmochowski. The second half of 1980 also sees Daniel make a new attempt at a live concert. Between October 1980 and spring 1981, the band gives a few concerts and plays for the first time on the continent. The adventure begins with Joe Foster and Mark Empire, before the replacement of the bass guitarist. During the mainly British tour in the spring of 1981, Ed Ball completes the trio, whilst The Times fill the first half of the programme. At this time the two men are inseparable. Ed Ball works with Daniel in the studios during the summer in order to record the band's second album, *Mummy Your Not Watching Me*, and accompanies him again in August for a series of concerts in Holland. However, the first signs of strain at the label appear when Ed complains of not being sufficiently consulted on the choice and selection of the bands whose records are released by Daniel. Ball would let it be understood that he thought his friend to be easily led and to have signed up (bad) bands for (bad) reasons. This would result in Ball quitting the label's management in early 1982. The official reason was to have more time to concentrate on his own band, The

Times. In reality, the risky and probably overheating approach, taken by Daniel, could be the real reason why Ed Ball kept his distance, even if he didn't leave the band for good.

Foster replaces Ball, who's unavailable, for a German tour to Berlin and Hamburg, until Mark Flunder takes over as bass guitarist in the autumn. It's at this time that the format emerges of a chaotic and turbulent live band, alongside its more intimate, gloomy, and psychedelic studio version. The album *Mummy Your Not Watching Me* reinforces this feeling of a band torn between different poles of attraction. Released in January 1982, this second album is the label's third release, after *The Gifted Children* and the record made by The Times. It sells a little less well than *...And Don't The Kids Just Love It*, but the operation is satisfactory and profitable for the label, which means that it can carry on with its programme of releases, reinforcing the feeling of freedom dear to the hearts of Ed Ball and his pal. The fans are surprised by the psychedelic aspect of the record. The production is slapdash, yet sophisticated and intricate. The vocals are distorted, garbled, and mixed into a blur, often overwhelmed by the guitars and other echo-laden effects which give an impression of unreality and alienation. There are big gaps between the tracks, so the music breathes and extends beyond itself, a technique seemingly inspired by *Metal Box* sung by Public Image Limited, the band of former Pistols singer John Lydon.

If the first song, *Adventure Playground*, is resolutely attractive and conquering, the next three magnificent pieces generate anxiety and are filled with apprehension. A striking contrast springs up between the Daniel who in: *"To The Adventure Playground / I'm coming out to play"*, bravely announces himself to be the champion of straight talking and risk taking, and the Daniel who carries the burden of the bleakness of his generation and the premature sacrifice of his dreams. In *A Day In Heaven*, Daniel hands the mike to Saint Peter high up on his cloud, and sees a young girl in tears who dreams of becoming a star. It's a heart-breaking picture, full of poignant melancholy. The naive dreams are gradually replaced by more contrasted and sombre visions. The young woman dreams of kissing Charles Manson and admits that she idolises Christine Keeler.

The addition of this new feminine figure to Daniel Treacy's gallery is no accident. The former call-girl became notorious for having had an affair with the Secretary of state for War, John Profumo, whilst being at the same time the mistress of a military attaché at the Soviet embassy. In the midst of the Cold War, the matter is not taken lightly. Alongside the pale Profumo, it's obviously Keeler who steals the limelight and attracts all Treacy's attention. Brought up in a converted railway carriage by her mother and unpleasant step-father, the young girl becomes a model in Soho at just 15 years old. At 16, after several unbelievable adventures, she stands out as one of the best topless dancers in Murray's Cabaret Club and meets Stephen Ward, who is thirty years her elder. The previous year, she had fallen for an American soldier a few weeks before his return home. Finding herself pregnant, she had tried unsuccessfully to abort, before giving birth at home after having concealed her pregnancy with the help of her mother. Her son would die six days later.

Ward is a former osteopath who moves in British intelligentsia circles. He works from time to time on the relaxation of such prestigious clients as Winston Churchill or Elizabeth Taylor, and paints portraits which even hang in the gallery of the Queen's art dealer, Leggatt. He paints Douglas Fairbanks, Sophia Loren, the Prime Minister Macmillan, but also the Duke of Kent and Prince Philip. But Ward is mainly a go-between and an organiser of orgies, specialising in the supply of very young girls for his prestigious clients. The Profumo scandal originates in this way during a weekend arranged in a property belonging to Lord Astor. It is here that Profumo, having indulged his fantasies with several girls

TELEPHONE 673 8228

DANIEL TREACY
WHAAM RECORDS
9, POYNDERS COURT,
POYNDERS ROAD,
LONDON, S.W.4

Dear

Thanks very much for your enquiry about our forthcoming compilation lps. Firstly let me explain our organisation and what we plan to do.

WHAAM is run by myself and members of my own group TV PERSONALITIES, you may possibly know or us. WHAAM is an independent label which manufactures and distributes through the independent network of distributors and shops. This has distinct disadvantages for bands wanting a wider exposure through such channels as radio who are not that keen on independent product. We have so decided to form a subsidary label called METROPOLIS. The idea is to encompas a greater variety of bands and artistes particularly those that may be thought of as too commercial to be considered independent. Our intention is to secure a deal with either a major distributor or label whereby they will manufacture our product. We aim to compile a good compilation album of the most interesting artistes around and then to work more closely with the best of these groups for future releases on METROPOLIS. We have the use of two s top London studios to record in. At this stage we are not intending to spend huge amounts of money on groups. We intend to provide a service for artistes rather than aim to become another huge corporate. We intend to run the new label on the same principle as our independent label WHAAM. On WHAAM we aim to act as a stepping stone for new bands. Our own group have been Independent and producing our own records for a number of years and we have always been able to advice groups from our own experiences. We do not make bands sign contracts and we do not promise silly things. We have the facility to press records and to offer a top promotion service through shops and radios and television. Bands who have benefited from our help include MARINE GIRLS and 1,000 MEXICANS who both went on to sign good deals after having records on WHAAM. Because we do not sign bands and our involvement is short term we insist on bands supplying their own recordings. We do this because the money invested in groups is only usually made back in a long term deal. If artistes believe in their own talent they should be prepared to invest in their own work so let me explain how our compilation will work.

1. Bands will supply their own finished recording, the quality we leave up to you, after all you know what way you want to present yourself. Remember it is basically a demo you are presenting, a good a&r man will be able to assess how a top recording will sound.
2. Each band will contibute £150 towards the album.. we will guarantee that you will receive 50 FREE ALBUMS that you can sell plus 75 PER CENT of profits from sales will be split between the artistes. The album will be offered to foreign labels for possible licensing. A licensing deal usually means the foreign label paying an advance on royalties of between £800-£1,000 plus a royalty of between 12 and 15 PER CENT. There are about twelve possible territories where the album can be licensed. Again 75 PER CENT of all advances and profits will be split between artistes.
The album will be given personally to the top 200 record companies, media people and publishers. It will be promoted at all local and major radio stations by a representative of the I.L.A who are specialists. They will inform us of all airplay received. You will of course receive Mechanical Royalties which are approxiamately £30 per songwriter per 1,000 records w we have pressed. If your song is not published we can put you in touch with a number of publishers who may be interested. We can offer help in an number of ways. We will then invite bands to record on our new label but their are absolutely no strings attached. We are a band ourselfs and the last thing we need is a bad reputation. We do not discriminate between bands. We will work for you if you want us to.
Please do reply if their are any questions.   best wishes /AA

and finding himself in pleasant company falls in love with young Christine. In 1963, the scandal breaks, embroiling evidently the whole government. Profumo makes a bad job of defending himself, but can count on the help of the intelligentsia who, by protecting him, keep the lid on his private deviancies. Ward tries to justify himself by pretending to have organised an exchange of information with the USSR in order to avoid a nuclear crisis. The system closes ranks on him and leaks information clearly implicating him as a pimp. Christine Keeler and a few other young women admit that he paid them as escorts, which hastens his fall. This flamboyant character, esteemed by high society, is sacrificed by his own caste. A few hours before the jury sentences him to fourteen years in prison, Ward swallows barbiturates and goes to sleep for ever. Christine Keeler unwittingly becomes an international celebrity. She would spend a few months in prison for perjury in a grim gang-land shooting and die in relative obscurity after yielding her secrets in several autobiographies. The picture taken of her in 1963 by photographer Lewis Morlay sitting completely naked in a (fake) Arne Jacobsen 3107 chair is so excruciatingly erotic that it would end up (along with the chair) part of the Victoria and Albert Museum collection, in London.

Scream Quietly and *Mummy Your Not Watching Me* complete the gloomy picture. The first song conjures up domestic violence and abandonment. The text is short and sufficiently elliptical to be interpreted in different ways. *"Someone stole her dream today",* sings Treacy. *"She saved it for a rainy day. Scream quietly or the neighbours will hear".* The idea that distress is embodied by a cry that nobody hears or is supposed to hear, is a regular theme in the Television Personalities' works. In *Mummy Your Not Watching Me*, this overwhelmingly simple song which gives the album its title, Daniel evokes the plight of a child who, even as an adult, still seeks the attention of its mother. Frequently performed in later years, the song is often accompanied by words dedicated to the

singer's own mother. The piece refers both to childhood anxieties and to a lost golden age when a child still has the shelter of a mother's love. In 2009 and 2010, the song figures quite often among the titles on the band's setlist. Daniel attaches such value to this piece that he often sings it alone, asking the band to go backstage. Sung *a capella* or accompanied by a feverish guitar melody, Treacy seems to hand out each evening one of the keys to his existence. Surrounded by his family, but no doubt deprived of that exclusive attention he wanted from his mother, owing to the presence of his father and sisters, Treacy craves the attention of the woman who represents the ideal feminine figure, the warmth of the home and unflinching support. Quite often he is unable to get to the end of the song and gives up. *"I try my hardest but I always get sent to bed. I don't know why, that's why I'm crying".*
— Enough of that shit, he often breaks off. That's enough, he scowls.

Mummy Your Not Watching Me is followed by five songs of the psychedelic school which explicitly reflect pop-art aesthetics. After a period of painting rather gloomy social canvases, Daniel Treacy offers a fanciful way out. With *Brian's Magic Car*, the rather *avant-garde* production takes us off for a ride in a magic car driven by Brian Wilson, the Beach Boys' lead singer. There is a feeling of some enthusiasm, partly endangered by the oddity of the driver and the soundscape, so we are not surprised that it all quickly falls flat. This song is the only explicit reference which allows us to make a comparison, albeit fleeting and rather unsatisfactory, between two of pop history's disturbed geniuses. In *When The Rainbow Ends*, one of the band's the most classically sad songs, Daniel laments on his inability to find the pathway to truth and love. His quest ends in desolation at the end of a rainbow whilst a few spontaneous piano chords repeatedly emphasize a sad refrain *"This is where the rainbow ends"*. The feeling of failure is even more obvious in the long litany which constitutes one of the most impressive titles in the album: *David Hockney's Diaries*. Here, the narrator deals with stardom and glory, the epitome of which for him, beyond material wealth, would be to figure in the diaries of the painter David Hockney.

Revealed in a short thirty-minute documentary broadcast in 1970, David Hockney's diaries are a collection of photographs, and notes, documenting the artist's activities and recording the people and things which have crossed his path. The diaries are less of a society address-book, than the future framework of one of the most modern and expressionist works to develop within the pop-art movement. His work is partly based on a fictional autobiography, partly built on portraits of friends, travel notes, more or less erotic visions of smooth sweet boys. Hockney meets Andy Warhol in 1963 and plunges into his famous swimming-pool series. Hockney paints the swimming-pools, mainly empty ones, of luxurious villas. The swimming-pool becomes the symbol of idleness and luxury, but evidently conjures up a certain vacuity. Hockney strikes up numerous relationships and is a frequent visitor to gay clubs. He comes back to live in London twice, tries out Paris, then settles in Los Angeles, where he takes up residence in a house once owned by Anthony Perkins, the star of Psycho.

The song lasts more than six minutes and gives marvellous expression to the narrator's frustrated and almost desperate desire for success. The violent music, conveyed by throbbing and cavernously echoing guitars, makes this desire almost dangerous and morbid, while insinuating that it will never be achieved. *David Hockney's Diaries* perfectly illustrates Daniel Treacy's inherent ambiguities and the stubborn impression at this precise moment (the second album) that the Television Personalities are already has-beens. The album would sell reasonably well, but a bit less than the previous one and a bit more than the following one, confirming the band's position on the side-lines. Unlike Lawrence, an oddball and leader of the independent band Felt,

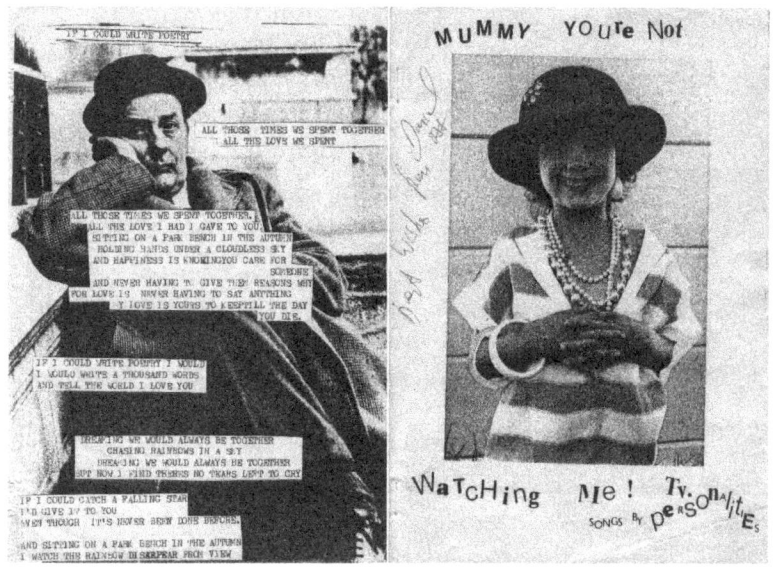

who would often be compared to Daniel Treacy and who, like him, would have severe addiction problems, the Television Personalities' vocalist is not obsessed with success and seems rather to accept the band's fate: to become a recognised independent band with little or no commercial success. The title of the Television Personalities' next album would be devoid of all ambiguity in this respect, resentful but above all ironic: *They Could Have Been Bigger Than The Beatles*.

In the meantime, *Mummy Your Not Watching Me* ends with two classics: *Magnificent Dreams* and *If I Could Write Poetry*. Both titles are astonishingly optimistic. In both cases, Daniel Treacy expresses great sensitivity and a capability to commit himself sincerely and unwaveringly to friends or lovers. *Magnificent Dreams* is a song full of hope and at the same time an incentive to go your own way, to express your freedom and personality. In many respects, with its generic lyrics and its childlike warm music, it is a manifesto full of idealism and attention for others. *If I Could Write Poetry* is probably THE great love song of the Television Personalities. The bass line carries the piece while the guitar plays in a folk register which is perfectly adapted to the simplicity of the arrangement. Daniel Treacy sings in "Bob Dylan style", like a traditional storyteller, down to earth and sheltered behind a production which somehow distances him from what he has to say. *"If I could write poetry / I would write a thousand words to tell the world that I love you",* he continues in a show of helplessness, while decking himself with most of the characteristics of a poet. With this last song, the Television Personalities seem to want to open up a radiant future, even if it is evident further on in the song that love has vanished and that the author is left alone to mourn his memories. *"Hoping we would always be together / But the rainbow disappeared from view."*

The mirage fades away, leaving in its place a haze of sadness. The band would continue for some time yet to navigate through these straits, as if torn between the temptation to admit its failure, and the continuing hope of a bright future.

NICO Life is a tsunami. Daniel Treacy is the wave which carries everything off in its wake, the roller, and the breaker.

Ed Ball keeps his distance in order to get on with his own work. Each in their own way, the two men pursue their dreams by running away and finding second-hand havens. Ed Ball's career would take on a certain lustre once he had distanced himself from Daniel and the Television Personalities. Ed Ball would prosper in his own way with The Times, and afterwards, as manager at Creation Records, he would accompany several bands on the road to success while treading his own path. He was to line up three albums in 1992, 1993 and 1995 under the original Teenage Filmstars name and without any help from his former friends, before achieving the beginnings of success with his solo albums, notably *Catholic Guilt* in 1997. Between an album dedicated to Edgar Allan Poe and permanent references to literature and the pop world, Ed Ball leads his life much along the same lines as he did as a teenager with the King's Road gang. Compared with Daniel Treacy's, and though it's merely an alternative path towards independence, Ed Ball's life would take on over the years the look of an academic career. Of these two pals, Ed Ball would be the one who would manage to keep himself afloat and to protect himself, when necessary, whilst Daniel took unimaginable risks.

The craziest guy is never the one you imagine and it would be a mistake to think of all this as just the opposition between what is reasonable or not. It would be 2004 before the two men got back together again. For different reasons, both are out of business. Ed Ball is pissed off with everything after the Creation fiasco and wants to pursue other interests. Daniel can't take it any longer. So, the two friends resume their activities: Ed Ball in order to save Daniel Treacy and in the hope of turning the clock back twenty years, Daniel in order to keep on walking and breathing. But there's still a lot of water to flow under the bridge.

Between 1982 and 1985 Daniel is here, there, and everywhere. He manages his Whaam! label, leads his band from album to album, writes, composes, and tours Europe to promote his music. As if that weren't enough, Daniel meets Emilee Brown and falls in love. He takes it into his head to promote the music he likes and takes responsibility for organising the programme of a club called *The Room At The Top*, which meets on the first floor of *The Enterprise*, a pub in Chalk Farm on the Northern Line. For a man who is often presented as anti-social and unstable, you could find worse. There is concordant evidence to describe the determination and immense charm which he displays during this period. Daniel is on cloud nine and piles up ventures and projects. He makes use of his systemic intelligence and his former taste for maths to develop his particular method of management, based on memory, rational organisation of chaos and permanent improvisation. Seen from the outside, the world which springs up around the Television Personalities is loosely structured and organised in the most amateurish way. In reality, Daniel, who is at the heart of all the decisions, is the driving force of one of the most interesting "Do-It-Yourself" experiments of the time, by extending the scope of the band, as yet still makeshift and low-scale, into a machine for the production, promotion, and organisation of evening events. Joe Foster is never far away and Alan McGee who, in the years to come, would lead Creation in an even more chaotic manner to the heights of the record industry, follows Daniel Treacy around the way he did at school. It has to be seen to be believed: darting from recording sessions with his own musicians, to hosting evening events at the *Room At The Top*. It has to be seen to be believed: taking a plane to Berlin, having tea with Nico, and then responding to a request from George Michael's lawyers. It has to be seen to be believed: recording a song, going to the cinema to see a French film, and ending the night making love on the sofa.

In 1980, the Television Personalities had given their first foreign concert in Germany. In May 1982, they are invited again for two appearances in Hamburg and Berlin. The first of these two billings is the one which motivates them to go: they are to open Nico's concert at the *Berlin Freie Universität*. Daniel and Joe Foster, who has replaced Ed Ball at short notice, are excited beyond reason at the idea of spending a few moments with the woman who remains for them the unmatchable beauty who enabled the Velvet Underground's music to find a niche in Andy Warhol's circle. Rough Trade is the instigator of this double bill and nobody knows at this moment whether the show will really take place. Nico is 43 and has never met the band which is supposed to accompany her for the evening show. It's an unprecedented situation: there's also the question of whether Christa Päffgen is still up to it and if she is likely to manage to do a British tour later in the year. Rough Trade has arranged to send some lads from Manchester, The Blue Orchids, to meet up with her and act as her backing band.

The Television Personalities arrive at the hotel on the 6th of May in the late afternoon. They go out on the town to have a drink and meet up again for breakfast fresh as daisies the next morning, the day of the concert. In the dining-room they come across the Blue Orchids, easily identifiable by their British manners. The band is led by Martin Bramah and Una Baines, two former members of The Fall. The band's name was suggested to them by the Mancunian poet John Cooper Clarke, that same Clarke who, several months later, would share for a while the life and the syringe of the German singer without, (according to his own account), ever sleeping with her. At the time, The Blue Orchids is a band which has the wind in its sails. They have opened a concert for Echo and The Bunnymen, and just sold 10,000 copies of their first album. Rough Trade intends to insist on them being the singer's backing group for the British tour. The Blue Orchids will also open the concert for Nico, in order to reduce the costs. So, this first meeting between her and her future band takes on a certain importance. The Blue Orchids' sole reference is a cassette sent to them containing several songs by Nico and the Velvet Underground such as *I'm Waiting For The Man* or *Femme Fatale*. They have had two days to rehearse and learn them before setting off. Daniel and Joe find the situation amusing.

— We could stand in for you, they laugh at one point. We know all the songs by 'eart. It'd be child's play.

They think about it for a moment, but the Blue Orchids are here for a reason. They haven't seen Nico yet and have no intention of stepping down. The night before, the band members had gone out and brought hookers back to the hotel. They had had a good time. That's the way Manchester bands do things. They've been well trained by Mark E. Smith. They drink beer at breakfast. Bramah is a year or two older than Daniel, but these guys look like real idiots. They've no idea who Nico is. They ask Daniel:

— Who is this girl? Never 'eard of 'er before.

Daniel, Joe, and Mark tell them about the Velvet Underground. Daniel hums *All Tomorrow's Parties* and more or less admits that it's his favourite song.

— Your favourite ever?

— Yeah, well I think so. I like *I'm Waiting For The Man* too, but *All Tomorrow's Parties* is better.

The Manchester lads take the Londoners for snobs, they laugh and carry on drinking beer.

— Well, we'll see, they say. It doesn't look that hard to play.

The Television Personalities don't know what to expect. Why has Rough Trade hired these guys? Has anyone ever heard what they play? No. Even Joe knows nothing about them. Maybe they've never even set foot in London. And then Nico makes her entrance. It's eight o'clock in the morning. There's toast, bacon, beans, and cheese on the table. There's tea and coffee. Mark has drunk hot chocolate with bread and butter, black German-style bread. And now, Nico is right there in the room. She is towering and so slim, tall, and dressed in black, like a ghost. Her hair is loose and grubby. It straggles over her shoulders. She has remnants of beauty clinging to her that catch the eye. And nobody utters a word when she sits down on the other side of the room without a look or a word for anyone.

Joe and Daniel are spellbound. They almost expect to see Lou Reed or maybe even Andy Warhol drop in on them at any moment. The Blue Orchids fall silent and lower their eyes as if they were there for a company seminar and were trying to avoid the big boss at breakfast.

Nico drinks some milk and nibbles a piece of bread. Her movements are slow, but quite similar to anybody else's when they're having their breakfast just after getting up. Life is a miracle. In 1964, Nico meets in short succession Brian Jones, Bob Dylan and then Andy Warhol, who invites her to the Factory, to which she would return on a regular basis. Mother of a two-year-old child allegedly fathered by Alain Delon, who she would leave in the care of his parents, Nico settles in the United States where, in 1966, she signs an important contract with the Ford modelling agency. At the same time, she dreams of a career as an actress. The New York artist gives her a place of honour, sometimes next to him, in his *Exploding Plastic Inevitable*, absolute pageants, where the arts and disorder mingle together. When, on the advice of film director Paul Morrissey, Andy Warhol discovers Lou Reed and John Cale's Velvet Underground, the jack-of-all-trades artist has a flash of inspiration: Nico is just the touch of glamour which the band needs to attract attention and create a contrast between its morbid songs and her pure Germanic beauty. The most beautiful woman in the world sings with the gloomiest band in the world. Warhol, turned producer for the occasion, arranges for Nico to sing three of the pieces on the album. Lou Reed is furious but can't do anything at this stage to go against his cumbersome patron. Nico hums through *Femme Fatale*, *I'll Be Your Mirror* and *All Tomorrow's Parties* and enters the legend of rock music. Her deep cavernous voice is disturbing and quivers with sexually charged emotion. These songs would figure among the most frequently performed over the fifty years to come.

But Lou Reed, Nico and Warhol soon go their separate ways. There's no room for the young woman in the band. Lou Reed hogs the stage in order to establish himself as the Velvet's real boss. John Cale takes her under his wing and helps her to start out on a solo career. Her album *Chelsea Girl* is a masterpiece and *Marble Index*, the album which follows in 1969 is a top-ranking experimental work. With Nico you never know what results from her own determination or what springs from her ability to become other people's fantasy. Here lies no doubt her strength and her weakness: her beauty at this time is so intense, natural, and immediate that it expresses itself without her having to do anything. Her beauty takes over and most of the time relegates her to a place far within herself, as if she were her own hostage.

Nico appears in films by Philippe Garrel, her current companion, who introduces her to heroin. The drug highlights Nico's originality and soon becomes her main refuge, in which she ruins her splendour. The most beautiful woman of her time slowly begins to fade. Nico withers away, saying little, ghostlike, as if she enjoys burying her past and her beauty in a sarcophagus. Her humour remains intact and she still shines in her lovers' hearts. Nico is sometimes pleasant and frivolous. She is amusing and attentive to others when she has had her dose, but immensely sad when the effects of the drug wear off. The concerts she gives from the beginning of the 70's take on a mystical aura. Nico plays the harmonium and deploys a sort of shadowy and imposing grace which entrances the audience. Her eyes change shape and over time become really impressive. The beauty is still there, but there is an overall impression that is more terrifying than seductive. She had authorized the American label ROIR to work on a live recording of her European tour which she finished in March, in exchange for a small retainer. *Do Or Die: Diary 1982* would come out on cassette in November. A little later in the year, a video clip made at the Preston Warehouse would establish for all time the black legend of the fallen Valkyrie. Nico comes over in the video like a spectre, transfigured by drugs.

As nobody budges, the youngest of them all, Mark Sheppard, makes a move. Mark is not even an adult.

— Come on you lot. You should go and talk to her. You're her band after all.

But the Blue Orchids are glued to their seats, incapable of doing anything whatsoever.

Mark gets up and goes to introduce himself. Nico raises her head, smiles vaguely at him, and asks him to sit down. The Television Personalities' drummer has never been afraid of anything. Less than a year later, he would leave the band to settle in the United States and become a Hollywood star. For the time being, Mark Sheppard is totally wrapped up in his life as a young musician. His face is reassuring and likeable. He watches Nico having breakfast and pinches himself at the same time, conscious all the while of his mates' envious looks behind his back.

His gaze rests on the singer's face, on her long hands with broken fingernails and prominent veins. Nico looks like a character out of Snow White, pale and gloomy, but you can't tell whether she's a nice person or not. After a few polite words, Nico asks him if he plays in the band which is to accompany her that evening. He says no, but that the guys just behind him are at her disposal. Nico doesn't want to talk to them. She doesn't want to see anybody.

— Do you ...?

Mark says yes before she can finish what she was saying. He's perfectly aware that she is not going to ask him to make love to her.

Nico interrupts her breakfast to go and do what's now the most important thing in her life. Mark goes with her and both of them come back half an hour or so later.

The rest of the Television Personalities and the Blue Orchids have not budged an inch. Nico and Mark sit down again as if it were business as usual. And then Mark, as if he had become Nico's personal assistant, orders them to step forward and they all get up and gather around the drummer and the most beautiful woman in the world, and watch her finally eat her breakfast. She exchanges a few words with her band, but has absolutely no intention of hanging about with them, before it's time for the sound check.

Nico seems to have taken a fancy to Mark. She suggests they go for a walk and afterwards go back to her room. Daniel and Joe decide to go off with them to stroll around Berlin, to walk quietly through Berlin in May, and then have something to eat. In turn, Daniel and Joe do the same thing as Nico and Mark had done in her room, because it's now become a habit and they're all feeling perked up and pleased with themselves. Then, Nico comes back to have a rest, and all four of them have tea together in the afternoon before the concert. Daniel and Joe ask Nico a few questions about the Velvet Underground, but they don't glean anything interesting, and certainly nothing about Lou Reed and John Cale's secrets of composition. They content themselves with having Nico near them, which to a certain extent allows them to understand her importance in all that.

The Television Personalities play early that day. The set is played with care and aims to present the band in its best light.

That evening, Nico gives a colourless performance. She dismisses the Blue Orchids after three or four songs, preferring to continue the concert on her own, playing the harmonium in almost total darkness. Either out of provocation or ineptitude, she decides that evening to give a rendering of the German anthem *Das Lied Der Deutschen* (better known as *Deutschland Über Alles*), but sings the first verse, blatantly nationalistic and prohibited since 1945. Bottles rain down on her head, which puts a premature end to the concert. In the concert hall, some guys shout out "Nazi" and others run all over the place as if they had seen the ghost of Adolf Hitler in swimming trunks. Nico isn't a Nazi, but the recording which she would make of this patriotic song would remain controversial. The police take up position backstage and force the singer to beat a retreat, whilst the Television Personalities take refuge in their dressing-room. Fires are started and insults fly. Thus ends the fixture. A similar mishap would occur a few decades later during an international women's tennis match between German and American players. Official apologies would be made later.

In Hamburg the next day, Daniel would play *I'm Waiting For The Man* and *Where Are All The Chelsea Girls Now?*, a song played extremely slowly for the occasion, first performed the previous year in the band's set, and which would be rarely performed thereafter. *Chelsea Girls* was the title of Nico's first solo album, but also that of an Andy Warhol film made in 1966. In the Television Personalities' song, you can glimpse a direct response to Nico's song and its refrain where the famous Chelsea girls come running up.

"There was a girl that I knew
There was a girl so true
And now she's gone forever
And all my dreams came true", sings Daniel Treacy.
"Where are the Chelsea girls now?
Where have the good girls gone?
They say that your dreams will come true
But nothing lasts forever."

The girls and Nico fade into the past, youth, and health too. As always, the Television Personalities are there to keep a poetic and painful record of it all. It's time to release another record. Concerts, records, concerts, records, this is what constitutes from now on their usual unusual life and what keeps them going.

They Could Have Been Bigger Than The Beatles is released in the summer of 1982, just seven months after the band's second album. It's a mix between a compilation and an album, a rather strange product, which comes out obviously too quickly from a commercial point of view, but which offers Whaam!, a profitable release whilst allowing the band to get their hands back on a few songs from their first records. *They Could Have Been Bigger Than The Beatles* with its insolent, but probably lucid, title is made up of sixteen pieces amongst which can be found improved, more legible and incisive versions of *14th Floor, The Glittering Prizes, David Hockney's Diary* and a few others. The song which benefits from the most impressive treatment is undoubtedly *King and Country*, changed into a six-minute thrilling polemic, electrifying, and sizzling. The last two minutes are particularly powerful, tense and supported by an instrumental monologue where the guitars, the bass and the drums nervously converse with each other, prefiguring the use which would be made of them later by bands such as Pavement and a few others.

Alongside these one or two-year-old pieces, Daniel Treacy puts together songs recorded with Ed Ball during sessions for their new stillborn band The Gifted Children, as well as some cover versions of the then forgotten band, The Creation. This band, which performed essentially between 1966 and 1968, relied heavily on Eddie Phillips, one of the most skilful guitarists of the period, sought after by The Who and imitated by Jimmy Page, and on a few singles which would be great hits ... in Germany. Their only album would moreover be distributed in only a few countries including France,

Germany, and Holland, but not Britain. The Creation's career is short-lived but it has a great influence on Daniel Treacy and his associates, including the future founder of Creation Records, Alan McGee, who would name his band after one of the Creation's songs, *Biff Bang Pow*. It is *Painter Man* from the A side of this precise single that Treacy includes in the Television Personalities' third album, alongside a rather anecdotal version of *Makin' Time*. These remakes, together with the magnificent *When Emily Cries*, a song which could well have been one of Syd Barrett's own, establish the Television Personalities at the forefront of a psyche-mod revival which rocks the capital for a season or two. The gigs organised by McGee and later by Treacy himself, form the epicentre of a scene nurtured by the culture of the Swinging 60's, revering the Kinks, and attempting to redesign its way of composing in the post-punk environment of the early 80's. Handing out recreational drugs is encouraged, even directly organised by the promoters, in the same way as they plan shows, like Warhol, enhanced by pictorial, dramatic performances or video projections. Ten or fifteen years later, when mainstream bands were once again to complete musical performances with complicated stage play and giant projection screens, people would obviously forget that everything had started out here with what, in the end, was a fairly un-arty desire to create a real audio-visual experience, capable of offering an alternative to lives of gloom devastated by economic crisis. Here lies the true ambition of the Television Personalities. It's not so much a question of amusement, distraction or escape from the world. It's more a question of setting up an alternative reality in which the heroic or media figures at the centre of current events, men of politics and power, are replaced by authentic popular heroes, fictional characters, and eternal artists.

They Could Have Been Bigger Than The Beatles, when you listen to the old songs again, sheds light on the changing conception that Daniel Treacy has of his art. Like Dylan before him, he considers that the songs have no permanent form: he can rework them, make them come and go, sometimes at intervals of decades. Things would accelerate with the passage of time and Daniel's increasingly non-conformist behaviour. The songs are never committed to writing and the lyrics are dependent on his lapses of memory or his inspiration of the moment. Later on, some songs would be particularly suitable to such ad-lib improvisation on stage, notably *A Picture of Dorian Gray*, *I Know Where Syd Barrett Lives* and of course, *Salvador Dali's Garden Party*, whose guest-list would be renewed with relish at each performance.

The Television Personalities are a band constantly on the boil, which in its approach adopts the "handyman" codes of what would later be called the Do-It-Yourself movement: produce quickly, record as a matter of form, improvise and never rehearse the songs. In the decade from 1984 to 1994, the bass player Jowe Head would admit to having taken part in only two formal rehearsal sessions with the band. Two work sessions in ten years. Daniel, just like Mark E. Smith, leader of the Fall who died in 2018; after forty years as a mainstay of British outsider rock music, refuses to give his musicians a set-list before the concert. Where Smith generally slips them the list a few minutes before opening in order to keep up the pressure, Treacy most often lets them guess the piece to be performed by starting to play one or two chords of the song by way of introduction. This technique creates a few glitches, some backtracking and stalling, but impresses by its audacity and radicalism. What would be thought of later as ineptitude and lack of professionalism is based, at the outset, on a concept of art as an instantaneous and unrepeatable spectacle. Daniel Treacy launches into stage sequences which smack of trial runs or spontaneous inspiration. Is he testing the songs he has in his head? Is he thinking out loud? The list of lost songs, played several times or just once, mentioned and never seen again, would be enough to fill several albums.

The Lives Of Millionaires is introduced in Brighton in October 1984. It is played six months later in London before reappearing in Scotland in spring 1988. *The Saddest Day I Ever Lived* is born and dies on the 7th of May 1982 during the opening of the Berlin concert with Nico. *Sad Little Boy, Beyond My Wildest Dreams, Shadows That Haunt Me, Somebody Loves You* are tested the same day and all four again, during an acoustic concert given by Daniel and Ed ball in London in November 1988. None of these remarkable songs would ever be used again. Whole albums are drowned or lost or are preserved on pirate cassettes which circulate among fans. The lyrics are sometimes jotted down in notebooks, or afterwards to be found on the Internet where their existence is kept intact by some testimony or spectator's account. Flyers and posters change hands or are stored in drawers. Fanzines come into being where stars of the time speak out and talk about their careers. As in most civilisations, records are kept and jealously guarded. History is always written somewhere, documented by the feelings which it inspires and the trace that it leaves in peoples' lives.

They Could Have Been Bigger Than The Beatles is a strange compilation which isn't lacking in coherence, despite its sprawling make-up. The new pieces are remarkable, a mixture of frivolity and spirit of the times. Britain is at war over the Falklands, invaded by the Argentine dictatorship. It's a brief conflict which is won, and allows Margaret Thatcher to be re-elected the following year. The World Cup is being played in Spain. England is ousted after a pitiful second round, without having scored a single goal. Margaret Thatcher is in power, and would remain there until 1990. The IRA sets off bombs in Hyde Park and Regent Street, causing more than twenty deaths. Nine others are killed in Harrod's a few hundred yards away from the King's Road, in 1983. The country is slowly splitting apart, changing at the double and with pain and suffering. The conservative revolution makes people want to dance, to forget and to resist all at once. You can't separate the second psychedelic wave from the context in which it develops. A war is being waged against the poor and everybody tries to muddle through. The second psychedelic wave has little to do with the first one. It's a movement which is in touch with the reality of the times, a movement of starving people who, in the mid 80's, would have no other possibilities of escape or of building their lives, outside the prevailing system.

Of the two instrumentals in *They Could Have Been Bigger Than The Beatles*, *Flowers for Abigail* is the most beautiful and also the saddest. It renders perfectly that search for comfort and consolation which underlies the Television Personalities' music. The great breakaways are final, as if it were a question at present of leaving the world for good. *In A Perfumed Garden is* most certainly a reference to the Arabic work of Mohammed Al Nafzawi, written in the fifteenth century, and one of the most famous erotic books in the world. To slide into a scented and eternal sensuality, or disappear like Syd Barrett on his *Psychedelic Holiday*, a song which half frightens and half invites on a journey where Daniel drowns us in a gilded sea, before watching the waves change into trees, and the dolphins intone a song of welcome.

As always, escape is the great temptation. But the time is not yet ripe. In *Anxiety Block*, an old song rearranged for the occasion, Daniel goes to the doctor's to get treatment for the anxiety which gnaws at him and prevents him from composing. He asks for magic pills, the blue ones that he was given before, the ones that cure the illness.

In the last song in the album, faith and hope ring out in the midst of misery and desolation. Daniel holds in his hand a few of the famous pills which kill just as much as they cure, and empties a bottle of wine like a lone mourner.

"Faith in something
Well I'm so ashamed I laughed at you
But you reached out to hold my hand
Communication is the key
Candle burn brightly for me
A bomb's gone off at the BBC
The headlines say at half past three
But no one's claimed responsibility
For the 22 bodies in the mortuary
God acts in mysterious ways
God acts in mysterious ways"

"God only knows, Brian Wilson would say. *God only knows."*
Maybe the carefree days come to an end here, in this second half of 1982. Times are changing and not for the better. Something in the band's music is shifting as if you can't enjoy yourself in the same way anymore. Yet, it's the time for business, for concerts and successful bands, the time for love with Emilee Brown. It may well be that Daniel reached adulthood at this moment. Perhaps also, he glimpsed the constraints that weigh on modern man and the courageous or less glorious ways of avoiding them.

BRIGHT SUNNY SMILES

The Whaam! label's activities continue throughout 1982 and 1983 and Daniel can be proud of a few successes such as having released the first record by the Pastels, a band whose renown on the independent scene would keep on growing, or having promoted the incredible Doctor And The Medics, one of the most spectacular glam rock bands in Britain. Whaam! also launches the Marine Girls band by reissuing their early album *Beach Party*, recorded in In-Phaze Records boss Pat Bermingham's garden-shed mobile studio. *Beach Party* would be quite a successful release, allowing the group to record two Peel Sessions in 1982 and 1983. Their singer, Tracey Thorn, would be better known a few years later alongside her boyfriend, in a band called Everything But The Girl. A strictly female band, the Marine Girls are the missing link between the Raincoats and the Young Marble Giants, an ambassadorial band for a movement baptised twee pop because of its supposed naivety, and which would later include such bands as The Field Mice, Belle and Sebastian or Beat Happening. The Marine Girls would be indebted, moreover, to Calvin Johnson, back in the United States after a long stay in England, for having

introduced the girls' music to his colleagues on the American label Sub Pop. The album *Beach Party*, as well as several other albums on the label, including those of the Television Personalities, would thus find their way onto the turn-table of one of their most famous admirers, the young Kurt Cobain.

Daniel Treacy is like a mother to the bands he discovers. In mid-May 1984, the label goes out of business as the result of a fortunate coincidence. Daniel, who manages all the business over the phone, gets a call from a mysterious London solicitor, who claims to represent a very well-known British band. The lawyer has been hired by the Epic label, just a few months before the release of the second album by the band consisting of George Michael and Andrew Ridgeley. Daniel is a bit mystified. A meeting is arranged, followed by an exchange of letters. Wham! moves in circles that seem light-years away from those of the Television Personalities. *Wake Me Up Before You Go-Go*, released at the beginning of the year, had reached number 1 in the British and American charts. The hit is followed by *Careless Whisper*, presented as a solo by George Michael, but in fact, written with Andrew Ridgeley, and is also a huge success. The band is on cloud nine when it appears as a duo in autumn 1984, with the single *Freedom*. The song prefigures the release in November of *Make It Big*, recorded at the Miraval studios in France, their second album, and a phenomenal commercial success which propels the band to the very summit of the hierarchy of popular groups, alongside Duran Duran and Culture Club.

Behind the scenes however, and before the start of this triumphant commercial and artistic campaign, Wham! had encountered one or two legal difficulties and, with its new record company Epic/CBS, begun a clean-up operation which oddly enough crosses Daniel Treacy's path. At the very beginning of their career, Wham! had already been warned about commercial credits and proprietary names. In 1982 they issue their first single in the

United States under the name Wham! UK to avoid an American rival of the same name who would disappear shortly afterwards, leaving them a free hand. A few years later, Andrew Ridgeley is seriously worried about the terms of the contract linking the two men to their label Innervision. There follows a difficult legal battle which causes Innervision to admit to discrepancies concerning the band's royalties. The label loses and would later go out of business. In the meantime, Innervision has had the time to release a horrible *Club Fantastic Megamix*, an unauthorized variation and an absurd medley patched together from recording sessions of the band's first album. When Wham! joins Epic Records, one of the conditions fixed by George Michael and Andrew Ridgeley is that there should be no cock-ups. The label starts by cleaning up the band's image a bit, and moving it slightly in the direction of pop to ensure its lasting credibility. The duo would be sexy, even stuffing shuttlecocks into their skin-tight shorts to enhance their bulge, and asking girls to "make it big". But at Vegas they would put the main emphasis on their meticulous compositions, and a relatively classy image.

We don't really know how the band's managers discovered the existence of the Whaam! label, but they identify it as a potential risk. Given the celebrity of the band, might not these minnows take it into their heads to cause them problems? From Whaam! to Wham! there's only one little "a" between them. No doubt the lawyer dealing with the business doesn't know about the link with Roy Liechtenstein's painting. Otherwise, he would know that the term Whaam! is by no means the exclusive property of the band, but a borrowing from the title of the American master's picture, he himself having re-used an onomatopoeia frequently found in the world of American comics. George Michael and Andrew Ridgeley had ended up calling themselves Wham! for want of a better idea. The two men had begun their career with schoolmates in a band called The Executive. The venture goes amiss, and when the band breaks up, the duo carries on and manages to get noticed by Innervision, a recently established label set up by CBS, who signs them up on the spot. When naming their first single, the unbeatable *Wham Rap! (Enjoy What You Do)*, Michael and Ridgeley wonder what to call themselves and choose to adopt the first word of their first song *Wham! Bam! I Am! A Man! Job or no job, you can't tell me that I'm not.* It takes a bit of courage to listen to this piece more than thirty-five years after its release, but the song was revamped by H&M who used it as a jingle for a major advertising campaign in 2017. Difficult to get further away from the aesthetics and the musical world of the Television Personalities. Stylorouge, the graphic artists who work for the label, suggest that the band keep the exclamation mark. It'll be Wham! To be honest, everyone gently takes the piss out of the name of the band. But only the hits count. The hits and the little spray-on shorts stuffed with shuttlecocks that you can play with backstage.

Epic offers Daniel Treacy a small sum to relinquish the label's name and end its activity. It's an amusing business. It takes a bit of time for the guys at Whaam! to react. Daniel Treacy has no legal advisor, but asks for opinions here and there. There are still great things to be done, but the prospect of making a bit of money in such a way and to be able to reinvest it straightaway, clinches the deal. Whaam! has a little bit of notoriety, but nothing to stop the company which has no employees, no office, nothing to prove its existence other than Daniel's small flat, from starting up again under another name. Treacy informs Epic that the money on offer is not enough. He's bluffing, of course, but he wouldn't say no to getting a bit more. Each single issued by the label costs money. It's more or less only albums that bring in money, but you need singles to herald their arrival and make them possible. The top brass of the label raise the offer a little and a deal is struck. It's not certain whether George Michael and Andrew Ridgley had ever heard about this transaction. They were probably told during a commercial briefing the way professional labels used to do, that a "naming" problem had been resolved thanks to the judicious intervention of the legal department. The label's boss, anxious to keep well in with their new golden goose, probably played on it to highlight his professionalism and his total commitment to defending the band's interests. Be that as it may, while Whaam! is on its way out, Wham! takes off towards an irresistible interplanetary success. The single *Last Christmas / Everything She Wants* sells more than a million copies, four hundred thousand in the United Kingdom alone and remains several weeks at number 2 in the charts, just behind *Do They Know It's Christmas?*, a song in which George Michael also participates and which underpins the Band Aid fund-raising campaign against famine in Ethiopia.

When Wham! launches into a huge world tour in March 1985, Daniel Treacy is already busy setting up a new company. It is to be called Dreamworld. New label. New name and new intentions. It seems that Daniel had initially intended to set up a new structure without delay in order to reissue the Television Personalities' albums and release their future works. The band's activity remains buoyant after the release of *They Could Have Been Bigger Than The Beatles*. Busy scouting for new bands to produce, Daniel Treacy gives the impression at first, of having deserted his flagship. The relative failure of the compilation album leads him to think about dropping the name Television Personalities and to give thought to a new vector for his music, or even to give up composing for good. This period of uncertainty lasts only a few months before Joe Foster convinces Daniel in the summer of 1983 to work on a new project. Daniel is beset by doubts and wants to be something other that the figurehead of an amusing and identifiable psychedelic revival but which is going nowhere and threatens to become a caricature of itself. It's at this time that what can be considered as a real movement crystallises around the band and the *Living Room* gigs. Groups are set up, relationships are formed around an alternative, makeshift, and intimate form of pop. The Press describes them as psychedelic, although the term has no precise musical or cultural connotation. LSD and recreational drugs are never far away, of course, but that in itself is not enough to be a defining characteristic.

Daniel chooses to take a tougher line, abandoning for some time his British models, from Joe Meek to the Kinks in favour of a more personal, rougher, and gloomier expression, inspired by the chill and bitterness of the Velvet Underground. At this point, Alan McGee becomes a central figure in the way in which this non-movement is promoted. The Television Personalities contribute at first to the emergence of the phenomenon by playing several times at the gigs. Daniel spots bands there, which he ropes in for his label. It so happens that The Television Personalities, back from a German tour, take part on the 1st of March 1984 in the launch of the Union Tavern gigs, after having been banned from the Adams Arms. This would be their fourth appearance in the space of a few months at a concert organized by Creation's founder. The increasing success of the *Living Room* gigs pulls in a new crowd, allows certain bands to emerge, but ends up seriously irritating Daniel who derives no additional notoriety from them and who takes a dislike to all this hype. Worse than that, he would come to think, in his own discreet way, and without it leading to things being broken off, that his artistic approach was being copied. Later, Alan McGee would willingly recognize the role played by Daniel Treacy and his label, in the hatching of his own ambitions. It would be farcical to pretend that Daniel Treacy had taught him everything, but it's probable that his audacity was the driving force which gave wings to McGee's career. Treacy's example served to show above all, that with a modicum of application and intelligence, you could succeed in the world of pop. But McGee has an obvious competitive advantage over Treacy and his labels: he's got know-how. The Scotsman, who at first is no more organized than anyone else, realises the importance of communication and starts early on to publish information through the fanzines that he manages, and in particular *Communication Blur*. It's no coincidence if the first reference to the label is an item by Jerry Thakray, alias Everett True, a.k.a. The Legend, and in McGee's words, "the most un-enigmatic, boring, kindest, shyest person you could ever meet". McGee, in an almost ironic gesture, encourages this dreary guy used to dancing around at the back of the hall, to climb on stage, while embarking at the same time on a career at the New Musical Express, the country's foremost music magazine. He would leave the NME five years later for Melody Maker. The Legend, whose importance should not be overestimated, serves in his own way McGee's interests in the musical press. At the time, his articles are quite controversial, for through them, the journalist constantly takes the centre stage and casts himself in the leading role. But he is unswerving in his support for the bands under contract to Creation. He would also play a major part in bringing grunge music to Britain at the end of the 80's, and at the beginning of the 90's would remain renowned for having introduced Courtney Love to Kurt Cobain during a concert by the Butthole Surfers and the L7. He would later be a close friend of the couple, especially of Cobain, up to the singer's suicide. On the other hand, The Legend's musical career would remain anecdotal and never go beyond his second single.

When McGee, after a moderately successful attempt at taking direct control of the *Communication Club*, begins to organize the *Living Room* gigs, all the ingredients are there for things to take shape. The idea is nothing less than to merge psychedelic rock and punk music, punk subversion and the hippies' and LSD-takers' idealism all bound together in a single code of ethics. The in-crowd come in droves, the press observes their gatherings with benevolence and sees in them a sort of festive and generally harmless resistance against current trends. Synth pop, which dominates commercial music has become so unbearable that any alternative is worth having, even if it's sweetly anecdotal, like the music of the first bands signed up by the label. Creation works with The Revolving Paint Dream, The Jasmine Minks, The Pastels, and a few others who, at first, might seem minor bands. Whaam! and its successor label Dreamworld, work with the same raw materials. It soon turns out that McGee and Treacy share a common musical space. This rivalry would never quite become reality, both because for a time there is more than enough room for two, but above all because Creation would get itself organised much more quickly, even if that didn't give it an immediate commercial superiority.

In its endeavours, Creation has the advantage of the hard work and decisive contribution of Joe Foster, who manages the majority of the bands with much mastery for a guy of his age with little experience, but equally that of the conscientious Dick Green, the third member of the team, responsible for administration. At that time Joe Foster works day and night, keeping himself awake with doses of speed. His vast musical culture does the rest. He would later pay the price for this by vanishing from the scene for more than half a decade before returning to manage a label producing re-issues and oddities. McGee would hold firm until 1994 when, just months before the emergence of his latest and perhaps most spectacular discovery to date, Oasis, he would sink into a deep depression, be admitted to hospital, and committed into care.

With the departure of Ed Ball, Whaam! lacks man power and the capability to conduct an offensive commercial strategy while keeping its affairs in order. The lack of resources would be even more penalising for Dreamworld, and prevent the label from fully capitalising on the nonetheless fantastic success of certain bands signed up by them, such as The Mighty Lemon Drops. Creation takes the lead, first by the success of the Jesus and Mary Chain, a Scottish cyclothymic band with a revolutionary sound, then in the second half of the 80's and in completely different registers, by My Bloody Valentine and, above all, House of Love. McGee's ambition, stimulated by the early success of the *Living Room* gigs and his innate showbiz sense, propels Creation from the outset into an international and professional universe which bears no comparison with the world of tight budgets, limited issues, and still-born ambitions in which flounders Daniel Treacy. Where McGee negotiates with the Sire label American commercial distribution rights for his bands, the founder of Whaam! negotiates night-time tariffs so that his bands can record singles when the studios are closed.

From 1984 onwards, a rift can be seen between McGee's team and Daniel Treacy who, later, would show no mercy to the founder of Creation. Treacy accuses McGee of having robbed him of everything and turned it into a profitable business. If McGee admitted in later years his debt towards Treacy, it only took the Scot less than six months to nourish, develop and impose his vision of things, and thereby change divisions and move into a higher gear. The frictions would be exacerbated by a quarrel that would start with Joe Foster over a fairly common problem of divvying out royalties, fees, and proceeds of sales. In mid-1984, after a fine tour which had included Jowe Head in the band, Foster deserts the ship for good. By joining McGee's outfit for good, he and Ball have chosen sides. In fact, Foster, would never see Treacy again, occupied as he was by other business, and also because he spent a good deal of his life abroad.

Treacy, in turn, would explain in a few interviews that the guitarist had never written anything worthwhile and would try to minimize his contribution to the band's songs. If their early close friendship didn't entirely fade (Foster would always defend Treacy in later interviews) it didn't resist the transition into adulthood. The amazing story of Creation Records would be written separately from Daniel Treacy's, paved with success (Oasis, Primal Scream) and miracles, all kinds of excess and bouts of depression, but almost always in the forefront of the history of British pop music. From now on, Dreamworld and Treacy would play in the back-kitchen.

Although he had distanced himself from the band once before, Joe Foster had nevertheless been the musical mainstay of their last great effort, *The Painted Word*, recorded mainly in the summer of 1983. Loyal from the outset, Foster completely devotes himself to this new project, presented at first as a solo album by Treacy and at any rate, as an attempt to finally break loose from what had been the burgeoning stock-in-trade of the Television Personalities. It's a complicated time. Foster and Treacy are each going through difficult periods. The two friends lead lives which are no longer anything like what they were in 1977. Insanity and depression are lurking in the wings. The nights are short and the risk of everything falling apart is never far off, held at bay only by the desire to make progress and the succession of projects, gigs, records, and initiatives. Difficult to say if either of these two men, who are barely 25, are conscious that their future is perhaps being played out now, in the two or three movements to come. Treacy with his gut feeling, and Foster with his obsession for music, thrown together in the heat wave of the hottest summer in London for the last twenty-five years, in a studio, trying to do what they now know best: put a record together.

Treacy is completely distraught. After the lack of interest shown for *They Could Have Been Bigger Than The Beatles*, the departure of Ed, and success which eludes him, he's not sure of anything anymore. He's no longer got the determination he had five years before, is no longer sure of going anywhere. Foster has spent the first few months of the year trying to make a new start as an actor, and comes back to music in the hope of taking his mind off things, and drowning his personal problems in the studio's reassuring darkness. The period itself is even drearier than five years ago. In February, unemployment reaches its highest level since the Great Depression of the 30's, the Cold War is in full swing and Margaret Thatcher wins a landslide victory in the June elections, leaving Labour with less than 30% of the vote. On the 15th of July, the temperature reaches 33° in London and the capital is suffocating. The sizzler would go on for more than a month.

And then, there is obviously that magnificent blonde girl from Northern Europe, Swedish or Danish, who had occupied an important place in Daniel's heart and who has decided to dump him.
— I'd rather we went our separate ways.

Who remembers all that these days? You can see that pretty girl in a single picture taken by the great rock photographer Bleddyn

Butcher, sitting with Joe and Dan in a retro café, decorated with neon lights. The young girl who has ditched him is there, smiling in black and white like all love-sick girls at the time. She has no idea what she will be the cause of, a few months after turning her back on Daniel Treacy. Naturally, she has no idea of what she was to inspire, her departure adding to the Cold War, the economic crisis and total nuclear war threatening to redefine the contours of the world. Such is the atmosphere in which Foster and Treacy put the finishing touches to the fourth album of the Television Personalities.

Quite naturally, the lyrics become more sombre, but maintain the initial intentions: talking about reality, taking sides, particularly against war, and building dreams, whilst reflecting the anxieties of their creators and the times. Foster plays the part of the great architect and attempts to turn his friend's misgivings into reality. He's the one who packages the songs and gives them a semblance of musical coherence. *The Painted Word* is nevertheless a bit of a wacky album, fragmented and disturbing, which evokes a feeling of frustration and unease. Foster plays most of the instruments and acts as musical director. He summons Dave Musker to replace Daniel Treacy, who is a mediocre keyboard player, and gives free rein to his fanciful imagination. The fourteen items form a ragtag collection but they are unusually forceful, and in the end come over as the most impressive and outlandish collection of songs by the band. *The Painted Word* is an album which instils fear and brings things a step closer to that decisive moment when the artist lays down his arms, admits defeat and breathes out in a final defiant gesture, what remains of his hopes, illusions, and innocence. It's difficult to detect behind this sublime but ailing music, the joy and comic nonchalance of the early singles. Treacy sings now with his soul bared, and with unreserved emotional sincerity. He constantly writes almost infantile songs, full of nostalgic references, and makes

them coexist with nightmarish visions and deep-seated traumas. Foster's production technique of cutting up the songs and stitching them together with the seams showing, reinforces both the feeling of torn-up reality, and that of a fracture that could literally rip the individual to pieces.

The percussion, performed by different drummers in the course of the recording sessions, is pushed into the background to give pride of place to an organ and the guitars. The title is borrowed from Tom Wolfe's acidic book, *The Painted Word*, which takes an ironic look at the superficial and fake world of art criticism. The book sets out, in a rather grotesque way, to suggest that art criticism has hastened the decadence of modern art, by inducing it to abandon realism, figuration, then even the brush and finally the colours, and thus turn a painting gradually into a simple abstraction of itself, or even an umpteenth form of criticism. After the lack of interest aroused by *They Could have Been Bigger Than The Beatles*, *The Painted Word* seems to imply a desperate attempt to impose an incarnate, afflicted and socially committed music on a world which, from now on, yearns for fun and soon for dance music, a world that is now busy offering Treacy's dreams to somebody else.

Much more than in the previous albums, you can feel in *The Painted Word* the passage of time and the idea that something has changed. The theme of the song *Bright Sunny Smiles* is fairly explicit, Daniel explaining, against an ominously festive, then funereal background, how the members of the band have lost their smiles.

> *"There's me and there's Edward, there's Joe and there's Mark*
> *We're playing in the garden and we stay out till dark*
> *And we've all got bright sunny smiles*
> *And we've all got bright sunny smiles*
> *…*

But now we are grown up and life's not much fun
'Cause when we were children we sat in the sun
And We all had bright sunny smiles
Sometimes we are happy, sometimes we are sad
When we think of the fun and the laugh that we had
Now it's hard to find a bright sunny smile
But now we are grown up and life's not much fun
But now we are grown up, there's nowhere to run
No bright sunny smiles, no bright sunny smiles.

The age of innocence is drawing to a close. Joe Foster is nailing together its first-class coffin. The quality of the compositions on the album is impressive. It's gets off to a flying start with *Stop And Smell The Roses*, a title which seems to be a refugee from a forgotten Velvet Underground recording. It's one of the band's most beautiful songs of lost love and solitude. The percussion is impeccable and Treacy's singing movingly dignified. The next track, *The Painted Word*, tolls the knell of the psychedelic revival. It is a song about break-up and heartbreak which is later reminiscent of the sublime melancholy of *Someone To Share My Life With*, or of the irresistible beauty of a title such as *Say You Won't Cry*, perhaps the saddest and most shocking of all. Apart from the songs that evoke a lost paradise (*Bright Sunny Smiles* or *Happy All The Time*), *The Painted Word* conjures up ultra-realistic pictures which mingle the Velvet's metallic aridity and a Dylan-like capacity for social observation. *A Life Of Her Own* is inspired from the kitchen-sink dramas of the 60's, mentioned earlier, and introduces a new character, the loose woman: a single mother, alone and high on drugs, whose usual ploy is to ask her own mother to look after her kid for the night. *You'll have To Scream Louder* echoes *Scream Quietly* on the second album. Where once he told you to put a sock in it, Daniel now recommends that you shout your head off. Times change. Despair has to speak up for itself. It's the time of demonstrations, of marches for peace or against nuclear weapons. You'll have to scream louder, he insists. Because nobody's listening. You can scream, you can shout. Don't expect to be heard. The song mingles an intimate dimension, and a political statement which would be called anti-establishment these days. Anger is mounting and frustration is on the point of becoming hate. The best post-punk songs often have this ability to express intimate matters by giving them a much wider scope and political significance.

"'Cause I've got no respect for the people in power
They make their decisions from their ivory towers
And I feel a hatred, it's growing inside
And there's nowhere to run to
'Cause there's nowhere to hide."

Ruin doesn't even spare fairy-tale princesses. *The Girl Who Had Everything* is the tale of a poor little rich girl who has everything in life: travel, sports cars, upper-class parents and courtship parties, and who ends up in a drug-filled haze. She starts using drugs just for fun and then she's done for. They called her the girl who had everything going for her. If there's no comparison between this girl and Daniel Treacy, the possibility that a happy childhood and adolescence may end up in total collapse is obviously uppermost in the singer's mind when he invents this story. Such things happen every day: throwing good fortune down the drain. Not playing your cards right. They called her the girl who had everything.

The end of the album amplifies the theme, as if to ensure that not a single ray of light hits the smallest corner of the room, nor a grain of hope is left. *Paradise Estate* is a magnificent but dismal song. Like Will Eisner who had introduced this theme to comic strips, Daniel puts on parade the occupants of flats in a housing development ironically called Paradise Estate. And it's an extravaganza. The first person we meet is called Mrs. Brown who has to walk a mile to the launderette where she works (Treacy's mother's job, you will recall), while her husband has been forced into early retirement, his lungs eaten away by asbestos. The lady next door sends her kids to school on an empty stomach, because she can't always afford to give them breakfast. Her husband has run off with the barmaid from his local. She drowns her sorrows in pills. Then, there is the teenage mother, abandoned by social services. *Paradise Estate* is a sinister version of the small community on the *14th Floor* of the early days. Each day is just like the last. On Paradise Estate, paradise has come a day too late. We live in our boxes. Our little boxes. Brick boxes. Boxes for single mothers, boxes for the aged, boxes for the sick. Paradise has come to Earth a day too late. To our boxes devoid of light.

But none of this is comparable to the seven minutes and thirty-four seconds of *Back To Vietnam* which closes the album. Those who still saw the Television Personalities as a faintly amusing comic-opera band would have to think again. The finale is terrifying, discordant, punk. *Back To Vietnam* describes the life of a National Guard veteran who has frightening dreams at the idea of being posted back to Vietnam. The song progresses as through a sprawling and penetrating nightmarish scenario, no doubt stimulated by LSD and other drugs. The sense of time is muddled between the past, the present, and a conglomerate of current or future wars: Vietnam, the World Wars, the Falklands. Space stretches out in total confusion: Vietnam, its dark tunnels, the soldier's wife in her kitchen, the terror. The hero becomes a refugee, a victim, a cripple in a wheelchair. To some extent he's transformed into a war machine, a tommy gun, a "power", an institution, in a delirious sequence reminiscent of Burroughs' most inspired examples in *The Wild Boys*. You can feel in Treacy's song that fear of war in your guts, expressed by the distress and desperation of the voice, the chorus of cries and the feeling of disorientation created by the guitars and production effects. The piece bears worthy comparison with songs by Love, by the Doors or with the Californian rock music of the time, decidedly difficult to follow, and brings *The Painted Word* to a close in almost absolute discomfort.

The album embodies the sum of all fears. It's the band's black diamond, a miracle of balance but also a monument of instability, as if Joe and Daniel had built a house of cards, an edifice constructed of all that is black and frightening in society: loneliness, mental disorder, loss of affection, war, the collapse of the kingdom.

It's a sign that Daniel is still in touch with reality, that he chooses to contact Rough Trade to promote the first track on the album. He's aware that the Television Personalities' potential is greater than his own label's ability to promote it. *A Sense Of Belonging* comes out in December 1983. It's probably the most unifying of the fourteen songs. Openly political, it describes in detail the ills of the time, and can be interpreted as a summary of the themes to be found in the album. If the litany of woes which afflict man is frightening and overwhelms the rest in terms of quantity, the overall tone and the lively melody imply that a ray of light is possible, and that realising this could lead to a form of optimism. *A Sense of Belonging*, by summoning reality and evil in a Dylan-like style, works towards its goal while leaving humanity a fair chance. From whatever angle, the song's message is not irrevocable. Rough Trade takes on the title, produced by Whaam!, and releases the single with the jacket chosen and designed by Treacy depicting a battered three or four-year-old girl, her face disfigured by two enormous shiners. It's a good allegory of violence, perfectly adapted to the theme and a choice likely to attract attention. But in the weeks leading up to the release of the single, the label staff shy off. They are afraid of being accused of complacency towards child abuse, afraid of being accused of sensationalism. The release goes ahead, but instructions are given not to promote the record. In reality, the label is now into a new project, The Smiths, which, although not devoid of risk, has enormous potential and is going to mobilize the label's energies, so at least the other bands think, to their detriment. The emergence of this Manchester band went back to May, with the issue of a single, *Hand In Glove*, it too endowed with a daring cover: a photo taken from behind of a naked male model, lifted from Margaret Walter's book, The Nude Male. The second single, *This Charming Man*, illustrated by a photo of actor Jean Marais, comes out a month before *A Sense Of Belonging* and whets the appetites. Given the success of Aztec Camera the same year, Rough Trade no longer has any faith in Treacy and his band.

So, the release of *The Painted Word* is put off. Rough Trade isn't interested. Daniel ponders for a while on the idea of issuing the record on the Whaam! label which, at this time, has not yet closed down, but he doesn't manage to, held back by financial quarrels with a disc-pressing company. The label's extremely meagre resources are not compatible with large-scale distribution. Cash is short and time is running out. The band gives a few concerts before and during the summer of 1983, at which several songs from their future album are performed, including the impressive *Back To Vietnam* which doesn't leave the fans indifferent. It's March 1984, however, before *The Painted Word* is finally officially released, by a small label called Illuminated. Founded by a certain Keith Bagley and with premises on Fulham Road, Illuminated would go largely unnoticed during its five or six years of existence. Throbbing Gristle and other "weird" or "cult" bands like Sex Gang Children, Amon Dull II or Kevin Ayers would nevertheless work with this company dealing mainly with industrial, avant-garde, minimalist or even gothic music, with little following. The release itself is delayed by the financial problems of the label, whose days would soon be numbered. The NME review a few weeks before the release is good, but the general press doesn't follow its lead. The Television Personalities is an increasingly little-known band in its own country, while still enjoying good critical reviews. The album is discussed in a few fanzines, but not mentioned anywhere else.

The concerts given at the end of 1983 and beginning of 1984 bring about a change in the band's line-up. Jeff Bloom makes his appearance on drums, seizing the opportunity of an epic visit to Italy, where the Television Personalities go from one shady club to another, accompanied by stern-faced organizers, whom they suspect belong to the Mafia and extort money from the clubs where they play. The journeys are long and oddly silent as if some veiled threat were hanging over the organisation. The band members keep themselves to themselves, and hide their anxiety behind a polite amiability. The arrangements are chaotic, but the stay fairly agreeable, with no lack of spectators and concerts perfectly managed from A to Z in a five-man configuration which allows the band to produce a powerful and offensive sound. When the tour comes to an end, the band is given first-class air tickets for London which fool nobody: they have doubtless been concocted the day before and bear little resemblance to real tickets. But there are no problems during boarding. The airport staff make no difficulties, pretending not to notice the obviously counterfeit documents, unless of course, they were regularly party to such practices. The band is led with deference to the first-class cabin where they settle in as laid back as you like, at which point an agitated American business man, heavy and fat like a poor imitation of Donald Trump, and accompanied by his family, thrusts identical reservations into their faces. This smug guy tries to make a fuss, but the crew intervene in favour of the TVP's and make the flabbergasted millionaire change seats. The Television Personalities' caravan rolls by and arrives back home without any major difficulty, and perfectly relaxed, with another unbelievable tale to add to their list. Mark Flunder, the bass guitarist who has never really got accustomed to Joe Foster's and Daniel Treacy's strange and fabulous world, takes advantage of the homecoming to leave the band. He is replaced, in early 1984, by Jowe Head who would become the musical mainstay of the band for the next ten years.

The 1984 tour begins with a five-man lineup and continues the following year as a threesome. The concerts are globally a wow, perhaps the best ever given by the Television Personalities. The band sometimes plays for more than two and a half hours, occasionally ending the set with a medley, where Daniel and his accomplices pick their way through several dozen more-or-less well-known songs, playing the odd refrain or just a chord or two, to the greatest delight of the audience. As a band immensely into cover songs, on such occasions the Television Personalities usually shed precious light on their musical references. For the most part, the review is confined to classic songs by the Pink Floyd, the Kinks, the Beatles or the Who, but also includes more personal interpretations of the Velvet Underground, the Creation, the Rolling Stones or of more obscure bands such as the Seeds, Arthur Lee, Love, Jonathan Richman and the Modern Lovers, the Strangeloves or even Joe Meek, one of the major influences on Treacy. Alongside these often-well-known pieces, Daniel is not slow in launching into more exotic or unexpected songs or excerpts, singing for example the *Batman* theme, Madonna's *Into the Groove*, songs by Rod Stewart, Stevie Wonder, Bruce Springsteen or James Brown. The range of these medleys is widened over time to include old variety numbers (Sandie Shaw, Petula Clark), current hits (*Blue Monday* by New Order, for example, *Milkshake* by Kelis in later years) or anything else which enters Daniel's head. The medley technique becomes a regular feature during 1984 and the band's trade-mark. It's an excellent indication of the band's internal temperature, as the sequence, which sometimes goes on

for more than twenty-five minutes, requires a certain concentration and awesome cohesion. The medley opens a window on the way in which the compositions are organised and interact in the mind of the composer, since often it's a case of shifting from one song to another simply because they have a chord in common, or similar melody lines. Playing medleys on a grand scale requires the same ability to find harmony as the assembly of a DJ's setlist, and the Television Personalities do this without any preparation or rehearsal. Needless to say, that nothing is ever put down in writing. From one concert to another, more than 75% of the pieces stitched together are new, the sequences unique, and the transition from one song to another totally improvised. Depending on how the band is feeling, the medley can be brilliant or laborious. At its best, and often with the skilful help of Jowe Head, it's an astonishing and spell-binding show, which covers several decades of rock, pop and punk music, by grinding the songs into pieces and offering a sort of textual analysis and laying bare their inner structure. In the worst cases, Daniel seems to be constantly changing course, offering one or two phrases or chords of a song before jumping to the next, the medley giving the impression of a confused and inharmonious headlong rush. In the course of time, the band would turn out to be incapable of sustaining such concentration for ten or twenty minutes and would prefer to come back to a more traditional style of cover songs. The fact remains that the number of covers sung by the band, either live or in studio, would amount to hundreds throughout their career, testifying to Daniel Treacy's tremendous musical knowledge, and his desire not only to play around with other band's songs, but also to absorb their sap.

The middle of the 80's marks the official end of the band's infancy. At this time, the boyhood friends have left the scene and turned their backs on Daniel Treacy. No official break is announced. Nothing is final, but the bonds of blood and age slacken with the take-off of Creation. The Oratory gang no longer exists. Daniel is sole master of his destiny. Whaam! is dead and Dreamworld only just born. Drugs have taken an insidious importance in the singer's life, a situation not yet critical, but one which is seriously beginning to cloud the horizon. After the departure of the pretty Scandinavian who would be immortalized in the *Painted Word* songs, there is love to be shared. And the idyll with Emilee Brown.

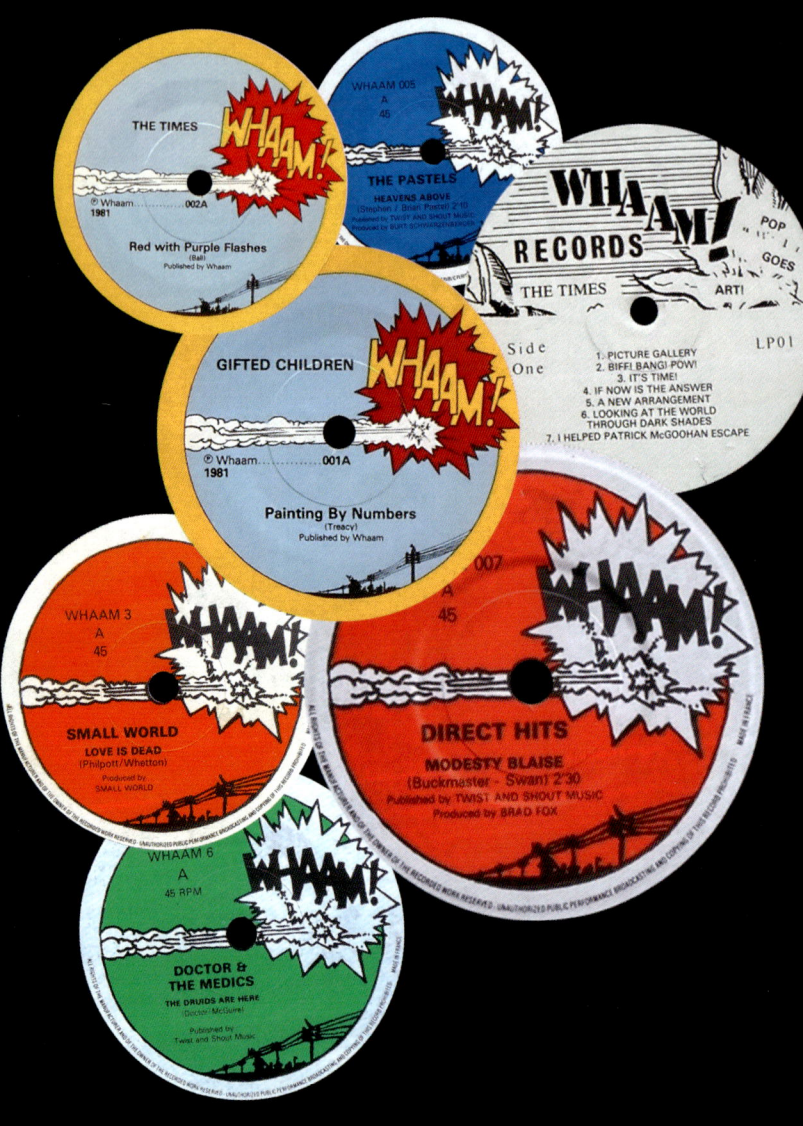

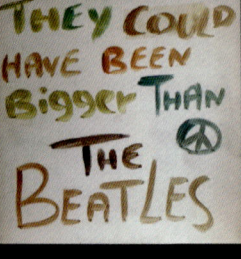

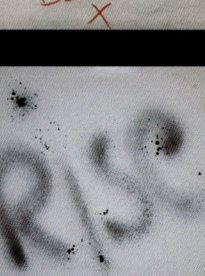

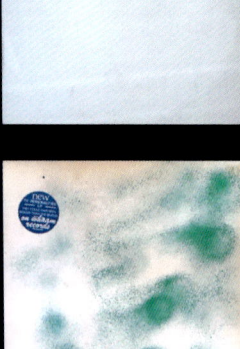

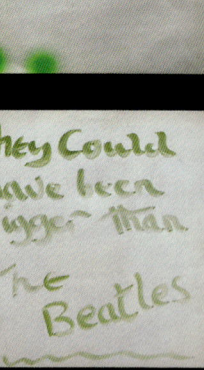

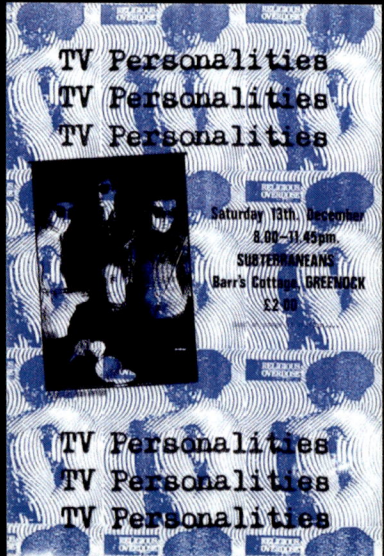

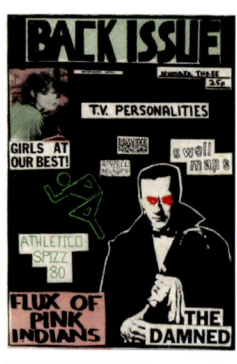

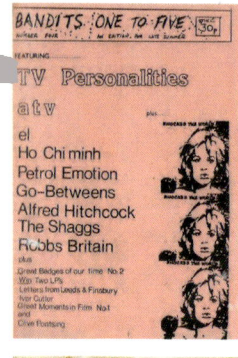
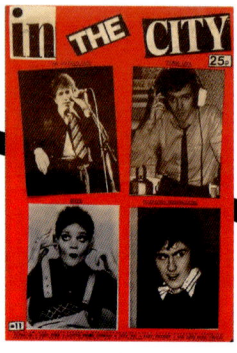
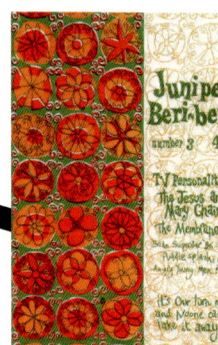
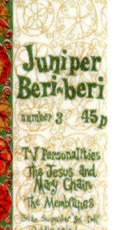

"BROADWA

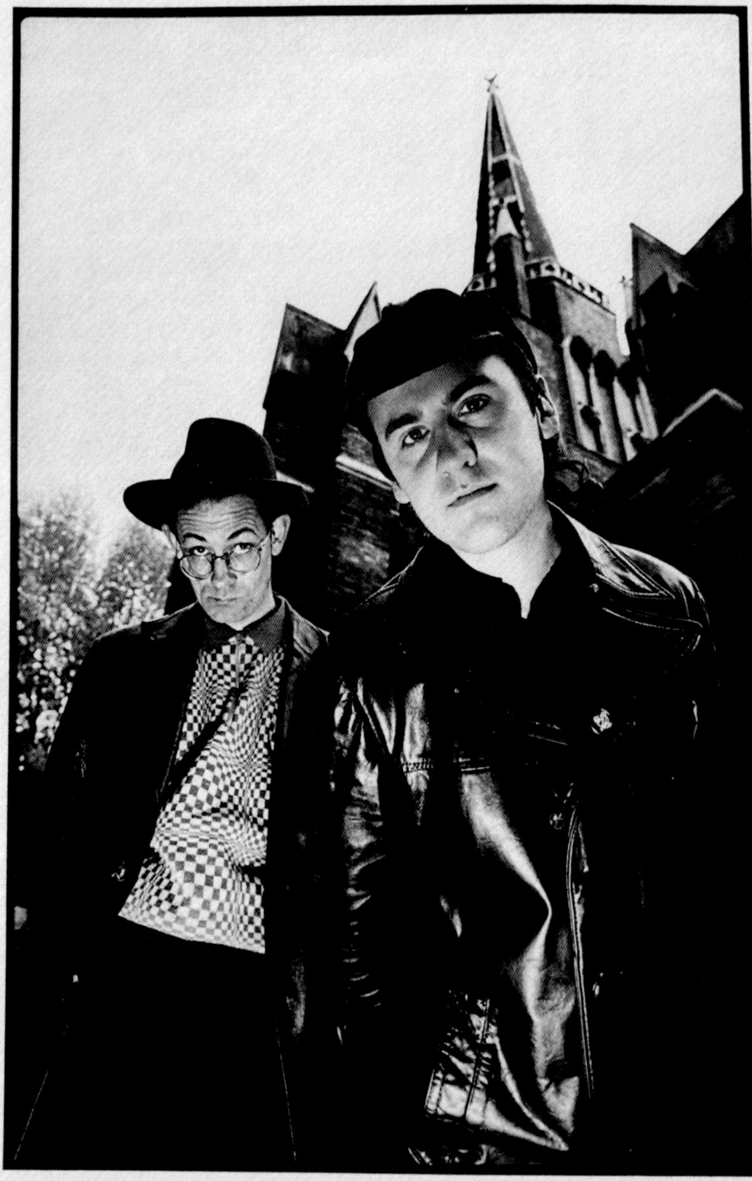

ED SIRRS

THE TELEVISION PERSONALITIES

FIRE RECORDS

FIRESTATION TOWERS · 9 HIGHBURY NEW PARK · HIGHBURY · LONDON N5 2EU
TEL: 01 359 6141-2 · FAX: 01 359 6641

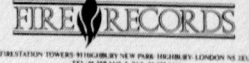

GEOFFREY INGRAM (2)

... Daniel is sole master of his destiny. Whaam! is dead and Dreamworld scarcely born. Drugs have taken an insidious importance in the singer's life, a situation not yet critical but one which is seriously beginning to cloud the horizon. After the departure of the pretty Scandinavian who would be immortalized in the Painted Word songs, there is love to be shared. And the idyll with Emilee Brown ...

— What do you think of that?

— Exaggeratedly melodramatic, but it doesn't come over as badly as all that, and you're right to make the most of it while the story is still not too sad. Some things don't ring true nonetheless. It all comes down to details and being exact is of no use when you're writing about somebody's life. I'm not very keen on your insinuations about the drugs, on the other hand. It gives the impression that you know something but that you have decided to keep things to yourself. What exactly do you know about all that?

— It's not an aspect that interests me particularly. I know that drugs were around from the band's earliest beginnings, or almost. It's no secret, everybody was using at the time, LSD, weed and anything else which could be smoked or sniffed. Daniel takes a liking to it just like others, but nobody notices or at least not many people. At the beginning of the story, it's a young guy who just takes drugs for fun. Just like everybody, I would say. Pills, mostly and then, as always, there's the moment when things go awry. You see: it's that moment which is quite difficult to identify. It doesn't happen on a particular day because he's gone onto another substance, or because he can no longer do without it. It's just something which happens ...

— You're completely in the dark, aren't you? I can see from the way you're beating about the bush. You say that you don't give a damn, but you know that in some way or other it'll be the only thing which will matter, starting from the 90's. It'll be an unavoidable subject. That's why you say that you're not interested in talking about it before …

— What do you want me to say about it? I'm not here to make a detailed record of his habits. I know he smoked crack and was hooked on heroin. That he smoked and injected all that junk. That he ended up stealing to feed his habit and that it made him go out of his mind. There's nothing new in that, nor anything very original, it's just sad.

— You're the one who chose to write this story. Was it the drugs which drove him out of his mind, or did he take drugs because he was going out of his mind?

— I don't want to go into that, Geoffrey. Not unless you have some information to reveal from a medical point of view.

— You know perfectly well that I wasn't his doctor. And then, medicine couldn't tell you any more about that than a nun could about making a porn film. From a medical point of view, anyone who drinks a glass a wine every day is an addict. So, drugs on the same basis … There are times when taking drugs helps you avoid other ailments.

— You're not going to raise that old argument again. Daniel used it himself in certain interviews when he made his comeback after the turn of the century. If he used drugs, he said, it was because drugs did him less harm than the misery which beset him when he was clean. I never believed a word of that. Junkies always tend to minimize the consequences of their habit and present it as something beyond their reach. In 1985, a journalist asked him what drugs did for him. You know what he answered?

— No

"A good remedy for my hay fever!" You see. In the music industry it's an illness which is often admitted to with hypocrisy. There's not a single pirate recording after 1985 where he doesn't make a joke when he's on stage about "going to the loo", or the imminent arrival of his "doctor". To me it shows how important drugs had

become in his life. I can hardly believe that he used drugs to stave off some sort of problem or mental illness. You've got to keep psychology out of it at all costs. Do people take drugs for pleasure, by mistake or out of spite? Do people take drugs to escape or to numb their minds? What can you reply to that? People take drugs and that's quite enough to explain the extent of their despair. Daniel fell into the trap and there are few more terrible ones.
— Care for a glass of wine?
— I wouldn't say no. How did we get on to this subject?
— You were telling me where you'd got to …
— I'm making progress, but there are still lots of grey areas.
— Well, I hope that there will still be one or two left at the end.
Geoffrey Ingram came back a few moments later with a bottle of French wine.
— Here's to Daniel!
— Yes, to Daniel. Do you think that he has any chance of pulling himself together?
— It's not very likely. I'm glad you accepted to come and see me.
During our first interview, Geoffrey Ingram had offered to be at my disposal if I needed anything whatsoever. It was a fairly conventional, but generous thing to say and which only referred, of course, to what he could tell me about Daniel Treacy, and nothing else. I had e-mailed him a few questions which he hadn't answered, claiming each time not to be able to particularly enlighten me. After all, he'd only seen Daniel episodically, even if regularly, and in quite unusual circumstances. So, I was surprised when he contacted me again to invite me to discuss things at his place. Geoffrey Ingram had invited me to come round after dinner and spend the evening with him so that he could show me some of his "treasures" as he put it, without going into details. He'd told me that he had lived for over ten years in the Clapham Common area, a few hundred yards from the flat which Daniel Treacy and Emilee Brown had shared from 1985 to 1988 and from where he

had managed the affairs of the Dreamworld label and organized most of the *Room At The Top* gigs. I had taken the trouble, on the advice of David Newton, songwriter and lead guitarist of the Mighty Lemon Drops, one of the most impressive bands discovered and produced by Dreamworld, who had given me the exact address and sent a photo, to walk casually past the house, before calling on Ingram. I had stopped to eat some fish n' chips nearby, and had been able to appreciate the difference of wealth and property between these South London neighbourhoods, often only a few hundred yards apart. The building in which Emilee Brown and Treacy had lived was intact, having only been slightly done up on the outside since the 80's, whereas the area had rapidly changed over the last fifteen years. Clapham had gone up-market. Long considered to be an ordinary neighbourhood for ordinary folk, the area had been adopted by a wide community of wealthy foreign residents, students and also young gays who had turned it into a burgeoning and trendy place to live. It was in an old traditional house wedged between a pastry-shop and a hair-dressing salon, typical of the new activities flourishing there, that Geoffrey Ingram had taken up residence, now living alone after having officially retired as a doctor, and given up any ideas of getting married again. The area was still home to a few celebrities such as J.K. Rowling, author of Happy Potter, Vanessa Redgrave and the designer Vivienne Westwood, who could occasionally be spotted in the local shops. It was a bohemian area, on the scale of a village, where such an effete, sophisticated and elegant man as Geoffrey Ingram could do no other than flourish. The house, of which he occupied the top floor, was spacious, elegant and furnished with a refinement not dissimilar to what the films had revealed of him. Since our previous encounter Geoffrey seemed to have got younger. To tell the truth, I had been stricken by his appearance when he had answered the door, as if the man opening it had been the younger brother of the one I'd seen the first time. His hair, which several months earlier had been thinning on top, seemed to have grown and strengthened. The crows' feet under his eyes had diminished and his face was less marked by age. I thought that perhaps he had had face-lifting surgery and simply made a banal compliment on his apparent good health.

— You don't know how right you are. You'll be surprised to know that a remake of *A Taste of Honey* is under discussion. For the cinema … It's a wonderful piece of news, if they go through with it. Even if it means I have to undergo a change of appearance.

Geoffrey Ingram continued to act as if his age depended on the interest accorded by the younger generations to his film character. A TV channel only needed to screen a replay of the film or a play in which he had appeared, for it to take several months off his age. The rumour of a remake of Tony Richardson's film had very much contributed to his new appearance.

— Come with me, he said, after pouring me another glass of wine.
— You're going to get me drunk, I laughed. The Burgundy was strong and my head was already spinning.

He showed me into a room which must have been his study. It was about ten square yards in size, but seemed much smaller as it was cluttered with piles of books and old souvenirs such as trophies (tennis, apparently), newspaper cuttings and illustrated albums that elderly bachelors tend to hang on to. There was also video equipment consisting of a TV set, a DVD player and an antique video-recorder.

— Take a seat.

Geoffrey motioned me to the armchair in front of the TV and leant forward to switch on the apparatus. He had prepared a video cassette which he slid into the recorder and sat down next to me, after refilling our two glasses which he had brought from the living-room.

— Ready?

I nodded, not really knowing what to expect.

The cassette crackled, flickered and wavered before the film settled on the entrance to a theatre or concert hall. The "cameraman" pushed his way through the entrance, winding his way around the bouncers and the blokes talking and smoking in the hall. I didn't recognize the place at first, but the camera paused on a poster which indicated that it was the Hammersmith Odeon in London. I could even make out the date. The recording was from 1984. The scene was undoubtedly filmed with a hand-held camcorder. The shots were clumsy and made you feel slightly sea-sick. The filmmaker made his way along the rows of seats, crossing the path of other creatures dressed in the style of the period, with far-fetched hairdos, Pink Floyd tee-shirts, brightly-coloured outfits and jackets with shoulder-pads. Most of the spectators had a glass in their hand and were casually smoking as people do while waiting for a show to begin. In the background, as the cameraman approached the hall, music could be heard. The Television Personalities were on stage. I thought I detected *David Hockney's Diaries*, but the song quickly changed to *Back To Vietnam* when the cameraman finally went into the hall.

At that time of the evening, ten or twenty minutes before the stage entrance of David Gilmour, the back of the Hammersmith Odeon was still quite empty, but the first rows were already filled as if ready for the parade. It was an impressive hall, able to accommodate over 3000 people which, since the end of the 80's was a favourite with international artistes for recording live shows. The art deco hall, built in 1932 by architect Ronnie Cromie for what was then known as the Gaumont Palace was magnificent, and one of the most famous in London. The first of the three concerts to be given by David Gilmour was eagerly awaited, the former Pink Floyd singer and guitarist having already toted songs from his second album *About Face* around most of Europe. After recording *The Final Cut*, the last Floyd album to include its founder Roger Waters, David Gilmour had had his fill of Pink Floyd. That little shit Waters had squeezed him out of the composition of this twelfth album, putting his name to all the songs and leaving him the vocals of just one cover. *About Face* would be the direct opposite of that, with David Gilmour in at every stage, the writing, the singing and the co-production. Written and composed in haste, recorded at the Pathé Marconi studios at Boulogne Billancourt, *About Face*, even though critically acclaimed at the time, was an album "of its day", full of mannerisms, relying on relatively poor compositions, apart perhaps from the singles *Blue Light* and *Love On The Air*, but enhanced by generally atrocious 80's style arrangements which kept the whole thing together. To make matters worse, the tour was grandiloquent, with an imposing band on stage and a semblance of "Moroccan" scenery with carpets and frills creating a strangely ethnic décor, which these days could be described as hippie chic. Three shows had been booked at the Hammersmith Odeon and all were sold out. David Gilmour's intention, at the height of an ego-trip (fuelled by cocaine) from which he would never really descend, was to draw attention to himself on this occasion by having the show, announced as being sold out, immortalized on video, just as Tears For Fears, Motörhead and a few others had already done. The Television Personalities, no doubt spotted by someone in Gilmour's team, had been called in as last-minute reinforcements, to open the great man's show. Had they been identified by their song about Syd Barrett? It's hard to say. The contract covered the London concerts plus a tacit agreement to accompany Gilmour on the rest of his British tour. Due to play that same day, the 28th of April 1984 that is, at one of Alan McGee's *Living Room* gigs, the TVP's had got themselves replaced and jumped at the opportunity. Gilmour was a member of the Pink Floyd, one of Daniel Treacy's all-time revered bands and this free-lance work was handsomely paid. At that time, Daniel Treacy had not lost hope of appealing to a wider audience in his own country. Whilst the Television Personalities played to audiences of thousands in

Germany, their adopted homeland, they continued to attract only a few hundred fans to their concerts in Britain.
— You like it?, asked Ingram.
— Did you film this?
— Yes.

Back To Vietnam was into its fifth minute. The Television Personalities were splendid, chaotic and violent, arrogant and amused by the hostile reaction of the audience to their music. Daniel was laughing his head off. Jowe Head was now throwing confetti into the air, but there was nothing joyful or festive in that. It was just a show within the show, a sort of morbid irony, a scathing ballet. Joe Foster was dead-pan, playing better than ever, looking straight ahead. And they played loudly, to shake people's certainties, to frighten everybody, as if their mission consisted in revealing something important about contemporary music. The message was:
— You don't get it!, You just don't get it, you fucking idiots.

The provocation came from the music, from the aggressive way in which it unfurled in waves of assault. The camera now panned over the first rows. The hippies had begun to whistle and cast reproachful looks, offended by the band's scruffy appearance, its offhandedness and its way of inducing, by its attitude, a distressing anxiety. There was a lot of indifference also. After all, it was only a bad opening performance. But what awful crap just the same. David Gilmour's album was copper-plated and full of good feelings. It spoke of love and break-up in reassuring and expected tones. The Television Personalities' music was lop-sided, clumsy and as if perverted by a twisted relationship with reality. None of the spectators at this moment were capable of realising that Daniel Treacy was perhaps the Syd Barrett of his generation, a lost child, a poet capable of composing great songs on a shoe-string. Here he was just a loser, screaming out this endless *Back To Vietnam,* whose anti-war message went over their heads. If only …

When the song ended in an electric cataclysm, there was total silence. One of the house managers brought a vacuum cleaner on stage and asked Jowe Head to clean up the confetti. It was unbelievable, but the bass-player complied willingly, wiggling his bum like a housewife in a porn film. He vacuumed the red, yellow and blue scraps of paper as if his life depended on it, while the others looked on and played scales on their instruments. The public jeered. Or was it afterwards? Then Daniel turned to Joe, nodded his head and, smiling and with a hint of emotion, launched into a medley of Syd Barrett's songs. Did he think that this would please the audience? Were they certain that the fans of David Gilmour and the Pink Floyd knew anything about Syd Barrett? Daniel strummed away at *Set The Controls For The Heart Of The Sun*. He scribbled his way through *The Gnome Song* and hummed *See Emily Play* which he could play perfectly, stammering through the lyrics in his out of tune infantile voice. The public had obviously recognized the songs. Not everyone, but they knew that here was something unusual. Some felt the fragility and the meaning. It was Barrett versus Gilmour. It was art versus industry. It was the 80's versus the 70's. Hit versus miss. You could see it in the film: there was surprise but also embarrassment, as if the ghost of the early days had suddenly slipped out from under the heavy Moroccan carpet. Treacy was singing of an alternative history, one of retaliation and people gone missing. Heroes are not the ones you imagine. This was more or less what he was saying, and what nobody could hear. Ingram's camera paused successively on each of the musicians before coming back to settle on Daniel Treacy, whose face, still juvenile despite his age, was aglow with pleasure and mischief. The guitar was slung across his chest and dropped slightly when he moved towards the mike again:

— Get a pencil and paper out. Make sure you make a note of the whole address. This song is called ... *I Know Where Syd Barrett lives*.

A murmur ran through the audience and a few cat-calls were heard. There was hardly anybody now who was not riveted to the happenings on stage. It's possible that some spectators had already heard the song or had heard of it, but most discovered it with intense interest. Nobody had come to listen to the Television Personalities, except perhaps Ingram, and you couldn't but wonder how he had known about it, and why he had turned up at that precise moment.

*"There's a little man
In a little house
With a little pet dog
And a little pet mouse
I know where he lives
And I visit him
We have Sunday tea
Sausages and beans
I know where he lives
'Cause I know where Syd Barrett lives
He was very famous
Once upon a time
But no one knows where he lives
And I visit him
We have Sunday tea
Sausages and beans
Jelly and ice cream
I know where he lives
At number 6 St Margaret's Square, in Cambridge
'Cause I know where Syd Barrett lives!"*

Daniel had waited to sing the refrain for the second time before revealing to the 3000 people now in the hall, most of whom were doubtless Pink Floyd fans, the real address of the little house in which Syd Barrett had taken refuge three years earlier. The author of *Arnold Layne* and *See Emily Play* had at first gone to live there with his mother before she left him the house and went off to live with her daughter. His mind was supposedly blown by LSD. Syd Barrett no longer inhabited it. On the scale of the Hammersmith Odeon that evening, it was no mean matter and certainly no minor scandal.  The audience rustled with dread, people exchanged frightened glances then carried on, as if nothing had happened. Daniel ended the song rather abruptly, and the band left the stage in silence. Ingram's camera captured them making for the wings, plus the slight ripple of applause which accompanied them. The picture was interrupted for a few seconds after that, before starting again with an unsteady back-stage shot, as if captured several yards in the air. It showed the corridor leading to the dressing-rooms and then went from one to the other as if there were no walls. In the biggest one, Gilmour was getting ready alone. Looking in the mirror, he was brushing his hair and adjusting his shirt-buttons. On a coffee table, there were one or two lines of coke waiting for takers, some French wine and grapes. His musicians were next door, downing a few jars and merrily playing the fool. The camera did a long track-shot across the corridor which resembled the ones characteristic of Orson Welles's films, except that here everything was in slow motion and slightly laborious. The Television Personalities had gone back to their dressing-room. They were sponging themselves down and laughing. Joe was bare to the waist and Daniel wrapped in a towel. He was laughing about his clever antics.

Jowe said:

— You 'ad it all planned from the start, didn't you, you prick? Admit it.

Daniel didn't answer. The camera zoomed in on his face. He looked pleased with himself. He always ended concerts either over the moon or deep in the dumps. There was never just the right balance. Drugs intervened just in time either to prolong or erase one or the other of these sensations. It was increasingly difficult for Daniel to cope alone with these mood swings and to get back into a state of stability compatible with daily life. Navigating between the two worlds took a toll that nobody could understand. And then the video came to an end.

— Well? I told you I had interesting things to show you.

— Incredible. I can't thank you enough. I never thought I'd get so close to this episode.

— Me neither. I've only seen the band live on four or five occasions which is not much over a period of thirty years. I'd arranged to meet Daniel that afternoon when he told me that the band had been invited to play at the Hammersmith Odeon. He was paralysed with fear, even though he wouldn't admit it. It was the first time that the group had played at such a big venue in Britain. Daniel was expecting the audience to be hostile. He put my name on the guest-list, and told me that he'd be really glad if I were there to support him. Unfortunately, I arrived very late. My surgery was packed that day and I had a hard time getting through all my patients. But in a certain sense, I arrived just at the right moment.

— I have a question to ask you.

— Go ahead.

— I don't understand how you were able to film back stage. I mean those shots. You would have needed to cut open the building and float through the air to see what you've shown me.

— The magic of films, dear boy. I have a few privileges unknown to common mortals. Don't worry about such trivialities.

Geoffrey told me the rest of what he knew about the concert with Gilmour. From the outset there was a difference of style between the Television Personalities' team and the former Pink Floyd singer's. On the one hand, the TVP's had unloaded second-rate equipment, used amps picked up cheaply, thrown any old how into the back of a van. On the other, Gilmour and his team had state-of-the-art equipment, carefully packed in numbered crates and arranged in unpacking order. Gilmour and his musicians had ignored them, pretending not to be able to distinguish the musicians from the roadies. Daniel, Joe and the others had taken refuge in their dressing-room, and had seen nobody before the start of the concert. Their sound check had lasted barely ten minutes. They had played the whole of *Part-Time Punks* and then a few bars from *Bike* as well as *David Hockney's Diaries*. The sound was remarkable, and he played too often to need to make many adjustments.

After the revelation of Syd Barrett's address, there had been no immediate reaction. Gilmour had played his set and it was only then that the decision was made known. The singer's manager and come and said something like:

— Mr. Gilmour doesn't want you to open the first half tomorrow. Nor the following days. Sorry.

Joe had asked why. The manager had replied:

— That's the way things go.

It wasn't so much this business about the address which had tilted the balance, as the style of the Television Personalities, which had turned out to be in complete contradiction with what Gilmour was trying to set up: pop that was classy, enthusiastic and at the same time, a little heady. He wanted to create commercial music which would not disown everything that he and Roger Waters had done with the Pink Floyd. Waters and Gilmour hated each other at present. Gilmour performed solo so that his vision of things would never again be contested. He wanted to sing with celebrities. Above all he wanted to play the guitar, to soar aloft with the notes and no longer be bound by endless lyrics. Gilmour hated bands that listened to themselves singing. He didn't like writing lyrics and sometimes called in friends to help him out when he couldn't invent a few idiotic lines to sing. The TVP's were not structured enough, too punk and disorganised to serve as a build-up to the trip and the movement that Gilmour wanted to instill. They seemed "spiritual". Gilmour detested that. There was no place for them in the decor.

It was now evident that Geoffrey Ingram was trying to get me drunk. He had filled my glass again while we were watching the video and I could feel that I was about to collapse. The French wine was strong. He brought some little biscuits and that did me some good, but I was pissed and slightly out of touch with what was happening. The room had closed in on me. I had slunk into my chair.
— You ready for another video?
— Of course.
Old pictures of the TVP's were rare. The Internet abounded in poor-quality recordings of the band between 2006 and 2011, but it was clearly not Daniel's best period. After what had happened to him, his voice had weakened and was even more out of tune. The band didn't always play well either. There were a few good moments, but often they verged on disaster. Some performances were quite unbearable. Daniel was not always able to come out on stage, and all this was splashed about on YouTube, to the point that it was hard to remember that the band had long been remarkable. They were at their most sturdy and brilliant when playing as a five-some, but the trio made up of Daniel, Jowe Head and Jeff Bloom was not without efficiency and charm. I was expecting Ingram to show me another video of a concert, but it was something completely different.

The video began in the park of a large house. From a technical point of view, Ingram had completely liberated himself from any fixed position. The camera floated in the air in a complicated choreography of high angles, pan shots, forward zooms, as if it were operated by a real film director, slightly tipsy, but terribly sure of himself. Crossing the park took half a minute or so. The camera paused to follow the ballet of luxury cars and the arrival of guests in all their finery or in fancy dress. The park was immense and hidden in the twilight was a sumptuous example of an English garden.

— How'd you manage to film this?

If the shoulder framing of the previous video could create the illusion, the means used to create this one, and the sophisticated camera movements could only have been done with the help of a whole film crew, or extensive shooting equipment.

— Being oneself a film character opens up possibilities that you can't even imagine, replied Ingram with a smile. That's not the most important thing here. What's important is that the film exists, isn't it?

As in the previous film, where the camera moved through the crowd, this time it moved towards the mansion and an area where what looked like a courtship party was taking place. The mansion was lit up in flickering red and orange as if on fire, majestic and at the same time, veiled in a disquieting intensity. The facade was wide and imposing, decorated in a late neo-renaissance style of dubious purity. A shadow cast on the main entrance by the trees in the park had the form of a skull, of which the door represented the open mouth. The "cameraman" or at least whoever was filming at that moment, handed an invitation to the doorman, who looked at it in a mirror to decrypt the inverted writing. Dressed in a smoking-jacket the man gave him a knowing smile and in impeccable French said that he hoped he would "enjoy himself". The cameraman went through the wide door and followed the monumental staircase that led to the first floor. On the right was a high-society couple in obviously made-to-measure costumes, completed by extravagant headpieces. The man, in evening dress, held his wife by the hand. He was wearing a fur hat topped by a wide tray on which had been fixed a still-life scene including a stuffed pheasant and other small animals. His wife was dressed in a magnificent lilac satin dress, and had her face hidden beneath an authentic stag's head. It was a spectacular scene with these people dressed in such ostentatious and decadent luxury, but it was nothing compared with what awaited the guests inside. The cameraman encountered other guests, their faces disguised or painted, wearing incredible jewels, absurd costumes and above all, a most extraordinary collection of masks and facial decorations. One woman, who looked like she might have been a Countess, was wearing a hat made up of three enormous black leaves from which there hung, hiding her face, a green, polished and shining apple worthy of a Magritte painting. One man had his face cut into white-painted slices. A woman was disguised as an Easter egg, with lace trimmings and wearing a sort of pair of bloomers. Some people had two identical heads (one was their own) and others had planets hung between their two ears. The orchestra, disguised as a Venetian fanfare, its musicians also masked, played a vaguely discordant lounge music, stirred up by a droning spectrum of electronics.

As the camera moved about, it filmed the orchestra, the cocktail table and the buffet, all characterized by the greatest extravagance. On the starters table lay a plastic female dummy, frighteningly realistically disemboweled and covered in blood. Between its thighs lay dying a battered baby cut in two, a theme repeated elsewhere, mixed with dead animals, copulating tortoises or baskets of fruit. The atmosphere was strange and totally surrealistic, but was based on rather sick imagery, albeit particularly creative, as if you had penetrated some secret society or come upon a vaguely satanic ceremony. At the end of the banqueting hall a sort of dark boudoir had been set up; in which huge seven-branched candelabra gave flickering light to a row of sofas. Cavorting on these, surrounded by Grecian statues depicting nude men and women as well as explicit sex acts, were smooching couples. A man with his face painted to look like clouds on a blue sky was touching up a blonde with a top model's figure and her upper body covered with copper and aluminium foil to look like an everlasting forest landscape. And all around there was that resounding debilitating music. The melodies were extremely repetitive and regularly interrupted by clashing cymbals, which disturbed the goings-on, and contributed to give everything an inharmonious and oppressing aspect. Was it a house-party, an orgy, the annual ball for the adepts of a sect? It was difficult to say. Ingram at my side was careful not to comment, leaving me in my drunken stupor to cope with what was filing past my eyes. I was terrified and fascinated at the same time by this documentary-type film, which seemed to relate to an event, a courtship party, a reception given several decades before. The film had a grain to it, reminiscent of the time of Visconti and a few film directors in the same vein. And then the mystery was partially lifted when the cameraman came upon Salvador Dali. He was one of the few people there who wasn't in fancy dress. His black curled-up moustache, which he twisted with his fingertips, was his only disguise. Salvador Dali was accompanied by a very tall model, a splendid blonde dressed in a light and almost see-through dress. The cameraman followed her into what seemed to be the VIP lounge, an antechamber off the main drawing-room, where the upper crust of financial and mass-media circles lounged on sofas. There was Audrey Hepburn, her head enclosed in a birdcage containing three cockatiels. There were also Jack Nicholson, Woody Allen and Mia Farrow, Debby Harry and Peter Fonda. As well as other show-biz and art-world celebrities whom I couldn't identify, but which Ingram named for me, as they filed past the camera with obvious relish. In the background, Dali welcomed the new arrivals with a vibrant "Greetings", rolling the "r" outrageously as he shook hands.

— Look carefully now, it only lasts for a few seconds, he warned me.

The camera pivoted through 180° to film a dessert table covered with mousses and creams in psychedelic colours and came upon two men standing opposite each other, talking in front of a mirror in which their faces were reflected.

— There, he said.

The first was Daniel Treacy. He was soberly dressed in a black suit and a paisley shirt with a Mao collar. He was holding a glass of champagne in one hand and in the other, a book with a title I couldn't make out. In front of him was a slightly bigger guy with curly hair thinning at the front. He was wearing a white shirt and cream linen trousers, that concealed a protruding belly. He turned slightly, having perhaps noticed the camera, and I recognized the former Pink Floyd singer, Syd Barrett, his face puffed up and his eyes bulging from their sockets. Syd Barrett and Daniel Treacy were chatting barely a few yards away from Salvador Dali but what they were saying was inaudible. And then, suddenly, the reflection of the painter appeared in the mirror, while he took the two musicians in his arms and hugged them. Dali kissed them on the forehead and pressed their heads together, until in the mirror you could think it was a unique two-headed creature from whose lower neck there now poured out, like in a Z-series film, a bloody raspberry-coloured froth. A woman fainted at the four feet of the two-headed singer, crashing noisily to the floor, while Dali, with his so characteristic voice shouted loudly to get everybody's attention:

— But zis it's horrible! Zis it's TRRREMENDDOUS!

Unable to believe my eyes, I turned to Ingram at the moment when the tape suddenly came to an end. What had happened after that? Impossible to tell. Just as impossible as the scene which I had just witnessed.

The song *Salvador Dali's Garden Party* had been performed live in the autumn of 1985. It would be 1990 before it would be included in the album *Privilege*. I was light-years from thinking that it had been inspired by real events.

— Nice bit of film editing, I laughed, finishing my glass for the last time. You really took me in this time.

— You don't think any of this is real, do you?

— How do you expect me to believe it? It just doesn't make sense.

My research was perhaps not as complete as it might have been, but I had quite quickly identified the famous *Surrealist Heads Ball*, organised by the Rothschilds. It was one of the most well known in the history of international high-society events. It had taken place in December 1972 at the Château de Ferrières and had brought together in a parade of masks and costumes, some of which had been imagined and no doubt made by Dali himself, a whole load of the well-to-do from aristocratic, business and show-biz circles. Photos of this mythical party for the Gotha had circulated a few years before, lending credence to what had been said about it. You could see the guests wallowing in mind-blowing luxury, their faces deformed by surrealist art, split up and fractured, walking lasciviously around in a fascinating and macabre setting. Men appeared as if everything were about to degenerate from one moment to the next, into a ritual mix of Satanism and a high-class orgy. Audrey Hepburn was in fact present, but to my knowledge, there had never been any other Hollywood actors. Woody Allen was at the beginning of his career at the time and no doubt was not yet acquainted with Mia Farrow. As for Daniel Treacy, he would have been barely a teenager if ever he had been in France at the precise time and place of the events. What Ingram had shown me could only be a fabrication, or at best a fantasy, even if the reconstitution is astonishing and the authenticity of the film shots, as shown to me, could scarcely be contested. But it would have taken a huge budget to fake such a scene. The tradition of the surrealist ball mentioned in the song *Salvador Dali's Garden Party* goes back, in fact, to the *Surrealist and Oneiric Ball* given in honour of Dali and his wife Gala in 1935 in New York. In a famous restaurant, a new kind of party had brought together the local intelligentsia wearing costumes as provocative as they were extravagant. Dali had turned up in a candy pink bra and his chest wrapped in a sort of glass casing. His wife had then started the fashion for morbid hats, having placed on her headgear the manikin of a dead baby, reminiscent of the Lindbergh baby kidnapped and assassinated in 1932, and whose murderer was on trial at the time. It's in the light of this tradition that the Rothschild's ball was to be seen and to this very ball that the Television Personalities' song was linked.

Stanley Kubrick had given a fairly realistic version of a similar perverse event in his last film, *Eyes Wide Shut* with Tom Cruise, (mentioned by Daniel Treacy as a guest at the party on the occasion of a concert in Linz on the 3rd of April 1990). A sort of Venetian carnival hosted a monumental decadent orgy, where the "upper crust" mixed with cohorts of shapely call-girls.

In the course of time and various performances, Daniel had extended the guest-list beyond reason. Syd Barrett was mentioned in it at least once during a concert given in Nuremberg on the 1st of April 1990, along with Roman Polanski, Dee Dee Ramone, Sonny and Cher, the Velvet Underground and the Television Personalities, which could substantiate the inferences of Ingram's video. For two decades, the list had been enriched with a whole assembly of film stars, mostly American, and other comic allusions. All of these had taken part and swollen the ranks of the *beautiful people* implicated in this pop-art party. Among the celebrities invited at some time or other by the Spanish painter were included:

— Actors: John Wayne, Steve McQueen, Warren Beatty, Paul Newman, Rock Hudson, Keanu Reeves, Denis Hopper and Jack Nicholson.
— Musicians: Fred Astaire, Mick Jagger, John Lennon, Prince, Michael Jackson, Jonathan Richman, George Michael, the Stone Roses, Oasis, the Charlatans, Julian Cope, The Jesus and Mary Chain, Simon Le Bon of Duran Duran and of course, Daniel Treacy.
— Politicians: Ronald Reagan, the Austrian president Kurt Waldheim, Richard Nixon.
— Top model Cindy Crawford, writer Truman Capote, painter Roy Liechtenstein, busty singer Samantha Fox and a few dozen others.

The Television Personalities' song had changed this sordid party, symbolic of the values of the intelligentsia, into a merry colourful birthday party. Where it was possible to imagine sleazy macabre costumes, power relationships, rapes and bewitchments, Daniel had preferred to see merriment, wealth and superficiality.

It's quite likely that this party was organized in response to the times, appearing or disappearing between one capital city and another, like a mirage or a travelling circus, into the past or the future. It replicated and reproduced itself in order to spring up wherever there were riches and ambition, beauty and arrogance, genius and the affirmation of class superiority. For Daniel Treacy, it represented a place of ultimate amusement as well as a cultural Valhalla where his personal or contemporary heroes came to enjoy themselves and then take their rest.

Just as I was about to ask Ingram for a few explanations, I felt my body give way under me. I felt two arms around me, hugging me tenderly, then I passed out. When I woke up, I was at home half-naked on my bed with a bitter taste in my mouth, and the impression of having been taken advantage of.

I tried to contact Geoffrey Ingram to find out what had happened, but for the following five or six days, I only got his answering machine. Since there was nothing else for it, I left it at that, incapable of making head or tail of this experience which was probably nothing more than a drunken night during which I'd wandered off the tracks, hallucinated and gone crazy. But to what extent? Only God and Geoffrey Ingram knew. He knew all about these sorts of things.

A few weeks later I received a visiting card which I took to be from the film character on which he had written: "Everything is covered by psychedelic immunity. Don't worry".

WITH EMILEE

At that time there was Dreamworld, a record label, the *Room At The Top* gigs, in a room above a pub called The Enterprise, like Captain Kirk's star-ship and also, above all, Emilee Brown. For many people who mention it today, it was "another time", something you refer back to with a certain nostalgia, but which could only spring up and exist in the context of a past that you don't really regret as much as all that. It was a time when there were still records, of course, but also one when brilliant parties, organised at the drop of hat and with little resources, could attract several hundred people. In 1985, Daniel Treacy, who is now over 25, is already a veteran of the London concert stage. The leader of the Television Personalities has seven or eight years' experience behind him, tours which have taken him to the continent and naturally, a halo from the First Saints' Psychedelic Church, which confers on him a certain respect. The commercial failure of the Television Personalities clings to him, but at this stage, it's neither a handicap nor a claim to fame. Independent rock doesn't exist yet. It would come into being a few years later and it would even be considered quite cool to be unsuccessful, but not for the moment. There are those who succeed, those who climb the ladder and become enormously wealthy and those who will never make it, and be left to wither. After three albums, the fate of the Television Personalities is sealed. Everybody knows it. It's very rare that things succeed late in the day. But it has been known to happen, so never say die. Meanwhile, there's still time to enjoy life and change the world or die in the attempt, as they say in American rap. The flat occupied by Daniel Treacy and Emilee Brown can be found at 9, Poynders Court, Clapham, to the west of Brixton. Situated on the ground floor near the posh neighbourhood of Abbeville Village, it's the perfect place to live for a young couple without children, in a quiet, wooded housing development, called Oaklands Estate, just opposite a row of very British semi-detached houses. At less than a ten-minute walk from Clapham South tube station at the southeast corner of Clapham Common, the flat is part of a three-story redbrick block surrounded by wide white balconies, one of a dozen such buildings in an open plan setting. It's the address of this flat which figures on the back of the Dreamworld record sleeves and from this flat, that Daniel and Emilee run their business. Indoors, Poynders Court is a little fortress of love, a bohemian refuge, sparsely furnished but comfortable, the very image of its occupants. There's not much space: a single bedroom with a bed, a small kitchen and a large living room containing a sofa, a small wooden table where Emilee works on her flyers and invitations to parties organised by the couple. A small corridor with film posters on the walls leads to the rooms, and is also used as storage space. The flat is nipping clean, but a little cluttered by the piles of books, magazines, and even records lying about everywhere, which are evidently not there just for decoration. In the toilet there are also books on a shelf and an amusing collection of National Geographic magazines. Just facing the lavatory bowl is a beach-volley ball, autographed by the Marine Girls, one of the bands produced by Daniel Treacy. In the main room, the table doubles as a desk. Near the key tray, there are post-cards and a birthday card sent to Daniel by his mother which, behind the cake and candles featured on it, says "Happy Birthday Son".

Dreamworld is an idyllic label, a place where anything could have been possible. A record company which would also be a bedroom and a love-nest. Daniel and Emilee work hand in glove. She is lively and sociable. Daniel does what's necessary and takes numerous initiatives, even if he prefers to keep slightly in the background when it's a question of getting down to business. Difficult to say who decides what. Daniel gives the impression of being the "driving force" but Emilee takes care of most of the practicalities, the promotion of the bands and all the graphic designs of the business. She's the one who takes care of the publicity for the *Room At The Top* gigs, who designs the flyers, and often stops by to ensure that everything is going smoothly at the studios. The bands who have signed up with the label deal directly with Daniel when it's a question of talking about music and seeking his advice on this or that approach, on a new song or an opportunity. The singer is always willing to share his time and his anecdotes. He's a good mate who gives advice, guidance and knows how to make decisions. Daniel is quite the opposite of the eccentric and dictatorial record company boss. He does what he thinks is right and is guided by his intuitions. In 1985, the duo manage the label's business affairs and organise gigs all at the same time, for the two activities are interdependent. Promoting Dreamworld's records is no easy matter. Allowing journalists to watch the bands on stage is a major advantage and reinforces the label's identity. Having a showcase such as the *Room at the Top* gigs also anchors the Television Personalities' activity on the London cultural scene, which is dear to their hearts. The place chosen by the couple is a small pub in Chalk Farm, ideally situated on the Northern Line and not far from Camden and its already famous market. At the centre of alternative and trendy city life these days, in 1985 Chalk Farm was less sought after, but already on the up and up. Situated at 2 Haverstock Hill, *The Enterprise* pub is on the first floor of a Victorian building constructed in 1865. Today, it's a stylish hotel with twenty rooms or so, which still publicises its former tradition of hosting concerts and alternative musicians. An "authentic" pub has been recently recreated on the ground floor to allow customers, mostly foreigners, to appreciate the best of British atmosphere without having to leave their hotel, or relinquish free Wi-Fi. In 1985, the first floor is just a room devoid of any equipment, which the landlord allows the couple to use in exchange for a share in the bar takings.

The gigs owe their name to a British film by Jack Clayton, which came out in 1959 and features, among others, the French actress,

Simone Signoret. *Room At The Top* is a showpiece of British cinema of the period, adapted from a novel by John Braine, itself largely inspired by Maupassant's novel *Bel Ami*. Acclaimed upon its release, the film brought to its Director, to Simone Signoret and Laurence Harvey, the leading actor, a whole host of awards, including Oscars. The film is a masterpiece that depicts an ambitious young man who seduces the daughter of a rich local industrialist. To avoid scandal and prevent things from going too far, Susan, played by the very pretty Heather Sears, is sent away by her family, which gives Joe, the young man, the opportunity to take up with an unhappy and sexy married woman (Signoret) and to fall madly in love with her. Alice (Signoret) is on the point of convincing Joe to agree to her divorcing in order to marry her, abandoning his dreams of wealth and glory, when Susan turns up again. Joe is torn between the two women until Susan reveals that she is pregnant. Whilst he intended going off with Alice, Joe is forced by the young girl's father into marrying her, and accepting an important job in his father-in-law's business. Distraught, Alice gets drunk and is killed in a car crash. Joe, resigned to his fate and indirectly responsible for the death of his mistress, steps back in line. He marries Susan and becomes the respectable man he dreamed of being. The social ladder is now his for the climbing. His wife adores him. He has the life he wanted, but takes it up in grief and despair. Dreamworld, as they say.

Room At The Top is served by a masterful scenario and remarkable performances by the actors and actresses. It's a film that fits in perfectly with the cultural references displayed by Daniel Treacy since setting up his band.

At Dreamworld, life is simple and easy. Emilee defines the graphic environment, designs and prints the flyers and jackets. She and Daniel choose the bands, mostly from cassettes which are sent to them, or after scouting ventures to trendy venues. Dreamworld begins its activities with singles by the Impossible Years and the One

Thousand Violins in the summer of 1985. The first is an American band from Philadelphia, which Daniel contacts directly by letter then by telephone, after having read an enthusiastic review of one of their first songs, *Attraction Gear*, released on a compilation album on the Bomp Records label, entitled *Battle of the Garages*. Treacy explains to Todd Shuster, lead singer of the band, who was later to become a teacher, that he has just set up a record company and would really like to sign up the band. The Impossible Years send him four songs including *Attraction Gear* and launches Dreamworld's activity with the EP *Scenes We'd Like To See*, a record which would go completely unnoticed, despite the quality of the Americans' song writing. *Attraction Gear* is a song with a tempo which is slow, but well packaged, and which testifies to the label's pop orientation. Dan and the band members communicate only over the phone which, at the time, is not always easy. Daniel has a few tricks up his sleeve to avoid paying the exorbitant telephone charges, and gives this band, which was never to come over to Britain, its finest and unique recording experience. Because of the records companies' lack of interest, The Impossible Years turn to producing their own records, but split up a few years later, each member going back to civilian life. The story of the One Thousand Violins is a little more interesting. Colin Gregory and David Walmsley are old acquaintances of Daniel who had released on the Whaam! Label a single by their first band, The Page Boys. With singer John Wood, and an inspired rhythmic section, the two men devise a colourful pop influenced by the 60's. Their first single, *Halcyon Days* (Dreamworld n°2) gets noticed for its B side *Like One Thousand Violins,* which gets them onto the John Peel show and into 49th position in the *Festive Fifty*, the list of the 50 best songs played by the British DJ, and acclaimed by the audience. In 1985 moreover, it's The Jesus and Mary Chain that hits the jackpot by reaching first and second place with *Never Understand* and *Just Like Honey,* ahead of the Fall's *Cruiser's Creek*.

The following year, the One Thousand Violins would have a mini-hit with *Please Don't Sandblast My House* (Dreamworld n°8), another airing on Peel's show and an unexpected 11th place in the indie charts. The band would leave a belated legacy at the end of the 90's, at which time its music would be rediscovered by diggers and nostalgic fans of the period. A Japanese compilation of their songs would thus become a minor success in the Land of the Rising Sun. But Dreamworld's recording highlight, apart from the repackaging of two of the Television Personalities' albums and one single by the band called *How I Learned To Love The Bomb* in early 1986, would be the discovery of the promising Mighty Lemon Drops.

Natives of Wolverhampton in the Black Country, The Mighty Lemon Drops are led by Dave Newton and Tony Linehan, the band's lead composers. Influenced by punk but also by psychedelic rock, the band has a vocal and melodic style reminiscent of Echo And The Bunnymen, post-punk, stylish and hard-hitting. Set up in October 1985, the Lemon Drops record five songs in a small eight-track studio, and start handing out a few cassettes to their entourage. Dave Newton takes the trouble to send out three by post. The first is to Alan McGee, but there is no follow-up. The second is addressed to Martin Whitehead of Subway Organization, a Bristol label that shows an interest, but is too slow in attracting the band. Daniel Treacy receives the third and gets in touch with Newton straightaway. He isn't exactly in a rush either to suggest releasing an EP. Of course, at this stage, Dreamworld doesn't officially exist. Treacy plays for time and asks for more information about the band. He suggests that the musicians keep in touch with him, before getting back to them a few months later to see if they want to appear at one of the *Room at The Top* gigs. By a quirk of timing, the invitation becomes a double event, as the Television Personalities enroll them to open their Deptford City show on the 12th of July, the night before their

concert with The Membranes at the Entreprise. The northern band drives down in a Volkswagen Dormobile belonging to Tony, the bass player. Between the 12th and the 13th, the band arrives in Clapham and parks for the night outside Dan and Emilee's flat on Poynders Road. Towards lunchtime, while the Lemon Drops are still fast asleep, basking in the glory of their previous night's success, Daniel Treacy in slippers and tee-shirt, knocks on the window of the van.
— Wakey wakey you lot! Live Aid is on the telly. Adam Ant is singing. You wanna come in and watch it?
When the Lemon Drops step into the flat, Adam Ant has almost finished singing *Vive Le Rock* on the Wembley stage. The organisers had invited him in order to add yet another name to the huge list of artistes brought together for this "good cause", but he is only allowed to play one piece. The big guys mustn't be squeezed out. Some would emerge enhanced from their appearance here. Others would be honoured, like Bob Geldof and U2. Long live rock music. Long live television. Many think, paradoxically, that Live Aid in 1985 marks the end of rock'n'roll and a new venture into the world of business. *Vive le Rock*. Adam Ant is one of the first to play, after Status Quo (17 minutes) and The Style Council (25 minutes). Costello would be allotted three minutes. Bowie nineteen, but around half past seven in the evening when the audience is at its height. Elton John, Madonna, Paul McCartney, Freddie Mercury would cover the London prime-time. It's a great event. The greatest TV success in history since Elvis's come-back. An apocalyptic success. There's no guarantee that the show is the stuff dreams are made of, as far as the Television Personalities and the Mighty Lemon Drops are concerned. Just the sight of these poor beggars watching television in the middle of the day, compared with the current elite of the profession, is enough to measure the gulf which separates them from that other world awash with money, where they make video-clips and sell records

by the cart-load. On the Dreamworld scale, the Mighty Lemon Drops are nonetheless the most promising and brilliant of bands. The concert at the Enterprise on the 13th of July goes off remarkably well and gives rise to a particularly enthusiastic review in the NME by The Legend!, a journalist who is close to McGee and his Creation label these days, and calls the shots on that weekly music magazine. Daniel Treacy reads the article over the phone to Dave Newton, who still lives with his parents. He makes him an offer of recording a single without delay. Things move fast in those days. Less than a month later, in mid-August, the Mighty Lemon Drops gather at the ElectroRythm studios in Hornsey, North London. The studio is well-known for the quality of its equipment, enabling rapid recordings of reasonable quality. It's one of the cheapest studios in London, way in advance of low-priced facilities such as the Alaska studios at Waterloo, frequented at the time by almost all the indie bands. Daniel is not there for the recording session, but Emilee stops by to say hello to the band in the afternoon and takes a few photos on the lawn outside the studios, one of which will be used for the record sleeve. In the evening, the Mighty Lemon Drops go to the Entreprise for a second *Room At The Top* gig, with The Trees band this time, before going back to the studio to mix the five songs recorded the day before. At the end of the evening, Daniel invites them to stay overnight at the flat. Daniel and Emilee are the kindest label bosses in the country. Daniel tells jokes and does imitations. Emilee makes them laugh to tears. The couple are in perfect harmony. Daniel gives the impression of being in control of the label's affairs, but Emilee is the more convincing of the two. When they are all worn out, the band occupies the living room as well as the corridor, where they have to bed down with the One Thousand Violins too, spreading make-shift mattresses, blankets and duvets on the floor.

The first single comes out in December, and is welcomed enthusiastically by the critics. Daniel is as proud as a peacock at a Janice

Long recording session on the 26th of January 1986, broadcast on the BBC the following week. The public is hooked. Business is booming for Dreamworld, which sells more than 15,000 copies of *Like An Angel*, released in two versions, and which has to manage, at the same time, the burgeoning craze for the One Thousand Violins, who are aired by John Peel in September. Things get complicated for the Wolverhampton group. Daniel and Emilee put every effort into promoting the band and its music. They work wonders to get articles and endorsements published left, right and centre, but the company hasn't the capacity to put the musicians on its payroll and enable them to live on their music. Two of the band members give up their jobs. Several major labels come courting the Mighty Lemon Drops whilst Daniel can only offer them the recording of a mini-album on Dreamworld. Weeks go by, and despite the spectacular sales of the EP, the Mighty Lemon Drops pocket nothing. Neither salary nor royalties. Understandably, they turn down Daniel and Emilee's offer and sign up with Blue Guitar, a subsidiary of the Chrysalis label, set up by Rough Trade boss, Geoff Travis. In January 1986, their last appearance with Daniel Treacy at a *Room At The Top* gig sets off a minor riot. Crowds gather at the doors of the pub and queue up, hoping to make their way upstairs, even though the band has already started to play. In August of the same year, they record their first Peel session under the banner of their new label. Success seems within their grasp. But it was to elude them. The Mighty Lemon Drops would never join the elite. With or without Dreamworld, they produce three albums in 1986, 1988 and 1989 that don't live up to Chrysalis's expectations and fail to capitalise on their excellent start on the independent stage. Sire, their American label, releases the album *Laughter* which reaches an honorable but insufficient 195th position in the famous Billboard 200 American charts. Little by little, the band disintegrates and finally splits up in 1992, leaving in its wake a few nice numbers, some live albums and one hit,

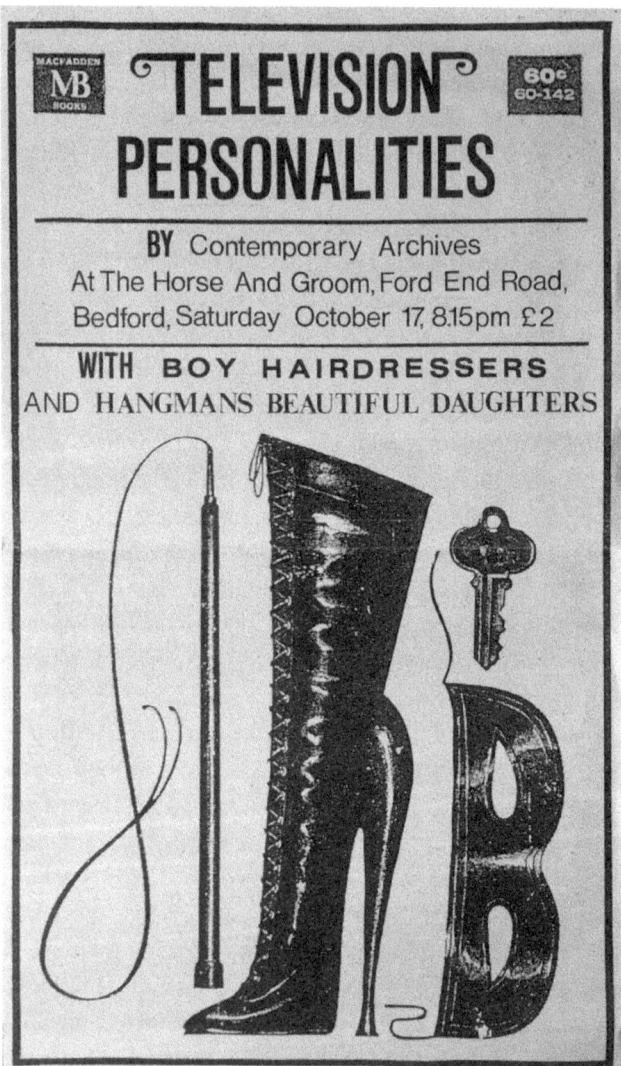

Inside Out, which would later be highlighted in the compilation dedicated to them in 1997.

The story of the Mighty Lemon Drops smacks of unfinished work and in its way symbolises Dreamworld's predicament. One or two satisfactory results are not enough to change leagues and be able to face the future serenely. Despite a few exploits, there would be no miracle for Dreamworld. In 1985, the door that had opened and allowed the emergence of independent labels such as Creation, 4AD or Mute Records, has slammed shut in the faces of the smaller record companies. It would be the early nineties before the re-emergence of a few labels dealing in electronic music, such as Ninja Tune and one or two others. The wavering financial management of the label only makes things worse. There is much evidence of this. If Dreamworld has no delusions of grandeur like Factory Records or others, its internal cash-flow is questionable. None of the bands signed up by the label seem to have received the slightest return on the sale of their records, neither the smallest bands, of course, that made a loss, nor the bigger ones like the One Thousand Violins or the Mighty Lemon Drops who, with one or two singles, contributed to a significant profit. Probably part of the money, as with all record labels, was used to fund subsequent recordings or promotional activities, but other expenses can't be accounted for. Daniel Treacy and Emilee Brown produced records only in economical studios and for very limited periods. Some recordings cost less than 100 pounds and achieved sales of over 10,000 copies. So where did the money go to?

It's probable that Daniel and Emilee lived from day to day on the admittedly modest income from the sale of the records. The couple went out a little, to exhibitions, concerts, but with no correspondingly lavish lifestyle. The economics of the *Room At The Top* gigs are rather vague and it's possible that even if they didn't cost much, they didn't bring in enough money to cover the advertising costs (printing flyers etc.) and the fees of the few paid artistes.

The rent on Poynders Court was naturally part of the standing expenses both of the label and the couple. In the end, Dreamworld's difficulties, such as they appear in 1987, can only be explained by part of the money starting to be, or ending up by being, siphoned off by other types of expense. Several things indicate changes in Daniel Treacy's life at this time. His absences and disappearances are more frequent, and in addition to organising gigs, to his work as a producer and record company boss, but also as singer and lead composer of the Television Personalities, he appears to be leading a second life of wanderings and visits to dubious neighbourhoods. One of the bands signed up by the label mentions their surprise when, after a concert in the North, they come to ask Treacy and Brown to put them up for the night at four o'clock in the morning. Without them even having knocked at the couple's flat, Daniel, fully dressed and smiling, opened the door and invited them in as if he had been waiting for them or hadn't yet gone to bed. It was only years later that they would ponder on his laid-back attitude and vaguely euphoric appearance. Another band recalls Daniel complaining at one point about a mysterious break-in at his flat. On this occasion, some equipment and the master tapes of most of the label's recordings would seem to have disappeared. It's true that the flat was on the ground floor, but few traces or memories can be found of such incidents in the area at that time. According to some sources, the master tapes had been quite openly offered for sale at Greenwich market a few days after this burglary, which seems strange if they had been stolen from their owner and not sold on by him. The most likely explanation is an increasingly pervading and costly addiction, probably due, notwithstanding the structural problems of the label, to the difficulties which complicate the couple's undertakings, and hinder the development of Dreamworld after eighteen months of existence. What with the £15,000 supposedly paid by Wham! in exchange for Daniel dropping his former label, and the accumulated income from 1985 to

1986, it's likely that with prudent management, the couple could have continued their activities for several more years. But this is not the case: Dreamworld's days are numbered. It's even becoming difficult to find money for the rent each month. As is often the case in such situations, Dreamworld counts on its driving force to bring the money in. In January 1986, the Television Personalities release an EP consisting of three new pieces, including the single *How I Learned To Love The Bomb* and the interesting *Then God Snaps His Fingers*. These would be the only original and previously unreleased items of the Dreamworld era. In June of the same year, the label repackages the compilation album for which it had been initially set up, *They Could Have Been Bigger Than The Beatles*, followed by *Mummy Your Not Watching Me*. These re-releases make no changes to the original records, except for the revamping of the jacket. In 1987, Daniel and Emilee add a new number to their catalogue for a 45rpm by the Television Personalities to include two new songs: *Privilege* and *Me And My Desire*. The album *Privilege* is also programmed for release on the label, but neither the 45 rpm nor the LP would see the light of day in Dreamworld's lifetime. The label plays its last cards in 1987 with an ultimate song by the One Thousand Violins and, in early 1988, with the first album by Emilee's band, The Hangman's Beautiful Daughters. The adventure would stop there. Dreamworld comes to an end, and with it the relationship between Emilee Brown and Daniel Treacy. The situation deteriorates quite quickly. The rent is no longer paid and the flat at Poynders Court has to be abandoned. Daniel moves into a squat and starts what would be politely referred to as his "alternative lifestyle". Some would say that this is the beginning of his downward spiral. Shut-down of the label, romantic break-up, eviction from his flat. Let's say that the prospects are bleak, but there's still everything to play for.

From an artistic point of view, the years between 1985 and 1989 are very different from the previous ones. The discographic production of the Television Personalities is almost zero, but the band carries on appearing live and cultivating its special relationship with audiences who still answer the call, especially in Germany, where the band now plays on a regular basis. Managed by Thomas Zimmermann, a young German encountered in London and who quickly becomes their official tour organiser for continental Europe, the Television Personalities travel in a lightweight format, as a trio, with well-defined roles. Jeff Bloom is an energetic drummer, whilst Jowe Head on bass is capable of improvising in almost any situation and filling in as lead singer when Daniel needs a bit of rest. In this line-up the band appears on dozens of occasions for a little less than ten months leading up to 1993. For a few months towards the end of 1988, Ed Ball reappears on keyboards for a few British concerts. On one occasion at the end of November, Daniel performs solo. Ed even fills in for Jowe Head on bass for a gig in Bedford where Jeff Bloom is also replaced by a local drummer. Apart from these rare exceptions, the line-up is solid, unchanging and offers sets which often reach two dozen titles or more and can go on for almost two hours non-stop. On New Year's Eve 1989, the Television Personalities play in Berlin, accompanied for two songs by Evan Dando, leader of the Lemonheads. It's a memorable concert which runs to no less than 49 titles, including a dozen incredible covers from the Rolling Stones to Mel and Kim. While hundreds of thousands of Germans and onlookers crowd around the Berlin Wall, chipped away since the 9th of November by chisels, hammers and all sorts of other objects, a few hundred spectators choose to ignore the rejoicings, preferring to listen to the band at the Ecstasy Madhouse in the Schönberg district. The hall is one of the spaces set up inside the international discotheque, a night-club situated at 30, Hauptstrasse which, in the post-war years was one of the most popular with Afro-American GI's. In 1989, the Ecstasy hosts a few fairly hard rock concerts. Nirvana gives a concert there on the 11th of November, two days after the fall of the Wall and the opening of the check-points. The main hall is converted into a discothèque. A second hall situated below and dedicated to electro-pop is largely patronized by the gay community. The Schönberg district is an area of counter-culture and resistance. At the time, it has yet to become the trendy place it is today. Towards midnight, whilst the Television Personalities are still on stage, movement can be heard outside. People coming and going. There is a general sense of elation. The setlist rolls along as if in a dream. *King and Country, Privilege, Stop And Smell The Roses.* Daniel Treacy performs his old songs, but includes a lot of new ones, songs which have now been waiting for long months to be brought together in a new album and which have been left stranded since the collapse of Dreamworld. Difficult to estimate the number of spectators present at this concert at such a peculiar time as this, when Germany is living through the frenzy of a changing world. A few hundred at most, even if the hall is full. The Television Personalities are in attendance at the bedside of a world which is opening up and collapsing all at the same time. The wall is a few hundred yards away, demolished and celebrated by a huge crowd. The concert is grandiose, fragile and just a stone's throw away from an event which it ignores but whose liberty and electricity permeate the atmosphere. At the same moment, or almost, the centre itself is filled by a quite different refrain. Invited by the organisers of the festivities, the actor David Hasselhoff, nicknamed the Hoff by his fans, and hero of the *Knightrider* and *Baywatch* series, climbs on stage to sing his hit, *Looking For Freedom*. The American is sporting a piano-scarf and a bright leather bomber-jacket. His athletic body, which would later succumb to alcohol and depression, is carried aloft in a surrealistic bucket lift from where he looks down on the hundreds of thousands of spectators. *Looking For Freedom*, composed by the German producer Jack White, had come into being ten years earlier. Written in English, it became a hit in the German version sung by Tony Marshall, *Auf der Strasse Nach Süden,* before becoming the official anthem of East Germans dreaming of freedom in summer 1989. Hitting number 1 in the German (and Swiss) charts in December 1989, it tells of the emancipation of a wealthy man's young son who decides to succeed in life by his own efforts. The song is mediocre and the singer, David Hasselhoff, manages fairly easily to emphasize its lack of subtlety.

The song lasts five or six minutes. Hard to tell what the Television Personalities are singing at that precise moment, but it's likely that the two concerts are taking place in tandem. The applause overlaps and a sort of electrical arc, caused by the clapping, the alchemy of the clamour and the jubilation, stretches in a momentary lightening-flash across the few hundred yards separating the two stages. For a timeless instant which only Mother Nature can explain, the two stages become one, putting Daniel at the centre of an immense crowd, whilst the Hoff disappears. David Hasselhoff and he merge into a mirage. The audience drifts from one camp to the other, as if it were pouring from East to West. At present, Daniel has donned the American's radiant cloak. He shines like a glow-worm and glistens like the Eiffel Tower on New Year's Eve. In a few seconds it will be midnight. Daniel feels the cool air in his hair. He swings his locks in tune with Hasselhoff's swaying golden curls. 1990 awaits. Daniel has never before played to such a crowd. Never before has he had the impression of so much power over the audience, and at this precise moment, he doesn't give a toss whether it's his audience or not, whether this whole scene is a mere misunderstanding. For the Television Personalities, it's an unconditional triumph. At last, they have what they deserve: an immense crowd to applaud them, a whole country joined in a peaceful and joyous revolution to celebrate the power of their music.

When he would later imagine, in one of his notebooks, a biopic of his life, Daniel would choose to be portrayed by the actor Gary Oldman. Christopher Walken would be Jowe Head. That's how he

sees it. Anthony Hopkins is the aging Syd Barrett. Only Courtney Love would play her own part at all ages. Later. The film is entitled *Drugs "Я" Us*, a reference to the well-known toy company. But for now, it's not Gary Oldman, but Daniel Hasselhoff, the famous actor-singer of *Baywatch* and *A Sense Of Belonging* who holds Berlin between his guitar strings. The Television Personalities are a committed band. Only Germany has realised this. Anti-war, anti-privilege. It's only right that they should be where they are.
The audience shudders when Daniel launches into a nine-minute-long version of *King and Country* and begins to cry when he plays the first chords of *Stop And Smell The Roses*. What an unforgettable moment! And then all of a sudden, as if someone had pulled out the plug, everything stops. The lights are suddenly extinguished. The glittering cloak is turned off and reverts back to the dark, worn-out leather jacket. Daniel shrinks an inch or two and is once again a club singer, deserted by the audience. He is enveloped in a dense and slightly eerie silence. The stage-lights go out, except for one spotlight which, a few yards away from the singer, lights up the young magnificent face of a thirty-year-old man. Daniel, who in 1990, has still fairly good eyesight, adjusts his gaze and recognises Johnny Depp, the Hollywood actor. Depp is leaning against a pillar sipping a pint of beer. Daniel comes over to him and asks him what he's doing there, what role he plays in the biopic of his life. Depp waits a few seconds before replying, just as he has been taught at the Actors Studio, in order to adopt a weightier tone. He relishes a swallow of beer and draws on a cigarette, tapping on it with his finger to drop the ash just there at Treacy's feet. Deep says:
— I'm the dealer.
He doesn't say "I'm here if you need me". But it's just as if he had. Daniel smiles but you can't tell whether he's happy or sad. When the curtain falls, he goes off arm in arm with Johnny Depp and the two men vanish into the darkness of the hall. – Treacy repeats:
— The dealer. Johnny Depp will play the dealer.

OPENING THE SHOW

He was perhaps nine or ten when they used to roam about together, her driving the scooter and him behind. He used to hold on tight and would either snuggle his face into his sister's back, or slide to the right so that the wind would slick back his hair and force him to screw up his eyes. Patricia drove confidently, and at what seemed to him an amazing speed. You should have seen how the King's Road and the 60's sped by. You should have seen how the people seemed to be running. There were the colourful clothes, the classy, eccentric get-ups, the blonde beauties and the sophisticated men. Sometimes the scooter would stop at a traffic light or behind a bus, and it seemed as if time stood still forever. Daniel would take the time to look at the sky and smile, and then everything would be mixed into one again: his heartbeat, his sister's breathing, the houses and the people. He could think back to childhood at will, with great ease, even if it pained him a little to come back to the real world afterwards. Many of his songs had allowed him to go back to when he was still a child. Although he didn't know why, these songs were always rather sad. Daniel had often felt unhappy. Born quite a while after his two sisters, his mother had not wanted him; and had often made him feel neglected or left him in the care of his big sister or his Irish family during endless holidays. His father was not an easy man and scarcely more affectionate. This status of last-born and unwanted child was long deep-seated in him and according to some, explains his lack of self-confidence and fragility. His family relationships had nevertheless left him with an immense affection and a great fondness for his elder sister Patricia, as well as veneration for his mother whose every movement was closely watched by him. *Everything She Touches Turns to Gold,* an 8-minute-long song from the heart, featuring at the end of the album *I Was A Mod Before You Was A Mod,* was an exceptionally lucid account of the situation.

> *"I Could never forgive you / I Could never forget you, he sang for his mother's ears.*
> *Mother didn't want me so she gave me to my sister like a toy*
> *A frightened little boy, big sister's little toy*
> *...*
> *And in the strangest way they made me feel unloved*
> *And Confidence came fleetingly and left as soon the same way that it came*
> *Slowly out the way and left me deep in shame*
> *I Wish I could love myself and tell myself*
> *There's more to life than this.*
> *I held it in my hands, I had it in my hands ..."*

Sometimes he was frightened and sometimes in pain. His mother had been a homeless child abandoned at birth by her own mother; and brought up by nuns near Torquay. He had often dreamed that his mother would protect and shelter him. He often sang *Games For Boys* on stage, one of the rare numbers for which he demanded an attentive and respectful attitude from the audience. They could insult and jeer at him, which happened quite frequently, but he didn't like that happening when he sang *Games For Boys*, because he felt that it destroyed the harmony of children playing. As pictured in the song, the family circle is idealised: the boys are playing in the rain, father is washing the car ("again", he insists) while mother is doing the dishes helped by one of her daughters. Then the children are given their toys: an *Action Man*, a bow and arrow for the boys, a doll and beads for the girls. This stereotyped image is turned upside down by the children's suggestion that they exchange clothes and pretend to be each other, inverting the assigned social roles. *Games For Boys* is a happy song. It's not surprising that it often features in the band's set list. Children's toys figure on the jacket of the band's last album, a teddy-bear and a toy box, and you constantly feel Daniel's nostalgia for those untroubled times, his need to plunge back into that childhood source of tranquility and warmth. It's not as if he needed to think of anything while injecting himself with heroin, but perhaps Daniel still saw himself back there in time, perhaps he conjured up pleasant images to make the chemistry work. It's not as if the drug gave you visions, hallucinations or gilded dreams. Its main advantage was to propel you into a timelessness devoid of all contingency, a chilly and gripping calm stripped of all emotion other than a hollow satisfaction. The needle switched everything off and momentarily interrupted your life with all its emotions, its trials and tribulations. With practice you could, of course, act as if everything were normal and still have the feeling of well-being and weightlessness. Either before or after the concert, there's never a bad time for it, nor a good one. Each day, if possible, and as often as the state of the finances allow. In many ways, heroin is useful to calm anxiety and heighten awareness. Heroin keeps success and failure at bay. It distances you from ethics and compromises, troubles and obligations. Above all, it keeps you away from yourself and all the shit that surrounds you.

It's Kurt Cobain's management team that had contacted the Television Personalities with a view to a concert at the London Astoria. When he accepted the offer, Daniel knew nothing of the band's music and even less of Kurt Cobain, its singer and leader. When he enquired around, his friends told him that the band was no small matter. On the 23rd of August 1994 Nirvana had pulled off a great coup by giving a thunderous concert at Reading, before an audience of 30,000 in early afternoon before the fans were even warmed up. The stage had rocked with the violence of the set, by its aridity and the feeling of acoustic aggression that it produced. A few songs from the band's new album *Nevermind* had emerged from the sonic magma and confirmed to the Anglo-Saxon world that Nirvana would be the hot event of that 1991 autumn. Cobain had seriously injured himself by jumping onto Dave Grohl's set of drums and wandered about everywhere with a huge bottle of cough mixture. A few weeks later, in September, the release of *Smells Like Teen Spirit* backed by MTV, had unleashed a critical and commercial tidal wave. In just a few weeks, Nirvana changed leagues and went from the status of a great prospect of alternative rock to that of a mammoth of mainstream, heralding the shift of grunge and a whole branch of guitar rock towards the wider audience. The band leader didn't care much for this sudden craze, which he thought a source of compromise and obligation to take on numerous responsibilities. Spurred on by his record company, and nevertheless attracted by the possibilities opened up by success, Cobain played things by ear, sometimes euphoric and sometimes directing all his rage against himself. Released on the 24th of September, *Nevermind* and its legendary baby swimming after an out-of-reach dollar, pushed Michael Jackson out of the number 1 spot in the American Charts several months later. In the autumn of 1991, having signed up with the major label Geffen, Nirvana would purely and simply invade Europe. Anxious to have a good time in the face of thousands of fans who he considered to have been brought together partly on a misunderstanding, Cobain decided to invite a few irreproachable bands to join him for the tour. It's for this reason that he sought out the Television Personalities, a band which he thought of as one of his early influences, after having already attracted for his British tour Eugene Kelly, his Vaselines hero, and his new band Captain America. After appearances at Reading, at the London Astoria and on other dates, Kelly's career would benefit from Cobain's helping hand and, thanks to his benevolence, he would even be signed up by Atlantic Records. There would be much less of an effect on the Television Personalities, who would gain no additional notoriety after this one date, apart from a visit by Courtney Love and Cobain to one of their concerts in America the following year.

Although they were in diametrically opposite situations, both winding along the spiral of success, but in opposite directions, Cobain and Treacy nevertheless had several concerns in common likely to bring them together. Among these was the question of the place of success in an artistic career: what worries or hopes could come of it, a sort of fear of being compromised and an attachment to independence. Treacy's fate was already sealed, whilst Cobain reproached himself each day with having left the discomfort of anonymity and lack of public recognition, for a gilded cage and murderous overexposure. Addiction was another point in common. Treacy was falling headfirst into his heroin habit, whilst Cobain would, for several months, walk a destructive path of alternating efforts to kick the habit and being tempted to drug himself into oblivion.

When they first met backstage at the Astoria, Tracy and Cobain hardly spoke to each other. Cobain asked the singer if he had everything he needed, which Daniel confirmed, though it's not clear what was meant exactly by this "everything" that each of them had. Although initially programmed to open the show, the Television Personalities ended up with second place in the set, that is to say the tough job of playing just before Nirvana, whose equipment they borrowed moreover, such a thing happening between an American top of the bill and an opening band being a rarity worth mentioning. On paper, it wasn't such a bad position, but it meant that they would have to confront the impatience of fans waiting for their favourite band. And things didn't go off wonderfully well.

The audience was abysmally young, knew nothing about the trio in front of them and, above all, was totally unwilling to give them a chance. Faced with a crowd expecting an overdose of decibels and brutality, the Television Personalities take a suicidal opposite stance and persist in a third-degree intimate rock. No need to remind you that nobody gives a monkey's toss about the lyrics and what they might be saying, and they care even less about why this band is here. Daniel plays the jester and lowers his head when the first whistles ring out. The band is in good shape and plays a subtle, yet powerful set, but it makes no difference. Treacy's voice is too weak to suggest anything other than a homosexual pop band. Cries of "Piss off" begin to be heard early on in the set, but they don't bother the band too much. Backstage, the fans of indie rock suffer in silence, whilst the majority of the audience wavers between indifference and hostility. "Oh, fuck off" shouts a guy. "Fuck off yourself" replies Daniel who continues as if nothing had happened. Towards the end of the set, Kurt Cobain leaves his dressing-room and comes to listen to Daniel, standing discreetly in the wings, hidden from public view. Dave Grohl joins him and the two men swing their heads, listening to a few songs. Then Cobain stays there a while on his own, moved by the band's music. He doesn't know what he's going to do with this *Beavis and Butt-head* style army which has made him their commander-in-chief. These morons are incapable of understanding why Treacy is a genius. Have they at least understood what Nirvana's music is about? You're always liked for the wrong reasons, thinks Cobain. This idea has haunted him for the last few weeks. This sudden success terrifies him. He has never wanted to be adulated by the masses, because the masses are dummos, who by definition listen to crap music. How can they possibly have become interested in him? It's what he wanted most but didn't really want. It seems to him that his whole life has been reduced to this one question. Why have these morons become infatuated with him? And what can he do about it?

The night before in Brighton, he had begun to screw up some of his fucking songs, playing them more slowly or deliberately sabotaging them, but that only made them even crazier as if they were witnessing something "special". His energy is sapped by that; and he's already worn out, even though this part of the tour has only just begun. How will he cope? He has a pain in the guts and he feels like he's living in another dimension. His only privilege is to be able to invite anyone he likes to play alongside him.

The Television Personalities end their concert by a cover of the song *Seasons In The Sun*, the English version of Jacques Brel's *Le Moribond*, popularised by the Canadian Terry Jacks in 1974. It's obviously a remarkable farewell song, but infinitely sad and even more sentimental and tearful in the English version. Daniel and his band leave the stage.

"That's funny", says the first roadie they come across, it's Kurt's favourite song. He's always going on about it. Daniel goes back to his dressing-room and comes face to face with Kurt Cobain who was waiting for him. He seems even shyer than when they met each other a few hours before the concert. Cobain shakes his hand and gives him a hug.

— Good concert, says Cobain.

— Thanks, replies Dan. Nice of you to invite us and to lend us your gear.

— Don't mention it, replies simply Cobain.

Cobain wants to tell him that he's sorry for the cat-calls and the dickheads for whom he's now a living god, but he says nothing, thinking that it would be churlish and impolite. Nor does he say that it's nice to see the Television Personalities in such a big hall and before such an audience, because he knows full well that it's the sort of hall in which the band should play every night if things were logical, but it's obviously not the case because the Television Personalities have become a bit of a cult band, precisely because they now are TOTALLY unsuccessful. Cobain wouldn't like people to say that he is condescending, as it's not at all his style. He doesn't give a monkey's about all that. The guy facing him is way above him and he knows that for a fact. At this stage, Daniel is head and shoulders above him.

— It was really great. Thanks.

Treacy is no innocent child. He knows that's the way things go. The two men say nothing for a couple of seconds, then Cobain changes subjects. He tells Daniel that he liked his version of *Seasons In The Sun,* the famous song.
— Yeah, a guy told me you like that song", says Daniel.
— You're joking. It's my favourite song. Do you know the B side of Terry Jacks' single?
— *Put the bone in*! laughs Dan.
And he begins to sing this unbelievable story of a run-over dog whose owner wants to give it a bone:

"Put the bone in
She yelled at the store
'Cause my doggie's been hit by the car ... "

— Hell, you know it?
— Yeah. It's a load of rubbish that song.
One chance in a million that two people who don't know each other talk about an obscure Canadian singer's B side, released 17 years before their conversation. One chance in one or two other millions that these two people should give a performance on the same evening before an audience of some 3000 fans. One chance surely, in several tens of millions that one of the two should be Kurt Cobain, don't you think?
"Don't let me keep you", says Cobain to Treacy as if it wasn't him who had a concert to give.
Treacy goes back to his dressing-room without seeing anyone else. He would keep an endearing and sincere memory of the young man he had encountered and who would in the following weeks become one of the greatest independent rock stars in history. "Cobain was a shy guy", he would say later.
Their second and last encounter would be in New York, on the 21st of July 1993. Courtney Love and Kurt Cobain would look

in on the Television Personalities' concert at the Wetlands, the first date of a ten-day or so tour centred on the East Coast. That evening, the TVP's perform at one o'clock in the morning. Debbie Harry is also in the hall. Cobain shakes hands with Treacy and introduces him to his wife. Not much is known of their conversation, or whether they do anything else other than take pleasure in seeing each other. Both have continued their fall or rise at this moment and the handshake has a strange tang to it. It wasn't obvious that the two men would meet each other at this precise point on the slope. Who's going down and who's going up? Who's dying and who's living? Since their last conversation, it's difficult to say who is the unhappier of the two.

The Television Personalities give a mediocre concert. Two days later, Nirvana's lead singer has a narrow escape from a heroin overdose. Just one of a series. He is reanimated amidst great panic by his staff, without needing to be taken to hospital. Things quickly resume their course: photo sessions, interviews etc. At this precise instant he has less than nine months to live. His daughter Frances is just a year old. He attends a sort of birthday party as if he were a stranger. Both men give the impression of being lost children caught up in a morbid and implacable adult routine.

The question is, which one will be the first to end it all? Cobain has died and Daniel … well … They've really made it.

ALISON WONDER-LAND

Six years after the issue of *The Painted Word*, the Television Personalities return to the 33rpm format with the album *Privilege*, released this time on the Fire Records label. The company had been set up five years before by Clive Solomon, a former acquaintance of Daniel and the Television Personalities. At the beginning, Solomon and the Television Personalities' lead singer hung around the same London venues which heralded the psychedelic renewal. Moreover, he had organised gigs inspired by the 60's even before McGee and others had thought of it, in a new club destined to become famous, the *Groovy Cellar*. At the time, Clive Solomon wasn't directly a member of the gang, but hung around wherever they were. His favourite band, among all those who trawled the scene, was … the Television Personalities, who he had seen a good hundred times on stage and for whom he had tremendous respect. It was thanks to them that he had talked to McGee for the first time, and certainly also thanks to them that he had decided to pursue his career. Producer and occasional musician, Clive Solomon's name figures, at the time of Whaam!, on *Sha La La*, the one and only single by the brilliant Jed Dmochowski, as executive producer. Whether that means he invested a few quid in the business, or that he was present during the recording sessions, is a matter of debate.

Be that as it may, in 1989 Clive Solomon is still managing Fire Records from his bedroom and is delighted to produce the Television Personalities' new album, initially promised to Dreamworld. At the time, Fire has not yet defined its strategy, nor emerged as one of the best-entrenched and interesting independent labels on the market. The model would be simple: produce young artistes, but also welcome older guys with a history, in order to try and take over their catalogue via meticulous re-releases and promotion of their new songs. The label establishes itself by crossing the path of gifted and challenging bands like The Blue Aeroplanes, The Farm, Spacemen 3, the main event of 1989, Pulp (the band before success knocked on its door) Eugenius, Mission of Burma, or even Evan Dando's band, the Lemonheads. It's a small world. Fire Records has a reputation for allowing its artistes great creative liberty and giving them long-term support. Some are more critical as regards the personality of Clive Solomon. Luke Haines, for example, doesn't spare him in the picture he paints in his book *Bad Vibes*. Solomon is described as a rather spineless guy, shy, bald and sallow, overplaying being nice to avoid conflicts. Haines, under contract to Fire with his band The Servants, quits in order to set up the successful band The Auteurs. If Treacy was to hold a grudge against Fire Records and Solomon, as he would against others later on, the release of *Privilege* and Fire Records' support of the band in the following years with two intermediate EP's and a further album, indicate clearly the attachment of Solomon and his team to the Television Personalities.

The label would moreover on several occasions re-release records by the Television Personalities, first in the early 90's, then again in 2002 to 2003, and continue to accompany the group up until the issue in 2017 of an album containing rarities, demos and other unpublished works, prior to the release of *Closer To God* in 1992. It would be a lie to say that the label was well thought of by those closest to the band, but everyone agrees that Fire put a lot of energy into making the most out of the band's reunified catalogue. Of the two albums released at the time on Fire Records, *Privilege* and *Closer To God*, it's difficult say which is the better. The band's fans usually place them a notch below their first album, which just goes to show the level of excellence achieved. The songs on the *Privilege* album, produced by Phil Vinall, one of the best British producers, were carved out and even recorded by the band in the course of three or four years of concerts. These are mostly remarkable songs, some even outstanding, which amply demonstrate the excellent health and the unimpaired genius of their composer. Phil Vinall replaces the insufficiently embellished parts, lightens the band's sound and gives it a clearly pop colouration never attained up to this point. Apart from the weird *My Hedonistic Tendencies*, a synthpop track which jars and has aged a little, the album is still as pleasant to listen to, after almost thirty years. Daniel Treacy offers one or two compositions which belong to his former psychedelic and arty inspiration, of which the record's signature song *Salvador Dali's Garden Party,* is the best illustration. But most of the record comprises songs with more personal lyrics, where the inherent sadness is offset by the inventiveness of the tunes and the agility of the guitars. Such is the case of songs like *Paradise Is For The Blessed*, the sublime opening song, or of the sumptuous *A Good And Faithful Servant* which follows. The texts are redolent of the singer's existential doubts, of the depression and solitude waiting in the wings, of the disenchantment (the terrible *All My Dreams Are Dead*) and of the fear of abandonment. The social and political aspects are always present (on *Privilege* or *Conscience Tells Me No*), but generally put aside in favour of sad songs which are among the most accomplished in all the band's discography. Vinall persuades Treacy to emphasize his voice more, which turns out clearly to be a winning card. Never has the vocalist sung so well as on this album, achieving first-rate performances within his register in pieces like *The Engine Driver Song,* or the very moving *What If It's Raining?* The studio work is fluid. Daniel is relaxed and receptive to suggestions. He knows the pieces by heart and doesn't mind having to go over them several times. He likes to work quickly, plug in, play without wasting time then move on to something else.

Vinall, who in later years, would be involved for several months with the emergence of Jarvis Cocker (Pulp) and Brian Molko (Placebo), is all admiration. He knows that several of these songs are gems, but he also knows that Daniel is aware of his limits and is not infused with the conquering spirit and aggressiveness which produce superstars.

"These are my songs", he seems to be saying as he deposits them at the feet of the producer. "They're for you. I'd rather you didn't return them to me".

The mixture of rockabilly (*Sometimes I Think You Know Me Better Than Myself*), of wild or psychedelic pop rock and of lo-fi, give *Privilege* extraordinary power and richness. A few stylistic waverings may weaken the whole, but in no way lower the quality of the compositions. *Privilege* is released in February 1990 and has a cool reception, despite the issue in October 1989 of a sound single on the theme of *Salvador Dali's Garden Party*. Fire Records does a low-key promotion of the album, accompanied by a British tour of five or six dates as openers for The House Of Love, which achieves little for the band in terms of notoriety. The House Of Love at the time is a band which has a certain success with the re-release of its first single *Shine On* and the release of their second album. However, the band is in disarray, having barely got over the sensational departure of Terry Bickers and saddled with Guy Chadwick, a leader sinking into a malignant megalomania weaned on alcohol and narcotics. It's easy to imagine the benefits derived from being yoked together with the Television Personalities.

1990 continues with an endless German tour, but the sales fail to take off, despite an album of the soundest quality. Fire Records and the Television Personalities are not disheartened and release two new singles in the second half of 1991 and the double album *Closer To God* in 1992. Between these releases, Daniel Treacy, in need of money, signs with the Overground Records label for a series of re-releases of the band's early singles. John Esplen, the founder of the label, owes his vocation to Daniel Treacy since it was during a conversation at the end of the 80's that he had seemingly encouraged him to work on re-releasing oldies and afterwards offered him the possibility of reworking his band's singles. Things would only come into being a few years later. *I Know Where Syd Barrett Lives*, then *Three Wishes* are thus revived, just like *Smashing Time*, *Where's Bill Grundy Now?* and *Favourite Films*. The singles are simply accompanied by new jackets, created most of the time by Alison Withers, Daniel Treacy's new girlfriend.

This frenzy of releases, for a band which is not necessarily often in the public eye, gives a strange impression to observers and blurs the communication connected with the new songs. Difficult to know, if you're not watching closely, which songs are re-releases and which ones are new, particularly as the band now mixes enthusiastic up-beat songs with almost acoustic numbers where Daniel plays solo in a totally different register. Where does such a band fit in? What are they trying to say? If, at this time, the band still had any hope of achieving recognition other than esteem and acclaim, it disappears into an often brilliant, but for most people, unfathomable mist. The re-releases of the first albums on the Fire label add to the over-production which, while making the band's music available once again, inspires the feeling that the Television Personalities have, in spite of themselves, become a nostalgic band of the past, bogged down in its own legend. Adding to that the live recording of a concert during the 1984 German tour, released apparently without authorisation from the band, it's the last straw. It's a false impression, since Daniel has never been so productive. Songs pour out like water from a tap.

When *Closer To God* arrives, Fire Records' usual strategy, which consists in rekindling interest in the band via revivals of its old albums, doesn't work. The signal is inaudible, as if jammed, and doesn't manage to provoke any response. The album which contains 19 tracks is nonetheless monumental and worthy of the greatest interest. It's easy to consider it as the band's last great album and a magnificent demonstration of their talent.

Phil Vinall, who is producer again, returns to the more rock sound, full of effects and echo of the band's beginnings, which, in the midst of the shoegaze and grunge wave, gives certain songs a really powerful impact. *Closer To God* is harsher than *Privilege*, but never departs from the melodic ambition and quality of the lyrics. The studio work is more extensive than for the previous album, since not everything has been written in advance. The music is meticulous, crafted, and once again, open to experimentation.

But for all that, it's not "where it's at" or in tune with what's "in" at this moment in time. Psychedelia has had its day and British pop is not in much better straits. Because of being ahead of their time, the Television Personalities are caught between two worlds and, for the first time in their career, almost anachronistic.

Stylistic coherence is not always maintained throughout the 19 tracks. Some songs are weaker than others, but without much impact on the density and power of the collection. *Closer To God* is a double album and a further occasion for Treacy to reveal the scope of his talents. The cover, designed by Alison Withers, is strange and relates to no known universe. It's not clear whether it does anything for the album which gets off to a cracking start with *You Don't Know How Lucky you Are* and *Hard Luck Story Number 39*. In these two songs, Daniel warns the listener (and himself) in prophetic tones, against changes in fortune, drugs and decadence.

> *"Would you like to see scars?*
> *My brand-new needle-marks? he sings like a show-off*
> *You've got a job, a house, a company car*
> *But you've still got shit for brains".*

The first piece is particularly violent, mixing biographical lucidity and anger directed against the well-to-do. The song ends with *"Open up your mind, it's an open door",* and like an ultimate cop-out, bids farewell to the world of escapism and psychedelics. Like the previous one, the album is a sort of patchwork of songs composed in the course of Treacy's wanderings and inspirations.

Between the releases of *Privilege* and *Closer To God,* Jowe Head and Treacy initially plan to produce a more intimate album which would only materialise twenty-five years later under the name of *Beautiful Despair*, a compilation of demonstration items and a few unpublished songs. Treacy literally forgets about the project, before re-injecting it by snippets into the monumental *Closer To God*. There's an obvious impression that the band want to give it everything they've got. Everything is sweetness and light. And it shows: Treacy is in love. His bouts of anxiety, awesomely expressed in *My Very First Nervous Breakdown* or *Very Dark Today,* are contained and overridden by peals of laughter, great moments of self-mockery (the incredible *Goodnight Mr Spaceman,* the very T-Rex-like *We Will Be Your Gurus*) and above all some very fine love songs. The benevolent optimism of *I Hope You Have A Nice Day* is pleasant to listen to, but it's the sentimental tracks which hit just the right tone that makes the album great. Even though he expresses a little clumsily his homesickness (*Coming Home Soon)* or his daft projects (*Me And My Big Ideas*) Daniel Treacy is no longer alone and drowns his sorrows in a one-to-one relationship which lights up his world. Few songs describe so well the ups and downs of love as *This Heart's Not Made Of Stone,* and even less dwell on the loved one's face with such attention and ability for amazement as *You're Younger Than You Know*. This lofty, contemplative and luminous song is perhaps the greatest on the album. It's a masterpiece of balance and delicacy in which the poetic images skillfully succeed each other, mixing naivety and sincerity as if it were a poem by John Keats.

> *"You're looking younger now*
> *Younger than the newest star*
> *That shines up in the sky*
> *Younger than the newest dream*
> *Baby dreamt last night".*

It's hard to tell if the narrator is describing the face of the girl he loves, or if he's talking rather of the effect of love on his own features. However that may be, *You're Younger Than You Know* leaves an impression of plenitude and fulfilment.

Closer To God ends with an autobiographical and existentialist eleven-minute-long title of the same name. Treacy comes back to his complicated relationship with the Catholic religion: his strict upbringing, a mixture of violence (at school and probably at home), of guilt and rejection. We know that his father was not a gentle soul and that life in the Treacy household was not always easy. We've already mentioned the nostalgic, but ambiguous relations that the singer had with his childhood. They are expressed here in a song carried by bass player Jowe Head, which is not entirely anti-religious, far from it, but transfers the issues of distress and depression into the realm of existentialism and the relationship with God. Maybe Treacy's career can be interpreted as an attempt to evince a form of original sin, to defile himself and sink to the bottom in order, like the *born again, to* rise back to the surface. The song suggests as much, but you can't be certain whether it's not all an attempt at theatrics. *Closer To God* , by its length, its intensity and its ambition, seems to be the spiritual and equally disturbed counterpart of *Back To Vietnam*. Despite the scope of its dramatic impulse, this final song would rarely be singled out as one of the band's best achievements.

With the release of two such important albums in less than three years and intermediate singles of this quality, at the end of 1992 the lukewarm reception makes things abundantly obvious: The Television Personalities are very unlikely to avoid their fate. British pop is at its lowest ebb. The American invasion is under way and despite favourable critics and reasonable sales, the band's revival turns out to be a partial failure for Treacy and Fire Records. That doesn't stop the trio from finally crossing the Atlantic for two successive American tours in 1992 and 1993, and going on tour in Japan the following year. But nobody is deceived by the band's progress which has all the trappings of a breakthrough which only exists on paper.

Things are starting to fall apart. Daniel Treacy manages to keep afloat thanks to the efforts of Alison Withers, one of the most important women in his life. Lover, best friend and colleague, Alison displays infinite comprehension. Daniel and Alison met up at the very end of the 80's. The young woman figures on tambourine in a single released in 1987 by a friend of hers, Jerry Thackray, a.k.a. The Legend! She moves in the same circles as Treacy and meets the singer several times at the heights of his splendour. The two meet up one evening in November 1988 during a concert by the *Spacemen 3*. Daniel has come with Ed Ball. Alison is there with a girlfriend. Like a teenager, she sends her friend like a scout to ask Daniel if he would like to talk to her. Daniel stammers a yes and away you go.

At the time, Alison works in a library in Kensington, not far from Treacy's parents' home which is now perched over a Council depot in a block of flats wonderfully named "Sky Gardens". Daniel had come back there to live after separating from Emilee and having spent several months of homelessness taking drugs and screwing up his head. Since then, he has sorted himself out a bit, surrounded by his family, even if he is still quite unstable. Alison also lives with her parents near Croxley Green, twenty miles or so from the centre of London.

Alison is young, knowledgeable, pretty too. She is free and lots of boys run after her. Daniel Treacy falls in love. And things continue, things go better than well. He comes to fetch her after work and presents her to his parents. His father greets her with a smile. His mother is more wary. Alison was to get on wonderfully with Daniel's elder sister Patricia, who she still sees even now. In the evening, his mother makes up two separate beds for

Daniel and Alison who wait until everyone is asleep before getting together like two secretive children. On Sundays, Daniel is sometimes invited by Alison's parents to share in the traditional family roast beef. He's not quite the ideal son-in-law, but he's on his best behaviour. He talks amiably and impresses them with his pleasant attitude. He spends hours chatting about this and that with Alison's mother. He has an evident taste for commonplace, everyday things, as if this normality at his fingertips is what he's always aspired to. A family, a quiet little life, maybe some kids: among the 1001 lives on which Daniel Treacy fantasises, this one has always hovered around him without ever managing to draw him in.

In the summer of 1989, they move into a three-room flat near Acton Town in West London. It's an old block, built in the 30's. They do some refurbishing, such as painting the entrance hall black and white. They have come into some of Alison's grandmother's furniture, as she has just died. Daniel begins to relax a bit. His drug habit is reduced to a few doses of speed on days when there's a concert. One day, Daniel comes across a strange bag forgotten on a tube train. Inside is the equivalent of three thousand dollars and five American passports in exotic names, two pairs of binoculars and a very expensive camera. From what he would relate later, the bag was just there at his side. It's not theft. The bag was calling for help. Daniel takes it and gets off the tube while it's coming to a halt. Officials arrive and seem to search the carriages and inspect the platform. Daniel makes off. Opportunity makes a thief. The money soon disappears. It slips between his fingers like a fistful of sand. But there's still the camera, and it determines Alison's career. Librarian and photographer from now on. The young woman takes her inspiration from pop art, does photos and collages. She goes to night-school. Like Emilee Watson before her, Alison becomes the graphic artist for the Television Personalities. Daniel encourages her with a sincere fervour. He encourages her to take the plunge and enrol at the School of Photography near Paddington, after leaving her job at the library. Alison lacks confidence, but her work gets better and better.

Alison excels at portraits of her boyfriend, group portraits and background shots. How many sofas, pale walls, pseudo landscapes, held up behind the tour bus, peanuts and aperitif tables? Pullovers, jackets, bonnets, whatever you like. Her approach is both distant and eager to grasp everything that is sensitive in humanity, in a corporal pose or the flash of a look. It's not an insult to other photographers to say that Alison "Wonderland" Withers is the photographer who has best captured what there was of poetic, beautiful and sometimes sadly dark, in Daniel Treacy's features. You only need to look at the dozens of photos scattered about on the Net to realise it: she created the mystery just as much as she was to reveal it during the seven or eight years over which they shared everything. For the band's record sleeves, Daniel often gives the impetus, the initial idea. Alison develops and exploits it. One of their greatest successes is the collage made for the jacket of the single *Salvador Dali's Garden Party*, which they compose lying on the floor of their flat while their cat Madonna rolls itself in the photocopies. Daniel never stops praising the *"little works of art"* produced by his girlfriend, which he would immortalise in the song of the same name.

There had been Emilee Watson and the flat at Poynders Court. From now on it would be Alison and Daniel, caught up in the eternity of these seven years from 1988 to the middle 90's.

The chronology wavers between the fits of depression, the moments of stability and the air-pockets. It comes in seven-year cycles. Such is the curse. At the ages of 14, 21, 28 and 35. The next one would be devastating, but there's still some time for happiness and love between the couple. Love is a breath of fresh air. You take refuge in your own little world. Failure is knocking at the door and addiction lurks under the carpet. The flat is a nest, an oasis, small, comfy, held together by the colours, the dreams, the piles of books, drawings and music. The main room is a workshop, based on the inevitable sofa seen on dozens and dozens of photos, on the kitchen table, which doubles as a desk, a workbench for cutting out and preparing the material, a place where they sit and work or just daydream.

Daniel and Alison would keep cats, two most of the time, called Madonna, Andy Warhol or, later on, Orangina. Sometimes their contribution is acknowledged on the record sleeves. Daniel plays the guitar, thinks up songs and writes. He writes texts which gather dust in shoe boxes, poems, dozens of pleasant little notes, short and lively like haikus. He sketches out of happiness. He plays records, reads books. Together, Alison and Daniel watch old British or foreign films, on VHS cassettes bought at the supermarket or second-hand, mainstream programmes or series on TV. They cook with Keith Floyd, the celebrity presenter at the time and gorge themselves on children's programmes and sitcoms. *The Brittas Empire* is one of their favourite shows. The series relates the life of an incompetent manager. His ideas are mostly half-baked and his life is boring. His wife has affairs, or swallows pills to keep her head above water. Gordon Brittas's deputy suffers from allergies. The receptionist is nuts and keeps her children in the drawers of the reception desk. The series is spectacular and wacky, absurd and slightly cynical. The Brittases are everything which Alison and Daniel will never be. Most of the time, Alison calls Daniel Treacy Mister Brittas. They like the humour of comedian Vic Reeves and his show *Big Night Out*, which alternates silly sketches and more serious items.

They play board games, frequently matching themselves at Mastermind. Daniel is clever at working out the combinations. He has kept the logical agility of his youth. Black and white key pegs for yellow, green and blue code pegs. There is a complexity and at the same time an inevitability in the trial-and-error approach and in the deduction which makes you think that one day, life will be as simple as the game. You just have to eliminate all the possibilities and have a bit of luck. Mastermind is an allegory of life: you make of it what you can. You reach your goal in one or two guesses, or miss your objective by a move or two. Everything comes down to that: getting there too soon or too late.

Daniel is the sort of guy who never arrives on time. It's best not to expect him at a rendezvous. Alison and Daniel nevertheless fix thousands of them. She starts by waiting. Then she gets into the habit of guessing when he'll arrive. She deliberately turns up late. It's their little unconscious game. It's obviously much easier to go out together and to leave at the same time so as to be sure of not missing each other.

The two of them go out a lot. There are concerts, of course, usually two or three a week. Alison and Daniel go to the *Camden Falcon* or the *West Hampstead Club*, the *Laurel Tree* or the *Boston Arms*, pubs and clubs which they frequent. They like to discover new bands and keep in tune with the vibrations of the audience when they first hear an up-and-coming band more talented than the others. Daniel would never lose this curiosity. After the concerts, they often finish the evening, although not systematically, with a few jars down at the pub. Daniel and Alison aren't keen on parties and are more inclined to spend quiet evenings at a restaurant or in a bar, rather than haunt the night clubs. They have their good addresses: the *Stockpot*, the *Brompton Troubadour*, the *New Piccadilly* or the *Honey For The Bears* (one of the Television Personalities' titles) in Acton. Their flat is at 37 East Vale on Second Avenue. They live there for two years before moving to Cambridge Court on Amhurst Road near *Finsbury Park* in the autumn of 1991. They eat Indian food, good or bad curry, or Mexican dishes in restaurants in Camden or Soho. In London you're spoiled for choice. Daniel and Alison walk all day long when they are alone together. They like romantic strolls, psycho-geographical walks where you discover the hidden treasures of the town. They linger around in Ravenscroft Park, in cemeteries like Brompton or Old Highgate Cemetery, where Karl Marx and George Eliot are buried. They follow the banks of the Thames near Hammersmith Bridge and explore the East-End back streets between Whitechapel and Liverpool Street.

Daniel and Alison are real townies. Hand in hand, they scour the record shops, flea-markets and charity sales. They know the markets well, and rarely go out without coming across people they know. They never miss a pop-art exhibition and go to the La Scala cinema. *Swinging London* belongs to the past, but London still vibrates to the rhythm of pop and culture. Their world is full of friends and relations who work in the sphere of the press, music, art: failed intellectuals, booksellers, former or future members of the band. There's Jowe Head of course, but also Ed Ball who is never far away. Alison avoids certain Television Personalities' fans who gravitate around Daniel and share bad habits with him. Over time, Daniel has become used to not being successful, and to his position as an outsider, revered by "those in the know". He can see the admiration in their eyes and takes a certain pride in it, which more often than not, he drowns in self-depreciation and alcohol. Between 1988 and 1995, Alison and Daniel's life is more a romantic than a bohemian one. Money is short, but the couple live modestly and feed on culture. When they're not going out, they eat a TV dinner off a tray. Daniel is now a vegetarian. He likes to joke and make love in the afternoon. He's a shy man but he explores his lover's body with the same serious attention as when he plays the guitar. Daniel is an intelligent man. He likes to stay in the background and do things discreetly, which is obviously a far cry from his exposed position as a singer. But his opinions are sound and often biting. He has a lively political awareness. He likes to support his friends, is generous and a brilliant imitator of singers or public figures.

In the strange life-cycle of the Television Personalities, everything isn't hunky-dory in those years. The songs bear witness to the presence of spectres, of shadows that take possession of the singer and cloud his mind. But the darkness has ebbed, and love keeps it at bay. Alison and Daniel's flat is like a sanctuary, a bulwark against doubt and evil. The exclusive relationship which he has with the young woman is what keeps him whole, keeps him together, prevents him from sinking and giving in to his self-destructive bent.

If someone loves you, it means that you are loveable, whatever you may think. We are all what others see in us. You don't need to be a great philosopher to know that. Life is good, but not for long. These eight romantic years would be a storehouse of happy images, of memories and regrets for the years to come.

HAPPY ENDING

The beginning of the end is nigh. There's nothing very amusing or spicy from now on. Just a story which ends badly and now only relies on a few selected anecdotes.

The light is fading.

Jowe Head's days with the band are coming to an end. Over the years, setbacks and mishaps have taken their toll. During the tour in the United States for example in July 1993, Daniel accepts to take part during the day in a promotional event organised by the magazine Creem as part of a seminar vaunting the vitality of the modern music scene. The concert is due to take place in the reception room of one of the New York Hilton hotels. Having accepted this event in the midst of promoting *Closer To God,* the singer changes his mind just before the concert, and hides in the toilets, from where he escapes minutes before the opening. Instead of joining Jowe Head and Lenny Helsing who are waiting for him a few yards away, Daniel takes to his heels, charges across the hall and makes off. He only returns later in the evening, without a word and with no intention of referring to the incident. Before the assembled professionals, Lenny Helsing introduces himself as Daniel Treacy, sings and plays the guitar, accompanied on bass by Jowe Head. The band plays for half an hour or so and finishes the set by an old rock number. Nobody's any the wiser. This amusing episode would be repeated on many occasions in one form or another.

Jowe Head frequently takes Daniel to task about the royalties from their contract with Fire Records, of which he's never seen the colour. The chaotic tours have taken their toll on the complicity between Daniel and the guy who is now his oldest and most loyal partner. During the second phase of the Television Personalities, the former Swell Maps player is the one who has had the strongest and most decisive musical impact. His contribution to structuring the band's sound, giving it power and precision and

a new punk energy, has been essential for more than ten years. The two men are now scarcely on speaking terms. When the band is signed up for a date in Edinburgh at the Cas Rock Bar, drummer Lenny Helsing discovers on his arrival that Jowe Head has not been informed. The rift between the two men is consummated. It would take Helsing years to bring the two of them face to face again. Jowe and Daniel exchange a couple of words in a pub called *The Birdcage,* where the drummer is appearing with his current band, then life goes on as before.
But without Jowe Head, as if it were now a question of living in a vacuum, of dispensing with the hope and affection still bestowed on him by friendly faces.

Alison and Daniel are a little less in love, or maybe it's just that Daniel is no longer capable of loving himself. The tours in 1995 and 1996 mark a definitive turn-down. Daniel's drug habit is out of control again. Alison can do little about it, especially as the tours get longer and he increasingly loses his bearings. The second tour is probably the more spectacular and tumultuous. In July 1995, six months after *Yes, Darling But Is It Art?,* an impeccable compilation of old or rare pieces, released on the Fire label, The Television Personalities offer Overground Records a new album composed during the previous months. The album, entitled *I Was A Mod Before You Was A Mod,* is as much a solo album as one by the Television Personalities. Daniel is alone, accompanied only by producer and occasional drummer, Liam Watson, the owner of the London studio in which he is recording. Watson would replace Jowe Head on bass for the coming tour. The record itself reflects how relatively destitute Daniel is at present. The titles speak for themselves: *I'm A Stranger To Myself, Haunted,* or *I Can See My Whole World Crashing Down.* The record is an avowal of personal failure in which the distress and the feeling of having screwed everything up, is palpable. If the tone is bleak and smacks of a confession, the album is astonishingly well done and stands pretty well the test of time. The production is skilful, light and typical of what can be identified as the lo-fi trend, of which Treacy can be considered to be one of the initiators. Later on, with a keyboard and not much else, he would push this concept to the limits. *I Was A Mod Before You Was A Mod* is nevertheless not lacking in scope. The opening track, *As John Belushi Said,* is a tribute to the American comedian and a splendid song about depression. Belushi died totally washed up in 1982, from a *speedball* overdose in his Château Marmont chalet. Robin Williams, who hanged himself in 2014 and Robert de Niro who made *Dirty Papy* in 2016 had visited him separately the same morning. Treacy is a little more in verve in the album's title song and in the lively *Little Woody Allen,* a hilarious song about the film director's childhood which is as good as any of the band's early successes. But the introspective songs soon take over and dominate the album. *A Long Time Gone* is probably the closest thing to admitting helplessness. It's a prophetic song which forecasts Treacy's imminent demise and which allows him to say sorry to Alison and the rest of the world. Despite the theme, the song remains quite lively and controlled. It's a tell-it-like-it-is song which also testifies to the singer's lucidity and the irremediable nature of his life-style.

> *"I'm sorry for being so f*** weak*
> *Ashamed that you could be so strong*
> *But I can't promise I will change*
> *'Cause I Don't know if I can change*
> *…*
> *Maybe I've had my share of luck*
> *I'm sorry for all the shits I've done*
> *But I haven't got a gun*
> *And I haven't got nine lives*

So I think I've had my time
And I'm gonna be a long time gone
Baby you might miss me."

In May 1995, the Television Personalities set off for Germany for what would be their last tour in nearly ten years. The band now features Graeme Wilson on bass and Sexton Ming on drums. Ming is a rather fascinating character, born in 1961. A minor artist and fellow companion of Billy Childish, the main proponent of what would come to be called "amateur art", Sexton Ming is a painter, singer, and actor. In 1999, along with a dozen or so other artists, he would sign the Stuckist Manifesto, a school promoting figuration instead of abstraction, a form of anti-conceptual art that would achieve some slight notoriety in the middle 2000's. The strokes are often thick and the contours imprecise. Stuckism is similar to naïve art. Ming shares a flat at the time with Liam Watson, owner of the Toe Rag Studio in which Treacy recorded *I Was A Mod Before You Was A Mod*. Sexton makes friends with Treacy although he doesn't know much about his work, and quickly gets a proposal to sing on the album (his voice, not very different from Jowe Head's, would be put on the astonishing *Things Have Changed Since I Was A Girl)*, and then to accompany the singer on his next tour. Ming, in need of money, claims to be a drummer, and is taken on without so much as an audition. After a first series in 1994 which is chaotic but which doesn't bother anyone, Sexton Ming agrees to take up service again in 1995. He saw Daniel in a contrasting light: a good mate most of the time, and then inhabited by a death-wish and self-destruction which got worse as the tour progressed. On the last day, on the point of returning to Britain, Treacy tells the band that he has met a girl in the Netherlands and intends to stay with her. Watson and Ming leave him behind and would meet up with him again five or six weeks later in London, drugged to the hilt and his tail between his legs, escorted by a gang of zombies who he would hang around with from now on.

The nightmare begins. Daniel is in a sorry state. The first two days of the 1995 tour are terrible. The singer has just begun to be treated with methadone and has withdrawal symptoms. He shares his hotel room with Ming and doesn't sleep a wink all night. He throws up everywhere and is bent double with pain. After two nights, to everyone's relief, he finally gives in and comes back with a packet full of cocaine and another of heroin. Ming himself is going through a violent bout of depression. Graeme Wilson is determined to try out heroin and the place is awash with alcohol. Treacy and Ming are running on Tequila and beer. Day and night. Night and day. The Television Personalities are living in another dimension. Wilson and Treacy get into arguments at every turn. One evening, the bass player accuses Treacy, usually meek as a lamb, of having stolen records from a friend's collection in order to sell them. Treacy gets uptight and breaks a bottle and brandishes it threateningly at his colleague. Ming gets them to stop, which calms things down. Treacy develops horrendous abscesses because of the injections, but refuses to seek medical help. Strangely, the concerts hold up and are not so bad. The band is in place and plays more powerfully than during the 1994 tour. Daniel is often hilarious on stage, sarcastic and bitter-sweet. The band plays notably a cataclysmic version of *Back To Vietnam,* coupled with *Closer To God* which lasts more than eleven minutes. This huge, ailing and dissonant piece has no difficulty in standing alongside the more pop and intimate songs in the set which Daniel increasingly performs alone on stage during this tour.

Backstage, catastrophe is never far away. Getting from one town to another each time is a feat in itself. During a radio interview, Sexton and Treacy are a hairsbreadth away from coming to blows. "I'm sort of the Godfather of independent rock", Treacy tells the

journalist. The exhausted drummer politely listens to Treacy holding forth on his place in the world of indie rock before a convinced radio presenter. Then, thinking to honour him, the journalist asks:
— It must be great to be a drummer with the Television Personalities, mustn't it?
Ming can't contain himself any longer. He doesn't reply to the interviewer and turns to Daniel to give him a few home truths.
— For fuck's sake, Dan, you're nothing at all. Stop talking rubbish. You're the guy who wrote *Part-Time Punks*, that's all. A one-hit wonder at best. You ain't never done anything else apart from that.
Treacy leaps up and the two men chase each other around the studio to have it out with their fists. The interview stops there. The tour ends in gloom and depression. The three men are ill, drunk and spend their time coughing and spitting into imaginary buckets.
Once back in London, Daniel is down and out. Sexton Ming, who still shares with Liam Watson (who now has a girlfriend), convinces his flat-mate to put Treacy up for a while. Watson is not keen on the idea, but is persuaded by Ming who says he will take all responsibility. Two months later, after a few upheavals, Daniel is invited to move out after having stolen a twenty-pound note from Watson's girlfriend's purse. Just as before, Treacy doesn't try to resist. He thanks his friends for the respite they have allowed him, says that he understands and vanishes, trailing his guilt behind him.
Years later, Vinita Joshi, boss of the Rocket Girl label would accommodate Treacy for long months, with similar difficulties.
It's during this period, and shortly after returning from continental Europe, that the Television Personalities appear for the last time on the stage of the Dublin Castle in London on the 21st of June 1996. Get ready for the come-back! The same morning,

Alison and Daniel had attended the funeral of Mathew Fletcher, one of his best friends and someone very close to his ex-girlfriend. Fletcher had committed suicide a few days before, following a severe bout of depression. He was 25. Treacy returns from Oxford just before the concert and, as he comes on stage, seems even more sombre and absent than usual. Technically speaking, the concert is a fiasco. The band just isn't with it and nothing is in place. At the opening and before launching into an unrecognizable version of *Stop And Smell The Roses*, Treacy stands before the audience, feverish and tearful.

"What a fuckin' life I've 'ad! You're 'ere tonight at the last concert of the Television Personalities. Yeah, for real. The last. It's my birthday on Wednesday. Guess how old I am ... (some guys make suggestions: 50? 48?) Not far off. I've got better things to do (than sing). It's time for me to settle down, start a family, that sort of thing. A legitimate family. Can you kill the spotlight? Thanks. I've 'ad an extraordinary day. I was at a funeral today. You probably don't know, but my friend Mathew of the Heavenly band committed suicide last week. It was a nice ceremony ... We 'ad a few drinks. I 'ad a good time. I'm next on the list".

After only eleven songs, separated by very few words, the concert ends with a shortened version of *Part-Time Punks*, with a few borrowed notes and lyrics from *To The End*, by Blur.

> "And it looks like we've made it to the end. Yeah, it looks like we've made it to the end".

Daniel doesn't hang about after the concert. He goes off into the night. Alone.

BLACK HOLE

Between June 1996 and October 2004, Daniel Treacy lives in a black hole a few miles from London. He only goes out to see a few friends, do a bit of shoplifting and get his supply. He has put a few personal effects in a corner and his injection gear well in view on the bedside table. His arms and thighs are ravaged by being pierced by the needle. The chewed-up flesh is dissolved and scattered around. A still distils pus as fresh as orange juice, and is served to guests. The gravitational pull is so intense that no music or light can escape from this place where it is alternately boiling hot or freezing cold, depending on the seasons and the years. No maintenance work has been done on the infrastructure since the end of the 19th century. The black hole is defined by the event horizon, that precise place beyond which nothing has any impact or influence. At the centre of the matter which forms the hole, a mixture of static electricity, burdensome memories and unhappiness, Daniel sleeps most of the time, waiting for life to pass by.

The black hole is a refuge and a tomb. You bury everything which is going wrong there, so why not hole up there yourself? The black hole makes you invisible. The human gaze cannot penetrate it. It's a one-way mirror, behind which you can close your eyes without being seen. By definition, a black hole is bottomless. It is the bottom itself. Daniel is arrested several times for petty thefts. He has never harmed a fly, but theft is akin to violence. As a subsequent offence it becomes aggravated theft and leads to prison sentences of up to 18 or 24 months.

One morning before he has even got back, three hundred men in dark suits come to arrest him. Daniel materialises in an instant and offers no resistance. He hasn't paid his rent and is threatened with eviction even from here. His life is a mirage. He no longer has any notion of time. He arrests them one by one and puts the cuffs on them.

— I sold music to buy drugs.
— That's your problem not ours.
— I 'aven't recorded anything for years. I swear it. I never touch my guitar these days.

He's haunted by the past. He's haunted by what is happening to him. He's haunted by Alison's tears.

Go back one space. Chance card. Go to jail.

BUTTERFLY

Number 7874 Daniel Treacy
A2 Induction Wing
HMP The Weare
Portland Dock
Rotherham Road
Castledown
Portland
Dorset
DT17 1PZ

Daniel Treacy resurfaces in public in June 2004 by sending a message announcing his return to a friend, Iain Baker, from HM Prison Weare, moored at Portland. This message is to be passed on to Andy Freiberger, boss of the Munich Label Little Teddy, and long-time supporter of the band.

"It's a long story, but not a long sentence. I'll be out on the 23rd or the 30th of June. I'm on a prison ship. It's a bit like going on a cruise except that we go nowhere …
I was sitting around the other day. I've so often sat like that these last years. I realised suddenly how much I missed music. Not the business that goes along with it. I don't even have a guitar or an amp to my name any more. It's been years now since I did. But these last years, I've written my best music and the music which's had the most significance in all my life. I want to make a new record of the Television Personalities. But I've had no contact for a long time with the people I knew before. I'd like to work with Jowe again (…) I'm stoney broke at the moment, but I ain't had any health problems or touched drugs for six months. Could anybody make up

a story like mine? I don't think so. (...) Tell all this to Andy. He can set up an official site for the band and I'll tell everything there is to tell. I could also give you the names of the songs that I'm waiting to record. He can also put my actual address on line. I wouldn't say no to a few birthday cards. Whatever happens, I want to think BIG this time. Pete Doherty spends three weeks in Wandsworth prison, for God's sake, and everybody sees him as the new Johnny Cash. If that's the way it is, I'm the new James Brown / Arthur Lee / Brian Wilson all rolled into one.
Cheers, Dan the jail-bird"

The history of floating prisons of the British Crown goes back to the end of the 18th century. Events like the American War of Independence, the French revolution or the Napoleonic wars make available for public use warships and troop transporters, which are ideal to turn into prisons for common-law offenders. These *prison hulks,* as they are called, are stripped of their sailing material, masts, sails etc. and changed into huge vessels incapable of putting out to sea, flanked by cells and appropriate equipment. Anchored in His Majesty's ports, these ships often provide good quality temporary accommodation before, for example, transporting prisoners to Australia or to other penal colonies. Although most of them were abandoned as prisons in the course of the 19th century, *Hulks* nevertheless carried on serving throughout the decades as residual detention centres. *HMS Argenta,* bought from the Americans in 1920, is notorious for having been used to confine the Irish Republicans arrested after the sinister *Bloody Sunday* of the 21st of November.

Last in a long list of prison ships, HMP Weare, built in Sweden in 1979, is first used to accommodate British troops stationed in the Falklands. After a first episode as a prison, the ship is sold to the city of New York which uses it until 1988, in support of its policy of massive clean-up of street crimes. Anchored to the north of

Manhattan Bridge on the East River, the ship turns out to be costly to maintain and is put up for sale by Rudolph Giuliani who gets rid of it in the 90's by passing it on to a European ship owner. Three years later, after crossing the Atlantic, the ship turns up on the Isle of Portland. Situated less than five miles from Weymouth, the southernmost point in Dorset, the island is in fact a peninsula linking the mainland to one of the largest man-made ports ever built. The port of Portland has long been a major military base in England and a strategic point in two world conflicts. Converted into a civil port in peacetime, the Bay of Portland is notably one of the sites of the 2012 Olympic Games. From the port, there is a splendid view over the bay, offering a rare vantage point from which to see the English coast.

It's in this rather surrealistic setting that Daniel Treacy emerges from a moonless night and comes back to life. A ship which no longer sails, a floating barge berthed on the edge of a bucolic green hill, with warships and merchant vessels cruising by, a country cemetery in the distance and the sea stretching out forever, a four-storey column of prefabs encircled by barbed wire. HMP Weare, which would be closed down two years later before being sold to a Nigerian company, then perhaps sold on again, is a prison coming to the end of its useful life. The concept of prison ships is criticised at the time. It's argued that the accommodation is expensive, that everyone lacks fresh air and exercise, despite the very positive reports of the prison inspectorate, which praises the quality of the food and the management. The ship is home to a little less than 400 category C prisoners, that is to say low-risk, and unlikely to try to escape. The men are mostly near the end of their time inside and serving sentences of less than a few months. Daniel Treacy spends some five months or so there. It's his third conviction, the most serious and the one which has given rise to this theoretical six-month stretch. His previous stays in prison at Brixton and Pentonville were shorter, but also tougher than this one. Inside those much larger prisons, the conditions are, by definition, harsher. Relations between inmates and warders are tense and the quality of the food more uncertain. Violence is omnipresent and the stifling atmosphere bears no comparison to the fresh air which blows through the corridors of HMP Weare. Above all, the view and the proximity of the sea are enough to keep anger and misery at bay.

As he would relate things later, no doubt embellishing the details, this enforced stay on HMP Weare is an illumination for Daniel. During these few months, the singer is supposedly clean. Things are probably not as clear as all that as far as drugs are concerned, but let's say that in general his health has improved. The abscesses on his body are healing up and he's recovering a bit of order and stability. With a bed, albeit in a cell shared with three other prisoners, and regular meals, the London wraith manages to pull himself together and is capable once again of envisaging a future for himself. If the majority of his acquaintances, from whom he has more or less voluntarily distanced himself over the last five years, don't know where he is and, for some, even if he is still alive, Daniel nevertheless starts corresponding again with his family and friends from his prison cell. He writes to Alison, for instance, and to a few others to bring them up to date, not without a certain touch of humour.

His situation improves towards the end of his stay, when a warder with whom he has made friends, gets him a guitar and allows him to keep it in his cell, in spite of the rules. Generally speaking, such instruments are excluded from the personal effects which the inmates are allowed to keep. It takes little for a suicide to occur. In subsequent interviews, Daniel would say (although the truth is difficult to verify), that a guitar and a piano had been given to him by a prison-visiting nun. It's a nice story, but hardly likely. Daniel becomes a local personality for a few weeks. He would say that the songs unveiled after leaving prison had not been composed while inside. Everything had been thought of and imagined well before, or after, but not during his detention. He is finally released on the 28th of June. It's at about this time that he starts to publish an on-line diary, first on a daily basis, but later at longer intervals. 2004 and 2005 are years particularly rich in information. The entries become scarcer after that, but the adventure goes on until May 2011, which allows people to follow the ups and downs of a back in business which is nothing if not chaotic.

The Daniel Treacy who takes up his career as a musician again in 2004, is a man who alternates phases of near-euphoria with bouts of deep depression. If humour abounds in the pages of his on-line diary, the obviously worrying surges of anger are also legion, and give the feeling that emotional instability is now deeply rooted in him. Daniel Treacy is enthusiastic about his future discographic activity and gives an account of the progress of his studio recordings, then vilifies the record industry because he's short of money or has no support. He imagines opening for Coldplay and earning a place in the sun, then decides to drop everything, before returning to the idea, as if there were nothing amiss. Reading the successive pages of this diary bodes nothing good, and confirms the struggle between opposing forces that are now at the heart of his existence. Looking for normality constantly collides with forces which nudge him towards giving up and plunging again. Although rarely mentioned in his on-line writings, drugs are clearly still there in the background. They sometimes disappear only to come back more present than ever. "I often stop using, he writes in his private correspondence. But I keep 'aving to check it out again for reasons that escape me". It's hard to say what he wants to keep on checking time and time again.

Then there's the poverty, the lack of money, the lack of a home which weigh heavily. Daniel, as always, can count on his sister Patricia, who once again bails him out and takes him in shortly after his release from prison. But living with Daniel Treacy isn't a sinecure. He's never stable for long and his drink problem isn't easy either. From his years of wandering, Daniel has maintained an ability to vanish without trace that continues to be a source of anxiety. His novenas worry his family, who have no illusions about how he's spending his time when he doesn't come back home. But a man of his age and in his situation has no real reason to step back into line or make a new start.

Six months after his release, Daniel Treacy has recorded more than fifteen new items. Contacts with the Domino label are well under way and a whip-round organised by his friends on the occasion of a "revival concert" provides the means to pay for part of the studio time necessary for the resurrection of the prince of twee pop.

Lawrence Bell, the boss of Domino, even if he was just a teenager when the TVP's were at the height of their fame in the early 80's, has long been a fan of the band, and is determined to give one of the heroes of his youth a helping hand.

After more than eight years of absence, the Television Personalities are back on stage at the end of 2004. Ed Ball is on bass again. It's his decision, after having voluntarily put distance between himself and the music world, to come back and help out his old friend. Ed Ball plays a major role in Daniel Treacy's musical resurrection. He does what he can to keep his partner on the straight and narrow and helps him develop his ideas for songs in the studio. Ed Ball is ever present. Chaperone, confidant, psychologist and official back-up composer, he needs few words to understand what Daniel is trying to express, and turn two hesitant notes on the keyboard into a melancholy miniature. The two men know each other well and share a great mutual affection. Old acquaintances of the singer rally around to get him back into the saddle. Among the credits on the *My Dark Places* album which would come out in 2006, appear the names of John and Gerard Bennett, the brothers present at the very start of this story. Alison

Wonderland is not far away either, even if she is careful now not to get too close to Treacy who dedicates most of his songs to her. When you listen to this album *My Dark Places,* sold by Domino as the revival of a giant of lo-fi pop, and its follow-up, *Are We Nearly There Yet?* made up, in fact, of songs recorded just after his release from prison and before the previous ones, you have to admit that Daniel Treacy's compositions are no longer the same. The singer on these records is a far cry from the young man who, twelve years before had composed *Closer To God,* a generous and ambitious double album. It oozes with suffering. The lyrics are sung in a voice often out of tune which strikes you mainly by its sincerity and fragility. The tunes are played with two fingers on the piano, or with a couple of chords on an acoustic guitar. The songs are often structurally incomplete, with repetitious retrograde themes, or a few clairvoyant notes offered up mostly without embellishments. Ed Ball, who works with Daniel at the time, plays the part of chief outfitter. He embroiders, darns the holes and tries to turn into something listenable, simple intuitions which reveal first and foremost the state of mind of their author. As a revival album, *My Dark Places* is a stupendous album, a success and a failure at one and the same time. Made up of sixteen songs, the record covers several registers: experimental and punk built around songs (*Special Chair, All The Young Children On Crack …*) which reflect a sort of latent insanity as well as a total inability to compose correctly, or more often, minimalist in a lo-fi confessional format which is overwhelmingly sincere. The album is light-years away from the ones for which the band was renowned. Gone are the cultural references. Everything is in shreds, but hangs charmingly at the windows. Apart from a few exceptions, (the superb *She Can Stop The Traffic*, the boastful *My Dark Places*), gone is the flamboyance, replaced by a biographical outpouring and an expression of infinite sadness. The memory of Alison is omnipresent as if time had not completely run its course, changing the eight years of life shared with the young woman into a sort of lost mythological tale.

Daniel contemplates the heap of ruins which his life has become, delving again into his own memories with morbid relish and the delicate and desolate look of a kid who has broken his favourite toy. A good half of the items on *My Dark Places* are of heart-wrenching beauty. *I'm Not Your Typical Boy, Tell Me About Your Day, Then A Big Boy Came And Knocked It All Down,* and *I Hope You're Happy Now* ring like a splendid and totally moving biographical quadrilogy. The singer bares his soul as never before, mentioning successively meeting Alison's parents, the bullying when he was a child and what is left of his dreams. The air is suffused with despair which contributes to a feeling of unease which the listener could do well without. The voice is not always in tune, derailing from one word to another, whilst some notes are more or less deliberately skipped in order to emphasize the effect of imbalance. *My Dark Places* is an album on a knife-edge, disturbing and admirable, but which despite itself, is clearly turned towards the end of the adventure.

With the release a year later of *Are We Nearly There Yet?*, this feeling is confirmed. The songs may well have been composed and recorded before those on *My Dark Places*, but there's no getting away from it; everybody is convinced that Daniel has relapsed and that his life has taken a sinister turn for the worse. The thirteen songs are assembled in haste and don't make up an album in the true sense of the term. Some of them aren't going anywhere and don't even seem to have been properly completed. The album's title song refers to a frequent children's question during a long journey. "When will we get there, mum? Are we nearly there yet?" The question only has a symbolic sense if you think about it. The lyrics seem to have been improvised. Daniel jumps from one subject to another and no longer seems capable of the slightest discipline. As in *My Dark Places,* the listener is stunned by the flashes of beauty which pop up here and there, the great moments of sincerity which are moving, and strike just the right chord, but equally disconcerted by the inconsistencies or the great moments of solitude which accompany complacent sequences, or which should have been eliminated during the mixing. Between a comic address to Peter Gabriel and an appalling tribute to Eminem, the Television Personalities do a perfect cover of Springsteen (*If I Should Fall Behind*) and have flashes of brilliance when describing grief and misery. *You Are Loved,* the most beautiful song on the album relates once again the break-up with Alison and the love Daniel has for her. The song is short. Three minutes and thirty seconds, but by its simplicity and absence of embellishment, the song is sculpted out of the tears and very heart of the singer. Over and above the pain and dramas of life, Daniel Treacy reveals himself here in all his beauty, loving and fundamentally kind, considerate to a fault and incapable of hurting anyone at all. The man describes himself through an uncompromising exhibition of what is left of him: a singing wreck, a beating heart and, in his own way, happily hopeful and astonished to be still alive.

The pages of the diary which cover these years give the feeling, apart from the confusion that they create, that Daniel has reverted to childhood. His singing is sometimes playful and in its best moments, the humour and irony of the young man he once was, are perceptible. Even in such a state, the Television Personalities still do better than millions of other bands. If the old assurance has completely vanished, the magic is still there. The huge sincerity of the lyrics, which some judge indecent, has opened up a new way of producing emotions, more direct and less sophisticated, reminiscent of the works of wise fools such as Nick Drake with whom Daniel shares his birthday, or better still, Daniel Johnston, the American lo-fi legend.

In 2005, the Television Personalities go back on tour again. The road team gets back together, drifting between successful and scuttled concerts. Entire tours are cancelled depending on the singer's difficulties. A German tour is struck off the list in May 2005. In summer 2006, the Television Personalities take sick leave from the Primavera Festival, the Route du Rock at Saint-Malo and the Green Man Festival. Daniel would reappear in London for an almost religious tribute given in honour of Syd Barrett in September 2006, notably playing, as a finale to the set, a sumptuous medley which enraptured the fans. The following three years are active ones. The band plays all over Europe, often for one-off concerts and in halls of varying size. The good concerts are as numerous as the ones which are complete failures. The band tries to hide the singer's shortcomings. Stand-in vocalists are pressed into service and on the bad days, Ed Ball wears himself out trying to convince Daniel to get on the stage or return to it. The singer's health wavers. After years of alcoholism and drug abuse, Treacy's liver is affected and he is handicapped by a hereditary kidney condition. His alcohol consumption has doubled to compensate for the decrease in drugs, bringing on problems with vision and mobility. The doctors tell him that sooner or later a transplant will be needed. The singer has black-outs and fainting fits for reasons which are not clear, resulting in accidents and falls. In May 2006, the doctors detect the first symptoms of multiple sclerosis as well as an excessive accumulation of cerebrospinal fluid in the brain cavities, otherwise known as hydrocephalus. Operations are forecast which would never take place.

The singer's living conditions are precarious. During the first years he lives in various flats, often small, but which provide him with shelter, and of which he rarely complains. Evicted in February 2006, he goes back to stay with his sister again before moving on. Keeping up with his movements during these years is not easy and of little interest. He comes and goes. Daniel sometimes lives with girl-friends. Some hitch up with him for a while, others are groupies met during the tours, Germans, Northern girls, real or imaginary. Over the years, Daniel often gets hooked, and the girls break things off, causing heartache and momentary crises which sometimes end up with attempts at suicide. One break-up is in May 2005. Another crisis in April 2006 leads to a voluntary overdose of diamorphine, pure heroin. Daniel pulls himself together. There are good and bad periods. The shift from one to the other is as sudden as it is unpredictable. Among his close associates, Ed Ball and Victoria Yeulet are his most loyal supporters. Daniel had met Victoria in 2004 in the Soho record shop where she worked. After his release from prison, he used to go there to get a bit of cash by selling records "borrowed" from the shelves of department stores. Daniel takes a shine to Victoria, who is unaware that he is a former well-known singer. The other shop assistant is also a girl, a very pretty punk with a Mohawk hairdo, called Gill. Daniel fancies Gill but she doesn't fancy him. The singer spends a lot of time in the shop, talking for hours on end about cinema and music. Daniel plays to the gallery, praising *Ray Of Light*, Madonna's belated masterpiece, passionately defending each song. Victoria overawes him and it takes him some time to be totally at ease in her presence. Little by little he becomes friends with the young girl. Ed Ball sometimes accompanies his mate and is just as eager to indulge in knowledgeable cultural debates. Victoria and Daniel have a few drinks together and go to concerts. The girl does photography and works on videos. She's an aspiring artist. She goes off for a few months on tour in America with *The Husbands*, a band she knows. Victoria does backing vocals on some songs and doubles as a roadie, groupie and friend. When she gets back, Daniel invites her to play along with him. So, together with Ed Ball and drummer Mathew Sawyer, she completes the line-up for the band's official revival. John Bennett replaces Mathew Sawyer from the middle of 2006. Ed Ball and John Bennett drop out in 2008, at which point Texas Bob Juarez moves up a step, to become the band's real musical director. After the departure of the old friends and Victoria, he's the one who keeps in touch with a Daniel Treacy who is increasingly unpredictable and difficult. Each appearance of the band is a balancing act where you have to be able to perform the songs and keep on good terms with the singer. The audience sometimes leaves the concert shaken and very often disappointed and dismayed. Sometimes the singer is taken to task by the fans and launches into more or less articulate exchanges with the audience which relegate the music to the sidelines. Lyrics are forgotten and chords are lost along the way. The dominant impression is one of waste. More and more London concerts are concocted in haste, motivated by the idea of making a bit of money, and do nobody any good. The team sometimes has a sordid look. Daniel comes on stage in a pathetic state, whilst the fans come to take a whiff of the disaster. On a more modest scale, the Television Personalities' concerts become freak shows which are just as bad as the shows given by the young Pete Doherty at the same period. Will he turn up or not? How will he be in the evening? On his feet or laid out? High on drugs or drunk?

As it happens, the former leader of the Libertines and Daniel Treacy would cross paths one evening in December 2007, at a concert at the London *Rhythm Factory*. The two men would only catch a very distant glance of each other, but that wouldn't stop the commentators from drawing a parallel between their respective destinies. During the fairly well-delivered opening by the Television Personalities, Daniel invites Alan Wass, vocalist with the Left Hand, a band on friendly terms with The Libertines also appearing that evening, to sing a piece with him. Completely stoned and incapable of awaiting his turn, Wass then refuses to leave, grabs the mike with every intention of singing instead of Daniel who, after a few minutes, loses patience:

— Get me this fucking arsehole off stage!

Wass screams out a few meaningless words before being removed by three bouncers and three staff members. Taken by force to the back of the hall, Alan Wass listens to the end of the Television Personalities' concert and comes back on stage to apologize, when his turn comes round. After somehow managing to struggle through only one song amidst the catcalls of the audience, he makes himself scarce, even though Peter Doherty has not yet arrived. Unfortunately for him, poor Alan would die a few years later at just over 33, after a series of scandals and dubious incidents, among which his presence at Doherty's house at the time of the fatal overdose of filmmaker Robin Whitehead, who shared pipes (of crack) with the two men while doing a documentary on the life of the British rock star. Wass narrowly escaped imprisonment for want of reliable witnesses among the users that evening, but was sentenced for possession of drugs. Victim of a fall described as spectacular though a "glass partition" at his home in Ladbroke Grove, Wass severed an artery in his right arm and lost a lot of blood. He had been in intensive care for two months, when his heart, no doubt deeply moved by all this havoc, stopped beating. Between Doherty and Treacy, there was no match played that evening, nor even a semblance of an encounter. "This is not a world championship." Daniel had moreover written himself when announcing the concert. The Babyshambles singer would later prefer to share the bill with Peter Perrett, a 70's idol even more stoned and diabolical than Treacy, who would have a dignified and classy flashback in 2016. Out of admiration and in order to approach him, Doherty would go as far as to take on Perrett's two sons in his band: Perrett is a thousand times sexier and more glamorous than Treacy.

You can't get away from the fact that Doherty has always managed to land on his feet until now. Some suggest that he knows his limits and has never gone beyond what's strictly necessary to keep his reputation intact. It's hard to believe in keeping anything whatsoever under control when it's drug abuse you're talking about. Doherty is only just 40. And according to what they say, he's in great shape.

In January 2010, the French gather at a rather serious concert by the Television Personalities during the *Mains d'oeuvres* Festival in St-Ouen. Daniel begins to wilt towards the end of a set of more than twenty songs, but on this occasion gives one of the most accomplished and consistent concerts of the period. With 25 titles and few incidents, the Television Personalities deliver one or two fine moments of emotion to an audience which treats them increasingly with sarcasm and disrespect. The fans from way back when are often grieved by the turn of events, whilst those who have just discovered the band take things at face value.

Daniel's health has not improved and that doesn't help matters. In 2009 and 2010 he talks several times of giving up live appearances, only to come back a few weeks later whenever an opportunity presents itself. In a few interviews he unearths his old dreams of painting, but turns out to be incapable of changing his lifestyle. None of this stops the band from producing a new album in 2010, this time on the independent London label Rocket Girl. Recorded once again with Simon Trought in his *Soup Studios*, *A Memory Is Better Than Nothing* is an album which is a wee bit more coherent than the two previous come-back records. Well supported by Texas Bob Juarez, Daniel Treacy applies himself admirably to the vocals and accomplishes a few memorable numbers. The band's limits are obvious and certain titles are weak (*My New Tattoo*) or not very sophisticated (*If You Don't Want Me*) but the collection is particularly efficient and infinitely moving. There are numerous moments of grace, especially when Daniel takes stock of his life, as in the magnificent *You're My Yoko,* which turn this album into a real winner. In some songs, Daniel is accompanied by female vocalists who add a gentle and maternal counterpoint to his own out-of-tune voice. Aimee Lockwood, Charlotte Marionneau, a French-born Londoner and former girlfriend of My Bloody Valentine's Kevin Shields, or Johanna Lundström contribute to making this album a little monument of fragility and sensitivity. Some of them would appear on stage with him to join in the singing. It's a far cry from Gainsbourg and the 60's, from Lee Hazlewood and singers for teenyboppers, but the presence of these women alongside Daniel rejuvenates his compositions. As in his previous records, sadness is omnipresent. The ghost of Alison Wonderland hovers over most of the songs as if, after all these years, the young girl remains the focal point of the texts and Treacy's emotions. In the centre of the jacket is a box of worn out and broken toys, a pointed symbol of what is happening behind the scenes.

The singer does his own promotion of the record by giving a few rare interviews. Vinita Joshi tries to save him from himself, but realises that it's impossible. His health has got worse since the beginning of 2010 and he makes no mystery of his despair of ever seeing an improvement in his situation. Daniel Treacy manages to survive three overdoses which can be considered as attempted suicides. A morbid routine interspersed with creative periods comes to a sudden end in autumn 2011. The band had played in London a few weeks before, for what would probably be its last public appearance. He is billed as playing a few songs in tribute to DJ John Peel at the end of October, when it emerges that Daniel has been taken to hospital after an assault, or a fall, on the night of the 7th or 8th of October. Having undergone an operation to remove a blood clot from the brain, the singer is placed by his doctors in an artificial coma, with a particularly reserved prognosis, given the severity of the blow to his head and his medical history. An inquiry into the circumstances of the accident leads nowhere and sheds little light on what has happened. Several hypotheses are put forward: a fall, following an indisposition or perhaps an assault, either gratuitous or in reprisal for something. There's talk of unpaid debts, but the police have no time to waste with this type of incident. According to several witnesses, Daniel had had an initial fall during a weekend of excesses in the company of a dubious character called Matthew. The following morning, it seems he complained of a headache and was persuaded by this same Matthew that going out for a breath of fresh air would do him good. It's during this outing that a second fall, this time when stepping off the platform of a bus, proved fatal, plunging him into a deep coma.

It would be late November, that is to say more than five weeks after the operation, before Daniel could react and open an eye for a few minutes. Little by little, he manages to move his right fingers at the expense of a Herculean effort. He leaves the intensive care unit at the beginning of December and can soon talk for an hour or two a day thanks to a valve in his tracheostomy tube. Fed by a pipe directly to his stomach and intubated all over, Treacy begins a long rehabilitation, of which the finality is far from clear. His recovery is frequently hampered by serious alerts linked to a series of infections or respiratory problems. From one institution to another, time goes by. His memory wavers and he has no real notion of the passage of time. He often thinks that he is back in previous years. The singer thinks that he is in a hostel for down and outs, and that in the morning he'll find himself homeless. He cries, says that he's going to die and can hardly see. His coordination is shaky, even if over the years he regains enough autonomy to feed himself and get through daily life. He gets random visits. In summer 2014, two and a half years after the incident, a photo taken by Texas Bob shows the singer in his room, sitting in a chair with a guitar on his knees. His fingers are placed on the frets and you would swear that he's about to play. The photo unleashes a bit of speculation on a possible come-back, but the next four years dash any hopes. His sister Patricia, who has had Daniel placed in a care and rehabilitation home near her, reports on his progress during the first years, before gradually letting the links peter out between Treacy and his army of fans.

In 2017, Daniel is doing mental arithmetic exercises during a visit by Alison Wonderland, the love of his life. He sometimes boasts to the other inmates of having been lead singer in a rock band, and sits up proudly when somebody plays him some of his old songs. Evan Dando is a friend of his, and one of the songs by MGMT, the youth of the day's favourite band, bears his name. The years go by. Two years, then another. Daniel is still hanging in there, but for the moment, the story of his life is at a standstill. He's alive, which at least is something, but life isn't worth much all the same when you can't make anything of it any more. Some have made a better job of it than him. His eyes hurt so much that he spends most of the day in the dark. The Television Personalities could have been bigger than the Beatles. You can get the gist of the idea. Daniel never had a taste for competition. He has neither lost nor won, but he has done one or two worthwhile things. There are better lives, but also millions of others which are much worse. Normal ones, short ones, peaceful lives and wasted lives. There are famous lives and anonymous lives. There are well-filled lives and others that are almost empty. There are lives which you talk about and others that you forget. There are lives which you would have wished otherwise and others which even surprise themselves.

You can be there and yet disappear. You can disappear and just exist. It's the principle by which artistes live. "We've now got to page 19 and once again, it would seem that the Indians are going to win. It's just like real life: the beginning is good, but there's no middle. So, while we're at it, we might as well cut the story short and go straight to the end. It's always the same old tale told thousands of times over."

MILLENNIUM DOME

I hadn't heard from Geoffrey Ingram for several months. Since our previous meeting, I hadn't tried to contact him. No doubt I was on my guard, given the way things had turned out the previous time. I hadn't had the chance to ask him about the fact that Daniel signed many entries in his diary under the name of Ingram. Had he met up with Ingram after his release from prison? I had one or two reasons to believe that the fictional doctor had prescribed him methodone several times during those years. One of his friends had shown me a prescription found among other irrelevant papers that Daniel had left lying about after having spent a few nights in his spare room. Just when my work was almost finished, I got an email from Ingram with a hyperlink to an FTP site. My connection was quite slow, and like in the early 2000's, it took me well over an hour to download the twenty-minute video. The film was a sort of documentary that might have been made by the BBC or some other channel, but it was interspersed, like the other videos that Ingram had, with hidden shots and angles that could never have been found in ordinary film editing. It was winter and the camera zoomed in on the Millennium Dome across the waters of the Thames from the Isle of Dogs.

"This will be perfect for you. Just think: the Dome is the entry to the new Millennium. A gateway to the future", Ingram wrote.

And he was both right and wrong. Built by the architect Richard Rogers to house the Millennium Experience, a special exhibition to celebrate the year 2000, the Millennium Dome was a structure of titanic proportions, organised around twelve-hundred-metre-high towers (one for each month of the year or each hour of the clock). The Dome formed a sort of circle 365 metres in diameter (one metre for each day of the year) and had an interior canopy 52 metres high (one metre for each week of the year). The initial exhibition, divided into fourteen zones, each sponsored by a major industrial group (L'Oréal, Marks and Spencer, Manpower, Tesco, British Telecom, Ford, etc.) was supposed to illustrate a primary function, or some fundamental symbolic dimension of human existence. Among these could be found a gallery called "Work". Others were called "Rest", "Talk", "Money", "Journey", "Learning", "Body", etc. Musician Peter Gabriel had composed a special piece of music to illustrate a show specially commissioned for the operation.

But for all that, in spite of positive feedback from the visitors, the whole business turned out to be a complete fiasco and a financial disaster such as Britain had rarely seen. The project had been largely paid for out of funds from a national lottery, set up for the occasion. The organisers had been banking on more than twelve million paying visitors over the year, but the figure was just over half of that. The building's future was soon called into question. Should the whole complex be sold on, since it couldn't be demolished? If so, to whom and for what purpose? Keeping up the building as it stood, estimated at a good million pounds a year, was no mean matter and called for urgent measures. The Dome was closed, then reopened, partly let out for concerts and a few prestigious events. In the winter of 2003, it housed the Winter Wonderland, including a funfair, a skating rink and other winter leisure activities. When Crisis, the largest charity association in the country, suggested for the Christmas period of the following year, to turn it into a huge shelter for the homeless, the idea caught on. This white elephant would finally be returned to the people, giving a social dimension to this futuristic temple, occupied up till then by all that was vile and pointless in capitalist industry.

In no time at all, the most fantastic communication campaign in the history of charity was put into place. An unbelievable marketing operation was devised in one or two months. Just listen to this: "One of the most costly buildings in the country, transformed into a huge welfare home for those who have nothing." A rallying point for all of the capital city's disinherited and neglected. 1200 places of accommodation in a cathedral of contemporary architecture, more spectacular and welcoming than the Ritz, Claridges, or the Dorchester. Thirty doctors and forty nurses would be on hand for treatment and checkups. Several hundred volunteers would organise leisure events and be on hand for the visitors. A sports centre to get people back on the right track, counsellors, social workers but also hairdressers, re-stylers, second-hand clothiers, estate agents and multi-media rooms. There was even a dog-care facility to take charge of your four-legged friend for the night. Open from the 23rd to the 30th of December in addition to the other shelters in the capital, Crisis would use the event to boost its "Be inspired" rehabilitation programme, a support structure aiming to get the visitors back into work, thanks to remotivation interviews and lessons in plumbing, maths or basic computer literacy. All this, then Daniel Treacy.

Six months after leaving prison, Daniel was living off and on with his sister. More off than on, to tell the truth, because he quite often preferred to sleep wherever he could rather than feel hemmed in and, to a certain extent, under surveillance in Patricia's house. Community life was rather to his liking. Shelters for the homeless often have sinister reputations, but have the advantage of removing the burden of having to be someone. It seems awful put bluntly like that, but it's possible to prefer that to anything else. After having had lunch with Patricia and her family, Daniel made himself scarce as he often did, and walked around the streets of London for several hours. The temperature was high for the season. It wasn't cold and there was no rain. People were in high spirits. He had drunk a little, but not excessively. He imagined himself arm in arm with Alison, and walked past the shop windows, imagining the things he would have bought for the flat they had shared. He was infinitely sad at this time, but not with that devastating sadness that sometimes makes you want to end it all.

No, this sadness was just curiosity to know what would follow and what would be the turn of events. He stopped to eat one or two bits of junk food, then caught a bus for Greenwich. The town was in jubilation. They had talked about the shelter facilities organised in the Millennium Dome on the telly, and that had attracted his attention. He had got washed that morning and was dressed in his usual style: a short, sailor-style woollen bonnet on his head, and a pair of wide trousers with pockets big enough to stash pilfered odds and ends, a thick pullover and a parka zipped up to the neck. Daniel had nothing with him, not even a small rucksack. Just himself and a monkey on his back.

The filmmaker was covering the Dome's facilities. The camera followed Daniel as he made his way along the busy passageways. From time to time, they stopped following him to concentrate on other down-and-outs and then caught up with him again. Daniel went to have his hair cut and queued up for an hour before a young redhead got round to dealing with him. In her hurry to get on with the other customers, she cut off four locks and decided that the haircut was finished. Then he spent a little time in the main hall watching the news. He drank two cups of tea and chatted for a long while with one of the volunteers, a middle-aged woman called Ruth, (it was the name marked on her badge) who seemed to find him to her liking. Daniel told her who he was, but she was sorry to admit that she had never heard of the Television Personalities. "It doesn't matter, he said to her. It's not all that important."

The kindness of the volunteers was sincere. Ruth was a pretty woman, but Daniel wasn't in the mood to chat her up. He wondered what to do, then he moved on, telling himself that he could see her again over the following days. Some people were singing along to a karaoke, but Daniel preferred to sign up for a quiz. Given the folk around him, he thought he might have a chance. There were lots of geography questions. Daniel had travelled the world with his band and had a good level of general knowledge. He won the first round with ease and was just beaten by a whisker in the second by a guy who looked more like a retired teacher than a person in need. He was nevertheless applauded by a few dozen people and he told himself that it wasn't so bad, even if it was a far cry from the satisfaction of appearing on stage before people who know the words of your songs even better than you do yourself.

Before the evening meal, Daniel went to the back of the Dome where the association had set up artificial sports grounds. He wasn't dressed to play, but he mixed with the other down-and-outs who were playing 10 aside football on a mini pitch. They gave him a blue jersey which looked like the Chelsea ones, then, even before he got onto the pitch, changed it for a neon green goalkeeper's jersey. He hadn't played any sport for years. He had a stiff leg and could hardly see.

— You can join in now, said the young man in charge of the game. There's a place as goalie. With the blue team, he added, seeing Daniel heading off in the wrong direction.

Daniel hobbled off towards the goal mouth. He was limping and had one shoulder lower than the other, but he felt like stretching his legs. His team was almost entirely made up of junkies or perhaps ex-junkies. He knew one or two from sight. If he was in the same physical shape as these guys, well shit ... It wasn't a pretty sight. They ran about on one leg, but their technique wasn't as bad as all that. These guys had maybe had some sort of life before ending up like this. In Britain, there weren't many guys who were totally clueless about how to play football. Daniel wouldn't have been able to run more than fifteen yards or so without collapsing, but in goal he could make a good show of things. Jumping on the spot, he touched the cross-bar, then moved sideways to intercept the ball kicked from a distance by an opponent. He set the ball down to clear it and felt a slight pain in the back of his thigh when he kicked it away. His shot reached its destination, twelve yards or so away and his teammate controlled the ball before taking a big kick to forward it for a header by a third player. The opposing goal-keeper kicked the ball clear. The ball got through the defence and Daniel found himself face to face with a skinhead charging directly towards him. The guy controlled the ball with skill, nudged it twice with his right foot and came directly up in front of him. Daniel bent his legs, but couldn't really crouch down. His movements were slow and his back felt like it was locked with a bolt. He stretched out his hand to the right, but suddenly sprawled onto his left side. The guy toed the ball under Daniel's belly and tried to leap over to avoid him. Daniel caught his feet with his forearms and the opponent fell to the ground whilst the ball rolled gently towards the goal mouth. Daniel and the guy rolled on the ground, the other guy performing a sort of pirouette in order to right himself. The singer turned and saw the ball roll and roll, almost at a standstill, then cross the line with its last spin. Daniel lay on his back for a moment before getting up. He looked at the metallic and airy ceiling of the Dome, which seemed a strangely majestic and beautiful structure. He had seen cathedrals and other monuments, but at this moment, the Dome seemed to him more gracious and imposing. It was a mix of church and barn, a prestigious official building and a concert hall. His eyes became blurred and he blew from his nostrils a few grains of sand which had landed there when he had flung himself to the ground. The game had begun again.

— You OK?, asked a volunteer, helping him to his feet.
— I think so.

Daniel now had a pain in the hip, but he kept his position as goal keeper for another quarter of an hour or so, without letting in another goal, which was a minor miracle in itself.

On the second evening, Daniel listened to a concert by singer Tom

Robinson in the great hall. Robinson had just turned sixty and sang most of his greatest hits, like *Glad To Be Gay* and *War Baby* or *Listen To The Radio (Atmospherics)*, which he had co-written with Peter Gabriel. Daniel knew how Robinson had been signed up quite young by Ray Davies of the Kinks for his Konk label before its scathing commercial failure. Robinson had been at the forefront of the gay liberation movement. *2-4-6-8 Motorway*, his best-known song, was about the life of a trucker on British roads in a tale "open to interpretation". Some saw a few smutty allusions in it, but the song was nevertheless a hit. Daniel had always hated Robinson who was a good singer, but who always tended to curry favour with his audience. He was thus more popular than his talent warranted, several of his songs having worked their way into public imagination. His backing band was a mixture of older guys and professionals, probably paid on a session basis. They all played with smiles on their faces and with the utmost diligence. The Television Personalities had never compromised themselves in such a way. Is that really what you call independence? Daniel thought that he might just as well have sung for the disinherited and derelict. He would have done it for nothing, but would probably have been thrown out after two or three numbers, since what people wanted, the destitute just like the others, was just hits and other well-known songs, not spiritual stuff, meaningful songs or fucking indie rock. And in their thirty-year career on this miserable planet, the Television Personalities had never really produced a hit. Sexton was right: he had never done anything worthwhile since *Part-time Punks*. Tom Robinson had the look of a successful sales rep or insurance agent. This sort of band was usually a deadly bore. There was no risk-taking, just an academic and almost exact imitation of original songs. The lead guitar did awful useless solos and everything was dampened by the debonair smile and the hilarious face of the singer. But the audience reacted with unmistakable enthusiasm. Robinson carried it off. He knew what he was doing. He was wearing a pair of jeans that were too big for him and a black shirt that did nothing to hide his bulging stomach. For a moment, Daniel thought that he looked like Morrissey and that made him laugh, then he let himself be won over by the warm Christmas atmosphere. The Dome looked like an enormous old folks' home. Once, during a concert in France, then on numerous other occasions, he had claimed that Morrissey was his lover and had constantly made jokes at his expense. Although they had never met each other, Treacy was convinced that Morrissey, whom he found ridiculous most of the time, was not so very different from him. The Smiths' lead singer was probably busy stuffing himself with costly vegetarian food in his Los Angeles villa.

It was the Christmas show. There were all these toothless guys, the poverty-stricken, the junkies, but also quite a few ordinary folk who had stopped by, and who had probably come to have a good time or to avoid being alone. There were a few women, but the audience was almost exclusively male. Daniel looked around him. It wasn't his usual public, but he felt in communion with this crowd of modern reprobates and outcasts. He had spent the last years trailing about the streets of London with them, sleeping in squats with them and now, for the first time, they were listening to music together, as if part of a huge community. These were not the hippies and part-time punks who had been his former companions. There were volunteers who represented the real world and who were having a great time, happy to share in such a fine initiative and to have a roof over their heads.

The camera roamed around and literally "looked" at the faces, lingering on them for a while, filming them straight on and at shoulder height. The filmmaker took himself to be Pasolini. He liked wide-angle shots and static shots. The colours were not as nice as those in the *Trilogy Of Life*, but there was that same idea of sounding the very souls of the characters. Daniel kept moving around the hall. The viewpoints varied, but it was evident after a while that the director had wanted to diffuse some sort of message by this film.

Tom Robinson left the stage and came back out after two or three minutes for the encore. His face, a little puffy, was still dripping with sweat, but he had just sponged himself down and changed shirts.

"Morrissey!", Daniel wanted to shout out again, but he stopped himself and left the hall, thrusting his way through the crowd.

All in all, what difference was there between Robinson and him? What difference between Morrissey and him? At that moment, Morrissey was probably in pyjamas, stroking his priceless cats in his millionaire's mansion. Or else eating goji berries with his boyfriend. What difference did that make? Love is everywhere and who cares who the object of it is? The camera caught him next at the entrance to a huge hall converted into a dormitory. He stood in the centre of an alley which itself was in the middle of lines of bedding, that is to say technically and graphically in the very centre of the hall. The camera rose and did a kind of zoom out, as if there were no ceiling. You could see the beds which seemed to mark out the ground plan of an American town, with the mattresses instead of the streets. And there was Daniel in the centre, in the midst of all this human misery, alongside these men preparing to bed down, getting rid of their outer clothes, scratching, hacking and coughing, farting no doubt, without bothering to say good night nor say anything else to each other. Life itself was a refuge. And Daniel was among them, right there and silent, his heart warm and at peace with himself, as rarely he had ever been on a Christmas Eve.

Could there be anything else to hope for after that? Were there still things waiting to be done? Through the windows of the Dome, the filmmaker captured the shadow of Robinson's impressive car gliding past the dormitory as if it were going to rush headlong into the Thames. The poet was in the centre of the Dome, inaudible and voiceless.

After three days spent at the Millennium Dome, just like other people spend a week's holiday, Daniel took his leave of Ruth and the hundreds of volunteers to go back to his life of freedom. When he stepped out of the door of the Dome, despite the mild weather, a few flakes of soft white snow fell and covered his halting silhouette. The camera captured him from behind. On his head he wore a red woollen bonnet to which the snowflakes clung. Daniel hesitated between right and left before heading due south towards the Millennium Leisure Park. He thought of taking the tube to North Greenwich, but remembered that he knew a guy near Charlton who could put him up. He hoped that he hadn't moved house and that he would remember how to find the place once he got there. So he walked on and that was that.

I thanked Geoffrey Ingram for sending me the film and wrote that it would be very useful for my work. I did that whenever anyone brought me new material, even if sometimes it was useless stuff, like old German articles or worthless documents, such as catering lists, or poor-quality photos. Everyone had to be thanked as if each contribution were valuable.

I told him that I was almost at the end of my research, that there wasn't much more to say, now that things were almost at an end. I had hardly sent my email when my cell phone rang. It was Ingram.

— I'm going to see Daniel this weekend, he told me. You can come with me if you like. I'll be leaving around 10 o'clock. Saturday.

— You think there'll be no problem with that?

— For whom?

— I mean if you go and visit him with a total stranger?

— I don't know. If he's feeling well, he won't mind and if he's not up to it, well, he won't give a damn either and won't want to see me any more than he will you. There's always that risk.

I thought about it for a moment or two. It was true that my work was finished, but I needed an interesting conclusion. I was aware that Daniel's last years were sad and could give the impression that his nevertheless oh so fabulous life had turned out badly, or else ended up in a fine mess. I told myself that a final, lively and uplifting scene might let me end on a positive note and make an impression on the readers.

— I'll be there, I said to Ingram. Once I've got my tickets, I'll send you the details of my arrival by email.

— We'll go by car, if you don't mind. The home is less than an hour's drive away and I don't care much for public transport.

I had had a brief conversation with Treacy in 2010 after the concert at St-Ouen, and then I had interviewed him by email a few weeks before his accident. But I had never met him face to face. It was an opportunity not to be missed.

THE PICTURE OF DORIAN GRAY

It's time to bring things to their conclusion, even if Daniel's story is not yet over. It's obvious that getting on for 60, almost blind and suffering from a host of physical ailments, his state of health will not permit him to reappear on stage and sing again, or even less, hope to make another record.
From a biographical point of view, an untimely or accidental death would have been easier to tackle than the fate of a hero sentenced to live out the rest of his days in a nursing home, surrounded by elderly people and road-accident victims.
The history of rock is filled with musicians stopped in their tracks by a premature or belated demise, even by a ridiculous death. Nico fell off a bike in Spain. Kirsty MacColl was struck by a boat off the coast of Mexico. Terry Kath lost a game of Russian roulette. John Bonham suffocated in his own vomit and poor Stiv Bators was run over by a Paris taxi. If you consider that it's always better to be alive than dead, then you have to admit that Daniel Treacy's life lives up to the image of his work, modest, tragi-comic and at the same time anti-spectacular. The obscure spiritual leader of independent rock, condemned to a sinister death from health problems. Out of earshot, out of mind: the singer who loved to disappear, ends up being forgotten by everyone.
The end is never funny and sometimes drags on for a long while. Independent rock is a tragedy whichever way you look at it. The only rockers still alive at almost 60 are forgotten rockers, or rockers who are no longer really rockers at all. Daniel Treacy lives in a state of weightlessness, suspended like his hero Syd Barrett, in a state dramatically different from what he was before.

Geoffrey Ingram was in excellent spirits when I met up with him that morning. I had taken the first train from Paris and had gone straight to his house after getting off at Saint-Pancras. We chatted for a few minutes and I told him of my doubts about meeting Treacy in his current state. I had refused up till now to say too much about his private life or reveal any of the really indiscreet things people had told me about him. It seemed to me that my work as a biographer, whatever people may think, obliged me to maintain a grey area in which the intimate confessions and family traumas would remain hidden for ever. Finding myself face to face with Daniel Treacy meant risking the disappointment of being confronted with someone that I'd spent months reinventing, but above all, with the reality of his decline. Alison Withers, and his sister Patricia had prepared me for the worst, the latter having described Daniel at the beginning of our correspondence as very diminished, often agitated and vociferously predicting his imminent demise. The latest reports that I had had of his health had reassured me a little, but all the same, I was apprehensive about meeting him and having nothing else to share with him other than my dumb admiration.

Don't worry, Ingram said, in an attempt to reassure me. Daniel is tough and rarely as out of touch with reality as all that. So long as you're not intending to interview him or whatever, things should go off all right.

The expression seemed odd to me to the point that I wrote it down straightaway in my notebook. For obvious reasons, I won't reveal here to which establishment we went. The care home was about twenty miles from London, not far from where Treacy's elder sister lived. The little town through which we drove was typical of the London suburbs, home to middle-class retired people or young couples of limited means. The house where Daniel now lived was in a rural setting. There was a shady park, surrounded by a wall fallen into disrepair, eaten away by ivy. There were flowerbeds, also in need of some attention. The main building was modern and probably quite functional, consisting of two storeys like most such facilities, in order to save on materials, and with no ambition

of lasting for centuries. The building had been constructed in the 70's and provided adequate quality nursing accommodation whilst remaining accessible to people of modest means or with basic health insurance. It cared for a mix of dependent elderly persons, a few Alzheimer patients, but also some young people with accidental mental or physical impairments, often resulting from road accidents.
Ingram left his Jaguar in the visitors' car-park and led me to the reception area. The weather was mild and most of the inmates who were capable of it, were strolling about in the gardens. Lunch had been served at eleven o'clock and those who could, were enjoying a walk outside, alone or accompanied. I noticed that very few of the inmates were in groups, most walking about on their own or helped along by one of the nursing staff. There were people on benches, others wandering among the foliage or along the pathways. Such establishments are places of great loneliness.
— Relax, Ingram said to me, as we walked up to the matron.
— Hello Doctor, she said, greeting him with a broad smile. We haven't seen you for a while.
— Yes, I've been rather busy. How's the patient doing?
— He has his ups and downs. More downs than ups to tell the truth. He's very often anxious and tends to get ruffled more than he should. He really can't see very well and I think that's what makes him so nervous. The doctor has broached the question of an operation with his family, but he doesn't know if he'd be well enough to undergo it, or even if it's worth the effort. There are only slight prospects of improvement.
— Where is he?
— Over there by the great oak tree. He's in quite good spirits today, you're lucky.
— Thank you very much. Come along, he said to me. It's this way. We walked slowly across the park. Ingram spoke in his medical jargon of Daniel's numerous health issues which, in his opinion,

would end up carrying him off sooner or later. With that detachment typical of medical men, he told me quite calmly that Daniel would probably no longer be there in two or three years' time.
— His life expectancy is limited. But as I told you, he's tough, so you never know. After his accident, nobody would have bet much on him pulling through. He's recovered far beyond the doctors' expectations, thanks, it's true, to a very good neurologist, whom I warmly recommend. Daniel?
Treacy was sitting at the foot of the oak and seemed to be waiting for us, even though it was impossible that he could have seen us approaching, given his poor eyesight. He was wearing his traditional round woollen bonnet, a navy blue one, and wearing, as a few years before, baggy khaki trousers and a cream linen shirt. When he raised his head to welcome us, I was amazed by his appearance. I had been expecting the worst, but the man who greeted us showed no sign of physical impairment. His right leg was paralysed and his foot strangely twisted towards the inside, but his face was smooth, relaxed and, above all, looked as if he were twenty or thirty years younger. Daniel's eyes were clear, even though he could hardly see anything and he seemed to me to be in better shape than on the videos that I had seen of him in the early 2000's.
— Nice to see you, he said to Ingram who leant over to hug him.
— How are you?
— You really wanna know?
Treacy remained seated and invited us to join him. Ingram was not the sort to sit down on the grass, but he did so all the same. As for me, I was stunned. His facial features were not the ones I was familiar with. Daniel Treacy didn't look like himself. He was much younger and in much better shape than he should have been.
— Daniel. This is your biographer. He's French and has just spent a whole year writing about your life.
There was no reaction from the singer. He muttered something which I didn't catch and looked down at the tips of his shoes. I had

already seen him make this sort of withdrawal in the Swedish TV documentary when Ed Ball had annoyed him, and I decided not to labour the point. But something bothered me, which I couldn't quite put my finger on. I had thought to read him a few passages from the book I was writing, in order to express my admiration and let him see that I had given him the leading role. But I didn't even bother to take the pages from my bag. It was a fantasy that now seemed out of place.

— I've talked to a lot of your friends. Jowe Head, Joe Foster, Mark Sheppard, Sexton Ming, Thomas Zimmermann. And Alison, of course.

— Joe ain't my friend any more, he said with a smile. 'E's forgotten me. And Sexton hates me.

— You're wrong. Really. All of these people have a lot of respect for you.

— It'd be better if they sent me some cash!

Ingram questioned him about his convalescence. He asked him if he saw the physiotherapist regularly and if he did his exercises. Daniel said that he did but that it was pointless.

— I'm done for, and you know it, he repeated. Done for.

He crossed his arms, revealing his scars, whitened with the passage of time. I wondered if it was being weaned off drugs and life in this institution which had given him this appearance or whether it was something else. Along the edge of his bonnet, his hair was curly and thick around the temples, whilst the Daniel of recent years was thinning and balding. Then I caught sight of Ingram who I found also even younger than on our last encounter, and realised what was happening.

I turned to Ingram, and without any consideration for Treacy, said abruptly:

— You've really taken me for a ride, Geoffrey. You know perfectly well that this isn't Treacy. Oh, for Christ's sake, I said, overreacting, don't tell me that it's an actor!

— Just listen to yourself, he smiled. I thought that you had understood the principle.
— You mean ...

Daniel had gone on hold and was pulling the petals off a daisy without paying us the slightest attention.

— ... Yes, he said, you're the one who's made him the subject of a whole book. In a foreign language to boot. What do you think is happening? You're the one who's done this.

— He doesn't look anything like himself any more.

— Of course not. He's become a character. Like Syd Barrett. Like Nick Drake, Like Ian Curtis. I warned you: things are never the same once you relate them. In your own way, you have done him a favour. Your admiration has helped to heal him. Your attention has given him importance and restored his colours.

Daniel looked at me in the eyes and I could see in his gaze that he was both the guy who had lived the life I had tried to write about, and at the same time, someone quite different.

— You know that Kurt Cobain just loved my music? he asked. And that I was friends with Evan Dando.

— Yes, I said. I know all that.

— I walked across Berlin arm in arm with Nico. Have you heard of Nico?

— Yes

— The most beautiful girl in the world ... after Alison, of course. Look.

From the pocket of his baggies, he pulled a photo taken at the same place where we were sitting, portraying a dark-haired young woman, magnificent and dressed in the 70's style with a navy jacket and a skirt just above the knee. I was sure that I had seen this photo before and that I knew the young girl.

— When was this photo taken?

— Last week, or the one before. When Alison came to see me. She's more beautiful than ever, isn't she?

Alison was well into her fifties. The young woman posing with him didn't even look twenty-five.
— It's not possible, I said turning to Ingram.
— Let it go, said the doctor getting up.
— Come on, added Daniel. Come to my place. We'll 'ave some lemon tea and I'll show you my collection of paintings. I did some of them myself. And I'll show you a picture of Dorian Gray. We can 'ave something to eat.
— Cucumber sandwiches, I added. Little cucumber sandwiches, I suppose?
— Emilee brought them yesterday.
— Emilee Watson?
— I dunno. Who's she?
Daniel pointed to a plush house which I hadn't noticed when we arrived, tucked away at the bottom of the park.
— Let's go. You could have brought a few friends. We'll go for a swim in the river. The weather's fine.
I began to smile and followed Daniel who strode off as never before. His club foot no longer hindered him and he was almost off at a trot. I turned towards Ingram who had changed appearances once again. He now had the look of a young man. I felt as if I were dizzy.
— What he has just said doesn't exist, and you know it Ingram. It's all just song lyrics.
— *A Picture of Dorian Gray,* I know. But why do you say that none of this exists? You only need to believe in it.
Daniel invited us to stay the night with him. The house was huge and I decided to let myself be tempted.
After all, I'd been asking for it.

THE END

CHRONOLOGICAL MARKERS

19 June 1960   Birth of Daniel Treacy

15 September 1961   Release of *A taste of honey*, a film by Tony Richardson, portraying the character of Geoffrey Ingram, adapted from the play by Shelagh Delaney.

15 September 1967   The Kinks release the song *David Watts*, which would inspire the song, *Geoffrey Ingram*. The song features on the single Autumn Almanac. A cover version would be released by The Jam in 1978.

5 January 1967   Photo session with Patrick McNee and the model Twiggy by photographer Terry O'Neill to promote the fifth season of *The Avengers (Chapeau Melon et Bottes de Cuir* in the French television version), as well as a collection of clothes by Alun Hughes and Pierre Cardin.

Mai 1968   Presentation at the Cannes Film Festival of *The Girl On A Motorcycle*, featuring Marianne Faithfull and Alain Delon. The festival is interrupted.

12 December 1972   *Soirée des Têtes Surréalistes,* organised by Marie-Hélène and Guy de Rothschild, in the presence of Salvador Dali.

10 May 1974   Led Zeppelin launch the Swan Song record label. The label has its offices at 484, Kings Road, London.

18 November 1976   Cindy Breakspeare is elected Miss World at the Royal Albert Hall in London.

December 1976   Malcolm McLaren and Vivienne Westwood's *SEX* boutique at 430 Kings Road is renamed *Seditionaries*.

1 December 1976   Bill Grundy interviews the Sex Pistols on the *Today* show (Thames Television), after a cancellation by the group Queen.

26 June 1977   Death of Karac Pendragon, son of Robert Plant, at the age of 5.

16 August 1977   Death of Elvis Presley.

August 1977   Recording and release of the Television Personalities' first single, *14th Floor*.

16 September 1977   Death of Marc Bolan.

November 1977   "O" Level record their début single *East Sheen*. The line-up consists of Dan Treacy, Ed Ball and John and Gerard Bennett and is identical to *14th Floor*. The 7" is released in May 1978.

March 1978   The Bennet Brothers, John (drums) and Gerard (bass, vocals) record a single of their own band Reacta (*Stop the World*), together with two school friends. The single is produced and financed by Daniel Treacy and released the following May.

11 May 1978   John Peel makes the first broadcast of the single *14th Floor*.

26 August 1978   Dan Treacy (vocals, guitar, bass) and Ed Ball (drums, vocals) record *Where's Bill Grundy now?* at IPS Studio. The single is released in late November on Treacy's King's Road Records label.

18 May 1980   Death of Ian Curtis.

22 May 1980   First authentic concert by the Television Personalities at the Clarendon Hotel, London.

February 1981   Release of the album ...*And Don't The Kids Just Love it?*

March 1981   Daniel Treacy's first release on his Whaam! Label, signed The Gifted Children, *Painting By Numbers*.

January 1982   Release of the album *Mummy Your Not Watching Me*.

February 1982   Ed Ball leaves the band. He would return for one or two gigs in 1988, before joining up with Treacy again between 2004 and 2007.

7 May 1982   Concert in Berlin, opening the show for Nico.

August 1982   Release of the album *They Could Have Been Bigger Than The Beatles*.

August 1983   Release of the first EP on the Creation Records label, *73 in 83*, by The Legend.

March 1984   First *Living Room* gig organised by Alan McGee at the Union Tavern. The TVPs appear there after having played on three occasions in 1983 at the Adams Arms, the original venue for these gigs.

March 1984   Release of the album *The Painted Word*.

January 1984   Jowe Head joins the TVPs for a tour through Germany and Switzerland. The band at this point consists of Dan Treacy, Joe Foster, Jeff Bloom, David Musker and Jowe Head and they travel via train. Jowe will be part of the band until the Japanese tour in 1994 making him the longest serving band member next to Treacy himself.

28 April 1984   The Television Personalities open the show for David Gilmour (Pink Floyd) at the Hammersmith Odeon. On this occasion, Daniel reveals Syd Barrett's address.

June 1984   The Whaam! Label closes down following a naming transaction with Wham!, George Michael's band.

Mid-1984 Joe Foster and David Musker leave the band.

September 1984 TVPs embark on their 1st long Euro tour. Over three weeks they pass through the Netherlands, Germany, Liechtenstein and Switzerland supported by Fenton Wells and Go! Service.

April 1985 Release of the first record on the Dreamworld label, *Scenes We'd Like To See*, by the American band The Impossible Years. The label is run from Daniel Treacy and Emilee Brown's flat at 9, Poynders Court, Clapham (London).

26 January 1986 The Mighty Lemon Drops record a BBC session with Janice Long. It's one of the biggest successes of the Dreamworld label.

July 1989 Daniel Treacy and Alison Wonderland move in together near Acton Town.

31 December 1989 A concert by the Television Personalities in Berlin, with Evan Dando. At the same moment, David Hasselhoff is singing at the foot of the Berlin Wall.

February 1990 Release of the album *Privilege*.

23 August 1991 Nirvana give a concert at the Reading festival.

5 November 1991 The Television Personalities open the show for Nirvana at the London Astoria.

October 1992 Release of the album *Closer To God*.

5 April 1994 Death of Kurt Cobain.

January 1995 Release of the compilation album *Yes Darling, But Is it Art?*

July 1995 Release of the Album *I Was A Mod Before You Was A Mod*.

21 June 1996 Last concert of the Television Personalities in London (Dublin Castle) before the temporary disappearance of Daniel Treacy.

June 1998 Release of the compilation album *Don't Cry Baby … It's Only A Movie*.

28 June 2004 Daniel is released from prison after detention on the prison-ship HMP Weare, moored opposite Weymouth Bay in Dorset. He makes his reappearance.

February 2006 Release of the album *My Dark Places*.

7 July 2006 Death of Syd Barrett.

February 2007 Release of the album *Are We Nearly There Yet?*

September 2007 Fire releases *Beautiful Despair*, an album of previously unreleased recordings from 1990.

June 2010 Release of the album *A Memory Is Better Than Nothing*.

October 2011 Daniel Treacy has an accident. After falling from the platform of a bus which puts him in a coma for several weeks, the singer is placed in a care home and remains severely handicapped.

8 November 2018 A benefit concert for Daniel Treacy is organised at the London 100 Club and brings together many grateful former members and musicians.

April 2019 Fire releases two compilation albums of singles, *Some Kind Of Happening* and *Some Kind Of Trip*.

September 2020 Fire releases a 3rd compilation of singles, *Some Kind of Happiness?*

June 2021 Fire continues its series of RSD releases with *Another kind of Trip*, a double album of live recordings.

ACKNOWLEDGEMENTS

The author would particularly like to thank the following for their availability and their considerable contribution to the project: Joe Foster, Jowe Head, Alison "Wonderland" Withers and Phil King, but also Sexton Ming, David Musker, David Newton, Phil Vinall, Victoria Yeulet, Clive Solomon, Lenny Helsing, Charlotte Marionneau, Mark Sheppard, Mark Flunder, Vinita Joshi, Thomas Zimmerman, Gregor Kessler, David Marshall and Patricia Ann Mellars for her kindness.

The author also wishes to thank the administrator and contributors to the *A Day In Heaven* website (www.televisionpersonalities.co.uk) which supplied a chronology of events and documentary resources often indispensable to the writing of this book.

PHOTO CREDITS

Cover: PA Images / Alamy Stock Photo

p. 50: "Where's Bill Grundy Now?", first released in 1978 in various covers on Daniel Treacy's own Kings Road label, later on Rough Trade.

p. 59: Handmade with copy cover and pinking shears: Both 'O'-Level-7"s and the first Teenage Filmstars 7" with a faked Merton-Parkas-sleeve

p. 64: Early gig flyer from October 1980. This was Ed Ball's first gig outside of London. Support act were the Cinematics featuring future Razorcut-members Gregory Webster and Tim Vass. Tim courteously supplied the flyer from his collection.

p. 69: Lyric booklet LP »And Don't The Kids ...«

p. 83: Promotional letter from Daniel for a planned compilation on a Whaam! sublabel. Neither record nor label came about.

p. 87: Lyric booklet LP "Mummy Youre Not Watching Me"

p. 117: Lyric booklet LP "The Painted Word"

p. 126: Dan Treacy, Living Room, February 10th 1984, © JC Brouchard

p. 129: Dan Treacy 1983 Starforce Studio, London Battersea during the session for "A Sense Of Belonging" 7", ©Mark Flunder

p. 130: Collectors Corner 1: rare 7"s (clockwise):
– "Still Believe In Magic", Caff, 1989
– 'O' Level, "East Sheen", Psycho, 1978, one of the 25 copies hand decorated by Ed Ball
– 'O' Level, "The Malcolm EP", Kings Road, 1978, red sleeve
– "14th Floor", Teen 78, 1978, Santa sleeve
– "14th Floor", Teen 78, 1978, 4 pics sleeve
– "Three Wishes"; Whaam!, 1982, red sleeve

p. 131: Clockwise:
– London, The Dive, 25. August 1982, with a just of age Mark Sheppard on drums, ©Thomas Zimmermann
– Dan Treacy with Gina Hartman (Marine Girls) and Gillian Elam (Co-Founder of Bi-Joopiter Labels) while shooting an unfinished video for "Smashing Time" in the summer of 1982. Dan and Gina (as "Cousin Jill") visited places mentioned in the text such as Carnaby St, Tower of London, and ate ice cream in Hyde Park. The 16mm footage shot by film students is considered lost. ©Mark Flunder
– Dan Treacy and Alan McGee in McGee's Living Room Club, June 30th 1984. That night on stage: The Pastels, The Legend and The Jowe Head Experience, ©Paul Groovy
– Living Room, June 4th 1983, ©Rob Mack

p. 132: Collectors Corner 2: Whaam! Labels

p. 133: ©Alison Wonderland
p. 134: Collectors Corner 3: handmade "They Could Have Been Bigger Than The Beatles"-Cover
p. 135: Promo pic "The Painted Word" 1984, ©Alison Turner
p. 136: Four of (approx.) 400 TVPs-posters
p. 137–139: Hamburg, Fabrik March 25th 1990, ©Moni Kellermann, www.kellerfrau.com
p. 140: Pressreview: fanzines
p. 141: Clockwise:
– London Hammersmith Clarendon, ca. 1984, ©Sushil Dade/Future Pilot Art
– Nürnberg, 1987
– Heiligenhaus, Der Club, Januar 6th 1984, ©Hans-Jürgen Klitsch
– Enger, Forum, January 7th 1984, ©Frank-Michael Kiel
– Dan Treacy and Evan Dando, backstage, New Year's Eve 1989, Berlin, Ecstasy, ©Thomas Zimmermann
p. 142: Promo pic »Privilege«
p. 143: Amsterdam, 1993, ©Alison Wonderland
New York, Hilton Hotel, July 1993, Creem Magazine Promogig, TVPs-drummer Lenny Helsing fills in as "Dan Treacy".
p. 144: London, Stamford Hill Park, January 1995, ©Alison Wonderland
p. 253: Self-portrait by Dan Treacy from issue #2 of German fanzine Orval, 1985.

Thanks for their support with photos and material from their collections:
Wolfram Bölian, Markus Wilhelms, Martin Schaefer, Christian Huhn, Jens Gerhard, Olaf Schumacher, Martin Cannert, Lenny Helsing, Richard Sigl, Raymond McGinley, Jed Livingstone.
Special thanks to Thomas Zimmermann for access to his archive and to Kai Becker for layout and graphics of the picture section.

Jimi Tenor
OMNIVERSE
Sounds, Sights and Stories
ISBN 978-3-95575-174-6

Beate Bartel / Gudrun Gut / Bettina Köster
M_DOKUMENTE
Mania D., Malaria!, Matador
ISBN 978-3-95575-155-5
(english/german)

Sub Opus 36 e.V.
SO36
1978 bis heute
ISBN 978-3-95575-165-4
(english/german)

szim
DEAD MOON
Off the Grid
ISBN 978-3-95575-173-9

www.ventil-verlag.de